I loved Amy-Jane Beer's *The Flow*. […] It is full of quiet wisdom and passion, and shows us what words can do when the personal and the ecological are blended organically.

Elif Shafak, *New Statesman*

A true masterpiece; generous, elega

Ch

The perfect commingling of deep
and quiet eddies of feeling, helmed
all-round adventurous soul.

Melissa Harrison, author of *All Among the Barley*

A quietly courageous, open-hearted exploration of Britain's becks, bourns and streams.

Patrick Barkham, author of *The Swimmer: The Wild Life of Roger Deakin*

Lyrical, wholehearted and wise, *The Flow* is a hymn for the rivers of Britain.

Lee Schofield, author of *Wild Fell*

Amy's prose is as captivating as the rivers she describes. I thought I knew what rivers were, but this stunning book is a powerful reminder of their infinity, their mystery, and their bewildering complexity.

Sophie Pavelle, author of *Forget Me Not*

The Flow moves deftly between deeply touching personal experience and carefully-researched erudition. It is a book of wit, of wonder and of wisdom.

Nick Acheson, naturalist and conservationist

Haunted by loss, *The Flow* is about the urgency of a life, land and love.

Nicola Chester, author of *On Gallows Down*

The Flow is passionately alive – a work of tremendous range and scope by one of our finest writers about the living world.

Caspar Henderson, author of *The Book of Barely Imagined Beings*

A gutsy biologist with webbed feet, Amy-Jane Beer plunges the reader into rivers the length and breadth of Britain. We emerge bathed in wonder and full of fresh understanding.

Derek Niemann, author of *Birds in a Cage*

The Flow is a tour de force: blending crystal-clear prose with mythic poetry and a cascade of lucid facts, washed down with uplifting insights into life, death and the water that sustains us.

Guy Shrubsole, author of *Who Owns England?*

From the incredibly moving opening scene, to a delightful conclusion, Amy-Jane Beer takes us on a journey on, in and through the waterways of Britain, in sparkling prose.

Stephen Moss, author of *The Robin*

An extraordinary book by an extraordinary author.

Chris Jones, conservationist and farmer

The Flow is a wonderful book: as passionate as it is knowledgeable.

Mark Wormald, author of *The Catch*

I have read dozens of books about rivers and *The Flow* is one of the finest.

David Profumo, *Country Life*

The Flow is gutsy and profound from the off, with exquisite evocation of place, dives into deep time, moments of humour and surging anger at what we've done to our rivers. In a golden age for nature writing, this stunning book is one of the very best.

Ben Hoare, *BBC Countryfile*

As with all the best books about nature, *The Flow* is a marriage of two things: a hard-won knowledge of the subject and a rare ability to write beautifully.

Ian Carter, *British Wildlife*

[Beer has] a poet's gift for description [...]. She's got an ability to make even a small moment resonate, such as her child's serendipitous discovery of a carnivorous sundew plant, with sharp prose and quick pacing. The result is an aquatic tour de force.

Publishers Weekly

An epic memoir that inspires awe for rivers and reveals their dual nature as both boundaries and portals.

Foreword Reviews

This erudite book is a joyous combination of science, nature, history, and mythology [...] a genuinely moving voyage of discovery of our ecological and personal place in the nature that surrounds us.

Yorkshire Life

THE FLOW

Rivers, Water and Wildness

Amy-Jane Beer

BLOOMSBURY WILDLIFE
LONDON · OXFORD · NEW YORK · NEW DELHI · SYDNEY

BLOOMSBURY WILDLIFE
Bloomsbury Publishing, Plc
50 Bedford Square, London, WC1B 3DP, UK
29 Earlsfort Terrace, Dublin 2, Ireland

First published in the United Kingdom 2022
Paperback edition 2023

ISBN: Paperback: 978-1-4729-7740-3; Hardback: 978-1-4729-7739-7; Audio download:
978-1-3994-0159-3; ePub: 978-1-4729-7737-3; ePDF: 978-1-4729-7738-0

6 8 10 9 7

Typeset in Bembo Std by Deanta Global Publishing Services, Chennai, India
Printed and bound in Great Britain by CPI Group (UK) Ltd, Croydon CR0 4YY

To find out more about our authors and books visit www.bloomsbury.com
and sign up for our newsletters.

For Kate, and all who loved her

Contents

Please help me build a small boat,
One that will ride on the flow
Where the river runs deep, and the larger fish creep
I'm glad of what keeps me afloat

Johnny Flynn, *The Water*

Only water, moving on

I know its depth, though not in feet

Nan Shepherd, *The Living Mountain*

Compared to their craggy Lakeland neighbours, the Howgill Fells are voluptuous. Where they stretch out between the valleys of the Lune and Rawthey, the bones of the Earth seem well fleshed, despite every curve along the tops being shaven by grazing. Lower down there are steep gills – damp, intimate, inguinal crevices, where life sports, water seeps and rivers swell.

On a cold, poster-bright morning, I step off tarmac onto a farm track and begin heading downhill. The change in gradient shifts tension from one set of walking muscles to another and, almost immediately, I hear running water. It's just a tiny rush-lined beck, but now I'm following it, I feel as though this thing I've resisted for nearly seven years has begun.

Autumn is well advanced here. The house sparrows in the farm hedges are unusually quiet. Last night brought the first hard frost of the season and it has silenced them – as though in their fragile bones, they know what is coming. Dog roses and hawthorns, heavy with fruit, have shed their leaves. While the rosehips are scarlet and vital-looking, the haws are the colour of venous blood spilled in the dirt: dark, deoxygenated, with a scabby crust on each little gout. I wonder if the sinister reputation of hawthorn stems in part from the appearance of the fruit. The contrast between wholesome hip and ominous haw intrigues me – I know I'm not the first to notice, and I pocket a little bunch of each as a reminder to read up on their symbolism.

I continue around a bend and reach the river. There's a footbridge next to a ford, and a yellow sign reading *Danger of Death*. It's a warning about overhead power lines, valid but somehow mundane. I turn my head so I don't have to see it, and give my attention instead to the water. It's sliding under the bridge, all of a piece and so smoothly it seems a solid, impossible thing. Staring too long at the ceaseless issuing of water, you could fear that the Earth is running herself dry.

The river is low, way too low to navigate by boat. As with most of the steep watercourses draining these relatively small catchments, it takes heavy rain to bring the levels up. Then, skeins of water thicken and merge, creating ephemeral navigations over and between the rocks. Plans to paddle somewhere like this always had to be made at the last minute. They would be mooted the day before on the basis of a weather forecast, but not firmed up until we gathered, early, kayaks strapped on roof-racks, usually in a layby cafe serving greasy butties and scalding tea. Then we'd agree a destination and drive, hopping out here and there to gauge water levels against known markers – bridge pillars, distinctive rocks. However, in ten years of running rivers all over the north of England, the Rawthey eluded me. It was never quite in condition, or its sister, the Clough, looked better, or we'd end up heading downstream to the Lune, further west for the Kent or the Leven, or back over the Pennines for the Yorkshire Greta or the super-reliable Upper Tees, which members of York Canoe Club regarded as a home run, despite the hour and a half drive to reach it. The Rawthey always remained a river for another day.

The water is the colour of weak black coffee, the channel broad and shallow. On the bottom I can see rounded stones and shelves of rock that chivvy the water into riffles. Upstream there are larger rocks, topped with moss. A few trees overhang, a leafless young ash with bunches of seeds like dirty hankies. There are alders too, covered in dark maroon catkins, and hazels, oaks, more rambling dog rose and hawthorn.

A path rises away from the water, jinking left and right and becoming little more than a narrow sheep track. I'm not sure it's the right one. I'm approaching my destination from upriver, quite simply because I don't want to take the route the emergency services took, from a layby and across a field, lugging their heavy packs of equipment. I want to go the way my friend Kate did, when she and a group of others, all highly experienced kayakers, passed this way heading downstream on the 1st January 2012.

Kate was larger than life without trying. Brown eyes, hair she never grew long, though her fringe sometimes swept past her brows, prompting her to rake it back often. Her hands were large and strong, the nails neatly manicured but unvarnished, and she had the seemingly effortless good posture that befits a physiotherapist and Pilates devotee. She made clothes look good and I can picture almost every outfit I ever saw her in because she wore the same few, well-chosen items nearly all the time. Her smile was huge and came easily.

I pass dense thickets of gorse – some of it in flower – dazzlingly yellow in the strong light. The hawthorns on the other side of the path mark a field boundary, and they are *old* – without their leaves they look sparse and windbitten, but sturdy, having grown slowly, carefully. A lot of them have lost their bark, and the exposed wood is bleached and skeletal. A robin is singing. Robins are always singing. A few rooks call. A sparkling rivulet of water hurries across the path and down the hill.

The river below me is silver in the sunshine. I can hear it – the continuous background rush of fast-flowing water, a music I have missed. I pass another farmhouse and the path heads downhill. It's steep, and gravity tugs at my feet until I'm among trees again. The oaks, beeches and sycamores are still in leaf, golden and fox red, but the air pings with the alarm calls of blackbird and wren.

The river has entered a gorge somewhere below and beyond these few trees. I know this is close to the place, that the water I can hear must be *that* rapid. The birds keep shouting.

Go away. Why don't you just *go away*?

As it turns out, I have little choice. There's a double barrier, robust stock fencing and several strands of electric polywire, live and ticking. No one wants me to go down there. Not the farmer, not the birds, not me. And then I'm past the gorge, still walking, telling myself I'll find a bridge, and go back up the other side. I cross a field and negotiate a farm gate next to where a shepherd is expertly manhandling some recalcitrant sheep. I fuss his dog.

'A grand day.'

'Aye, have to make the most of 'em.'

'Yes, we do.'

I rejoin the river, and here it's quiet – limpid almost, with no sign of any turmoil upstream. On that New Year's Day, it must have looked much the same. Flowing on, with the light gleaming just as beautifully as before. The sound as consistent as before. No regret, no guilt, but I can't say no intent, because a river is *all* intent, all progress.

I cross a stone bridge and head back up the valley road. I'm resigned to walking from where the paramedics parked, across the field where the air ambulance must have landed. From there it's easy enough to clamber over a fence and slither down the riverbank, and before I've gathered my thoughts, I'm in the gorge – facing the steep crags topped with the fenced-off woodland I skirted an hour earlier. The birds might still be calling up there, still warning me off, but I can't hear them over the rush of the water. Shafts of sunlight do reach down though, lending brilliance to the flow.

This should be the place. The river is constricted here – only about 5m wide. But there's more than one rapid and I'm confused because I thought I'd just *know*. From a kayaking perspective they're not steep, but they are intricate and technical, with lots of choices to make. The low water level makes it hard to read the flow. I can picture Kate in her boat in the eddy above, smiling, enjoying the winter greenery of moss and fern and lichen and woodrush.

Maybe she'd have scooped up a handful of water to splash her face, as we all did from time to time to sharpen the senses and feel more engaged with the river. It's not just water though. You can see that simply by looking. Little by little, the hills are letting themselves go, relinquishing the life they have fostered. That coffee-colour tint is a geological and biological essence of what was once land and living matter, but which no longer belongs to anything other than the river.

Kate announced she was pregnant around the time my husband Roy and I started trying for our own baby, but there ended up being a two-year age gap between the arrivals of her daughter Hannah, and my son Lochy. I sought her advice often in the early days, and two pieces of wisdom stuck. The first was to 'Embrace the mess', and has stood us in good stead, applied to all aspects of life, not just the sticky and chaotic business of childrearing. The second was, and is, harder. 'When a baby is born,' she once said, with characteristic conviction, 'that's only the start of your separation, so you have to start straight away getting yourself used to it. You have to put him in the arms of others and let them love him too. Because though our kids feel like part of us, they are people in their own right and they need us to teach them how to be that. Our job as mothers is to make ourselves redundant, when our selfish hearts want the opposite.' I definitely wanted the opposite. I still do. I want Lochy to stay close. To know that he is loved beyond measure. But like Hannah, he is an only child. And seeing them both grow and connect at their root-tips like trees in a forest, befriending the world beyond their immediate family, I know Kate would be proud.

Kate had a heart like a rising sun: huge, touching everything, and always on the horizon, in the pursuit of which she had sailed around the world – racing, not cruising.

After Lochy was born, I wanted to start exercising as soon as possible, and I sought Kate's expert advice about regaining some of my former physical shape. I remember her guiding my fingers so I could feel the gaps where my abdominal muscles had separated to accommodate the baby, and warning me against running until they had rejoined. There was nothing to stop me paddling though, within reason, and I was back on the water as soon as the C-section scar had healed. Several others in our circle were managing the same juggling act. Roy and I took our regular summer trip to the French Alps when Lochy was seven months old – friends taking turns to bounce and cuddle him on riverbanks while we paddled. Babies and kayaking – we could have both. We did have both.

As I confront the bones of the rapids in the gorge, my gaze is drawn from feature to feature, trying to make sense of it, envisaging the ways things might have gone wrong. That rock? That crease? Or that one? In this low water I can't even see what the line – the optimal route – might be. Everything is flowing through easily, little swirls of spume making patterns on the surface, as though it's being stirred by an invisible wand.

I don't really know what to do, now I'm here. I didn't bring flowers. It seems I didn't even bring words. But there are the two small bunches of berries in my pocket. Scarlet hips and crimson haws. I weigh them in my hand, then toss them into the water. The hips glow so brightly in the sun I can see them bobbing until the river curves slightly and they are carried out of sight. I start picking my way downstream. It's not easy. The bank is too steep and scrubby to move on, so I'm climbing over rocks and moss at the water's edge, grasping roots and tussocks. I pass the end of the second rapid, and realise only then that there is another below. The gorge narrows though, and I can't get to it, so I climb up and around, descending towards a wide pool a little further on. As I begin to scramble down again, I catch a glimpse of the rapid below, and it stops me in my tracks because I know that *this* is it. I know because it's a mean, tight space, with water piling in, relentlessly beating itself up, with a whole tree trunk stuck in it, roots uppermost. Sunlight doesn't fall in there and individual sounds are kettled by rock walls and subsumed into white noise.

Kate was under there for ten minutes.

I flinch and swear, and wonder aloud what good I thought coming here would do.

I turn my back but I can't unsee it.

Finding my way to the quiet water a little further downstream, I crouch on a rock shelf at the edge. This must be where they got her out, though how they managed it I can hardly fathom. They didn't stop CPR until the paramedics came.

I wash my face, smelling the water and feeling it tingle on my skin. There's almost more nostalgia in these sensations than I can bear. I realise how much I miss the water – *this* kind of water – icy, earthy and aerated, fresh and yet so very old.

I have tried to go back. We've used our open canoe on lakes and placid water and that has always been a joy. But when it came to white water, the paddling that always had my heart, I can't trust my vision to stay clear, my muscles not to flood with adrenaline, my heart not to race. For years, my kayak sat in the garage. Then it went to a friend's barn.

As the water I've washed with trickles down my neck and evaporates from my face, I look down … and there is something strange. At first I think it's a fine thread – fishing line, or a strand of spider silk maybe, floating on the water. It moves slowly, sinuously, then disappears. I cock my head and there it is again, catching the light. I reach out to touch it, and there's only water. But I can still see it, very clearly now, and I realise that it's not just on the surface. It's a veil, visible only as a perturbation of light, extending down into the depths. It has no substance and fragments of detritus in the water pass through it, as do my fingers, and it reforms when I take my hand away.

It dawns on me that I'm seeing an interface between flows – an eddyline. In my kayak, I used to visualise eddylines as curtains or walls – obstacles that required carefully judged power and angle to cross safely and under control, without the tension between one flow and the other forcing me off line, or even into a capsize. But I don't recall ever actually *seeing* one. I've seen surface flows colliding, curtains of bubbles, swirls and humps of water – other clues to where flows meet. But never this perfect, precise boundary between flow and return. The currents just here are slow, so slow that the water appears almost still. There's no disturbance at the surface to disrupt the slight refractions that are allowing me to perceive something that is normally invisible. It's like seeing the join between past and present, life and death. The tiniest nothing between enormities. The longer I look, the more subtle features I see. Micro-eddies, upwellings, swirls and little dimples. The latter must be the result of vortices, tiny ones, tugging at the surface from below. They look like fingerprints, as though someone had touched the water and it remembered. They move slowly, sometimes bumping into each other as they drift downstream. It's mesmerising, weird and comforting, this layering, mobile architecture of flow.

I remember the few hours just before the call that New Year's Day, when I didn't know. There was a pearly pink sunrise, a run up Arnside Knott, and lunch in a pub in Ambleside. For some reason I always picture the carpet there, from which I'd done an inadequate job of cleaning up the pasta and vegetables scattered by a less-than-cooperative eleven-month-old. But then there was a phone call, a drive back to Yorkshire in the dark, to a house packed with a lot of the people we loved best, where we waited for news of a miracle from the intensive care unit. Cold water can slow things down, can't it? We'd all heard stories of hypothermia lending a lifeline in circumstances like this, reducing the brain's roaring demand for oxygen. And this was Kate. Kate who never gave up. Kate who would never dream of leaving early.

We waited two days, dossing down together. Candles burned to stubs, more were lit. We cuddled our babies and hugged each other. We drank a lot. Then the call came from Kate's husband, Paul. A few strangled words, two unfinishable sentences. The world changed shape. Important parts ripped and splintered.

For a few weeks it seemed we just trod water. Did only what it seemed most needed to be done. The funeral was a riot of colour, a river of stories, an ocean of love. Weeks became months and by the time I realised life was moving on, it was like coming ashore after a long time at sea, landmarks in familiar places, solid ground under my feet, gravity doing what it always does. But by then I had sea-legs, and solid ground felt insecure. And of course I didn't have the worst of it. Kate's parents and brothers, Paul, and even little Hannah, were all doing her proud, leading by example. And while I felt sure that there must be more I could do for them, and for the friends who had tried so hard to keep Kate with us, at times all I could do was curb the rage at my inability to intervene in events that had already happened.

All our kayaking friends had stories of near misses, narrow escapes, epic fails, rescues. It's the same for any adventure sport – a folklore of daring, teamwork, grim will and sheer bald luck. Stories of absurd survival have always lodged deep with me. Vesna Vulović, the Serbian flight attendant who fell 33,000 feet in a fragment of fuselage and survived to wave and smile from the cover of my *Guinness Book of World Records*, 1981 edition. Skier and medic Anna Bågenholm, who in 1999 slid beneath the ice of a frozen river and was successfully resuscitated after 80 minutes' immersion and two hours' cardiac arrest from a core body temperature of 13.7°C. Bob Sandford, a novice mountaineer who was swept by meltwater down a moulin in the Saskatchewan Glacier, all the way to the bottom, where he washed clean along the river flowing beneath the ice to be reborn at the snout. When such things are possible, it felt outrageous for Kate to not be able to regale us with her own wild tale of beating the odds.

My grief was shot through with monstrous, inexpressible rage at my inability to make things better – to intervene in events that had already taken place – and with a sort of guilt. I'd let Kate down by not being there. We'd all trained in white-water rescue. We'd all practised, and in practices of course, the save was always made. Not having a chance to at least try was almost unbearable. We never discussed it, but I think this was intuited by our friend Ian, who was with Kate that day, who helped pull her out. In his part of a many-voiced eulogy he introduced himself and said simply that it had been his privilege to be there on Kate's last river trip. Ian is a man of relatively few words, who sometimes gives the impression he's not really paying attention. Then from time to time he blindsides you with something like that statement, which not only honoured Kate, but saw and accepted the snakepit of emotions I thought I'd done an OK job of concealing. It took me a long time to consider that maybe every experienced paddler in the room felt the same.

Almost unbelievably, we were back in the same crematorium ten months later, grappling with another shattering loss. Jason Raper joined the club aged 16, already a fully formed personality: kind, sparky and one of the most naturally talented paddlers we'd seen. Two months after Kate died, Jason paddled 160 continuous miles of the Rivers Ure, Ouse and Humber in three days, raising thousands of pounds for the air ambulance service in her memory. Less than four months after that, he too was gone, swept away on the River Raundalen in Norway. He was only 19 years old. It was weeks before his body was

recovered – three months before his mother could arrange a
funeral for her only child. There's a stained-glass window in
that crematorium, depicting a primitive square-sailed ship
under a starry sky. There's a crucifix in the shape of the mast
if you choose to see it that way; and a cosmic river in the
waves and the starry sky if you want that. I wanted neither.
No one was going to tell me that any of this made sense or
fitted some higher purpose.

Several months later, Paul shared a letter from one of the
recipients of Kate's donated organs. And then I wept properly,
privately, and with overwhelming gratitude. Because there
she was, somehow, making things better when we were
helpless to do so. The organ donation was a gift not only to
those strangers, but also to us. And after that, quietly and
undramatically, the rage just left.

I've always meant to visit the place. I had thought that it
might be on an anniversary of some sort – that a right time
would somehow suggest itself. Today I just happened to be
in the area and it seemed easier somehow, for not being
planned and not telling anyone. I've tricked myself into it.
But the fact that it's autumn does feel apt. Fecundity and
decay press in from either side, channelling life into a silver
stream with death on one bank, renewal on the other.

I'm halfway back to the car when I realise I didn't do the
thing I think I must have meant to. I haven't said goodbye.
And I haven't said it because Kate wasn't there. Of course
she wasn't. There was only water, moving on.

She'd regret that I've barely sat in my boat since, but
perhaps she'd understand why, after years of seeking
adventure with a spring in my step, I started baulking. Partly
of course, it's being a parent, partly it's growing older, and
becoming much less fit. There are plenty of adventurous
mums out there, still hitting it hard, but I've come to a point
from which I don't need to be pushing further, daring more.
I can look back on the endorphin-soaked days with pleasure.

I can see where I've been, and yes, it's a great view. But Kate, I believe, would tell me not to spend too much time looking back. She would insist that the more intriguing vista is always the new one just coming into view. The emerging landscape is hummocky and cryptic, and something is pulling, gently, but insistently, like gravity. Defying gravity is easier than you might imagine. You can do it with a puff of breath that keeps thistledown aloft. But for now, the river and I seem to want to just go with it.

To just flow.

I go back again a few months later, on New Year's Day, leaving home early to make the most of the short daylight. This time I go straight to the place, climb the rickety fence, and slither down the bank, feeling the abrupt angles of rock under deceptive cushions of moss. The water is even lower than last time, exposing the unforgiving anatomy of the rapid – a deep step into an undercut pot with a narrow outflow. Big way in, small way out – a classic trap.

The pool is deep and clear. I don't spend too long looking, because I'm already chilly despite my down jacket. I have to do it now or not at all.

I've been river-swimming for about five years. No great distances, and only in the warmer part of the year, and always in a wetsuit, even in summer. But I realise that the suit has reduced my inherent tolerance for cold water, rather than improving it. If I'm going to reacquaint myself with rivers, and do it properly, that separation has to go. Choosing the depths of winter to start wild skin-swimming goes against all the advice. But I'm not unfamiliar with cold water, and certainly not naive about the environment. While the rapid above is a killer, the pool is about as safe as a cold river gets – deep and slow with easy access and egress, running into a shallower section below. The only real risk is cold shock and I can mitigate that by taking my time.

I strip off and hurriedly pull on a swimming costume and a pair of old trainers. I have immediate full-body gooseflesh.

'Steady,' I tell myself, 'Go slow. It's going to burn, it's going to be hard to breathe at first. Let those things happen.'

They do happen. I step down into the water up to my knees, then my thighs, my waist and my chest, letting the gasp reflex have its moment. And then I'm pushing off. I'm swimming. And almost immediately, weirdly, it is fine. After 30 seconds I can breathe slowly and deeply. I take a lap of the pool. The water is golden, and it makes my legs and feet look buttery yellow. My chest feels weird though. I'm perplexed for a moment then realise that in my hurry to change, I've put my swimsuit on backwards, and the lower-cut back is, unsurprisingly, not covering what it should. Too cold to feel what was amiss, I had got in the water with my boobs barely covered. Now they have escaped entirely. Treading water, snorting and cursing, I wriggle the suit off and lob it onto the bank. In the unlikely event anyone does happen along I'd rather be seen naked than dressed backwards.

I circuit the pool again, trying to master my breathing, only now it's giggles that are convulsing me. I swim as close to the exit from the rapid as I dare, thinking I should rage at it, or address it solemnly about what it stole, but the wardrobe malfunction has flipped a valve. I can't find anything but a sensation of being vigorously, whoopingly alive.

I climb out on the sharp angled rocks, rub myself clumsily with a towel and pull on clothes, glad I remembered to leave them laid out ready. I can't feel my skin, but there's a furnace in my core that wasn't there before. I drink a flask of coffee and walk back over the field. A gaggle of rooks is pecking at a patch of grass when a gleam of sunlight breaks through, and they all pause and raise their heads – not to me, but to the light, as though astonished by it. I stop too, and for a few seconds we all stand there, bathing I imagine, in similar floods of brain chemicals. The light seems to mainline to a

deep, ancient brain, through Russian-doll layers of ancestry:
the reptile within the mammal, the amphibian within the
reptile, the fish within the amphibian. An unbroken line of
wily, cautious, opportunistic, tenacious, ferocious, scrambling,
wriggling, darting, striving survivors. I feel them all, my
ancestors, stirring in their sleep.

The tentative idea for which today was a sort of
experiment has solidified. I am going to go back. Not just to
this river, not necessarily to white water − I'm not 30
anymore − but to rivers in general. I've been thinking of
that hair-fine eddyline I saw here a few months ago; the
fingertip dimples; the scent of river-aerosol and of wet rock,
and I wonder what else I missed in all those years. So yes, I
will go back, but slowly, and this time I'm going to pay
more attention.

CHAPTER 1

Fresh and yet so very old

There are rivers in the sky, and they are vast.

We can't see them, because unlike clouds, rain, snow and fog, these rivers are made of gas, rather than liquid water or solid ice. Invisible vapour makes up around 99.5 per cent of the water in our skies at any one time, and it is always on the move, pouring along pressure gradients and around obstacles, just as terrestrial rivers descend under gravity. The largest of these flows are tens to hundreds of kilometres wide and thousands long, and they shift ten billion tonnes of water away from the humid tropics every day. That's up to 27 times the discharge of the Mississippi Basin, or a thousand times that of the Thames. These immense flows are part of the system that has driven water over and around and through the Earth for billions of years.

The term 'atmospheric river' is relatively recently coined, but the effects have long been familiar in places where they make landfall. Alaska and Chile receive conveyors of moisture carried north-east and south-east from the tropical Pacific; others cross the Atlantic from the Caribbean to bring rain to the British Isles. Some bring steady but essential showers, while more powerful versions result in prolonged deluges or epic dumps of snow. The impacts of landfalling atmospheric rivers vary hugely, not only with their speed, direction, size and intensity, but also with landscape topography: characteristics such as elevation and the shape and orientation of different river catchments are all important. Developing this new science into accurate forecasting and risk analysis for a given location is fiendishly complex. But the existence of these sky flows is a reminder that a river is not a bounded entity, not merely a ribbon of water in a channel. The naturalist, activist and writer Roger Deakin once wrote that 'a tree is a river'. But a river is also a tree, rooted not only in soil and rock but in the sky, with branches that spread into the sea. Science is only now beginning to unpick the ways tree roots interconnect invisibly via networks of mycorrhizal fungi, but the fact that water flows through every earthly life is more immediately apparent. There is a river running through you, now.

When I was nine, we lived in Germany, and the local swimming baths had what we'd now call a leisure pool – made for playing in rather than swimming. This suited me because I couldn't swim. I wasn't afraid there because I could just about touch the bottom and had full faith in my orange arm bands. The best thing about this pool was that it had a wave machine – quite a thing in the late 1970s. Every 20 minutes or so, a chiming *bonggg* would echo off the tiles, and water would begin to heave from the deep end and surge up the gradient to the shallows. The waves would get bigger and bigger until they formed real breakers, powerful enough to hurl a small girl bodily up the 'beach'. I loved it. *Bonggg.* I was there.

One day, as the waves dwindled, questions presented themselves. Watching the water slosh over my arms, I wondered, *What IS this stuff? How does it move like this? Why does it sparkle?* If you ask my son, now of a similar age, what water is made of he'll say without hesitation it is H_2O – molecules comprising two hydrogen atoms and one oxygen. I don't have any memory of being taught that kind of science so early. At that time I was already at my fifth primary school, so my early education had been, if not exactly lacking, possibly a little erratic. I certainly had no knowledge of molecules. Water was just water, elemental, much as it was to the ancients. But in that moment I wondered. And the wondering made me ask my mother. 'What if water is made of very tiny things we can't see?'

I recall the quizzical look she gave me. 'Well, it is.'

How the rest of the conversation panned out I don't remember, only the picture it set in my mind. The 'very tiny things' were silvery, with an oily rainbow shimmer. They had many different forms, they jostled and swirled and ran over one another, and they glowed where they touched. They were alive. Possibly I'd seen microscope images of plankton and not understood. For a long time these strange forms were how I imagined water to be, if only we could look close enough. And I still see them now, sometimes, when I try and imagine the very small. The molecular world and, smaller still, the quantum universe: all light and slither, collision and flow.

The truth about water is no less strange. The properties of dihydrogen monoxide are down to its molecular structure – two hydrogen atoms attached asymmetrically to one oxygen. Oxygen currently makes up almost 21 per cent of the Earth's atmosphere and around half the mass of all the rock in Earth's crust. It is the third most abundant element in the universe in mass terms. And there's even more hydrogen. Despite being the smallest and lightest of chemical elements, hydrogen makes up three-quarters of the mass of baryonic matter (that made of atoms) in the universe. The willingness of these copious ingredients to combine makes water very abundant stuff. The weirdness stems largely from the lop-sidedness and polarity of each molecule. The hydrogens carry a slightly negative charge, while the oxygen is positive, and because opposite charges attract, water molecules cling to each other. This creates the phenomenon of surface tension, which among other things gives raindrops their bulbous shape and allows pond skaters to walk on water. The self-attraction also results in capillary action which enables us to drink through a straw and plants to haul moisture from the ground in defiance of gravity.

Also of great biological significance is the fact that the oxygen atom on each water molecule has the capacity to bond with atoms of other elements, making water a uniquely effective and broad-spectrum solvent and a medium in which the myriad chemical reactions that make life possible can take place.

Another oddity of water is the narrow range of temperatures across which it occurs in solid, liquid and vapour form – a range that coincides with conditions on the surface of the Earth. Earth is thus the Goldilocks planet – not too hot, not too cold, but just right for life as we know it. Across these temperatures, water can freeze from liquid to solid, melt or thaw from solid to liquid, evaporate from liquid to gas, sublimate from solid to gas and deposit from gas to solid. Most unusually, the way water crystalises when it freezes means that ice is less dense than liquid water, so bodies of water freeze from the top down, leaving free water below in which aquatic life can survive. These characteristics of water are so familiar that they hardly need stating, but they are not 'normal' in chemical terms, and their implications for life are impossible to overstate.

Until relatively recently, the water that filled the first oceans was thought to have come from icy comets or rocks that struck the Earth 3.8 billion years ago, but remote analysis of samples from several comets suggests that their water contains too much of the 'heavy' hydrogen isotope deuterium to be a good match for Earth water. A more favoured scenario is that Earth's water has been here much longer, somehow surviving the early hot phase in Earth's history and the collision, about 4.5 billion years ago, of the young planet with another, which caused an ejection of material that subsequently formed the Moon. It is possible that superheated oceans remained liquid because of the enormous pressure of carbon dioxide in the atmosphere at the time. Whatever the truth, the water filling oceans, frozen in glaciers and polar ice, falling as rain or rising from aquifers and flowing through rivers and our bodies is almost inconceivably ancient.

The chemical character of this venerable, mobile, labile substance is also central to the way it is distributed around the universe and especially on Earth. The transformations and movements of the water cycle are now taught even in nursery schools, but it is one of those recurring themes in education that expands with each iteration. At its simplest, water evaporates from the ocean, forming a gas (vapour), which condenses into clouds and then rain, which falls on the land and drains into rivers to be conveyed back to the sea. Except it's not really like that. Roy, who was a teacher of Geography and Earth Sciences at the time we met and married, rolls his eyes if I refer to it as a cycle at all. Rather, he says, it is a system of barely graspable complexity through which water is looped, filtered, diverted, transported, sequestered, chemically bonded, split and reformed. One evening over a bottle of wine I challenged him to give me his version of Hydrology 101. It took more than one evening and more than one bottle, but what he described to me was a dance, or perhaps even a song, with some moves or phrases that repeat, but whose structure, rhythm and location are part of the freeform jazz that nature (which is to say physics/god/the universe) plays so well. It goes something like this.

Most of the free water on Earth (between 96 and 97 per cent) is in the oceans, and oceans are briny because for billions of years, salts have been dissolved from the rocks and minerals over and through which water flows on its way to the sea. The salts are left behind in the ocean when water evaporates from the surface into the atmosphere. Fresh water makes up around 2.5 per cent of global water, and around 99 per cent of that is either frozen in glaciers and icecaps or in storage or transit under the ground. The remaining 1 per cent (0.025 per cent of global water, if you're keeping track) exists in lakes, rivers and marshes, in the soil, in the atmosphere, and in living things.

Atmospheric water is a *tiny* fraction of global water –
about 0.001 per cent (0.04 per cent of fresh water). Even so,
this still amounts to around 13 trillion tonnes, suspended
above us at any one time. Put another way, around
580,000 cubic kilometres or 580 trillion tonnes of water
vaporise into the atmosphere every year. If all sky water
rained down at once, approximately an inch would fall on
every square inch of the Earth's surface, but in reality only
about 0.5 per cent of atmospheric water condenses or
freezes to form clouds or precipitation at any one time.
Eighty-five per cent of global evaporation is from the
oceans, most of that from tropical and subtropical latitudes,
from where it is distributed by air movement. These
movements take place because of pressure gradients resulting
from differential heating of the Earth by the Sun – low
latitudes receive more solar energy than high ones. Warm air
rises and cold air sinks, creating circuits of air, known as
convection cells, above the planet's surface. The spinning of
the Earth means that there is a longitudinal element to
convection as well as a latitudinal one, and this offset is
known as the Coriolis effect. These factors combine to
move air (and hence water) around the lower atmosphere in
a broadly predictable way, along jet streams and other
currents. Moisture is diverted from some places, sprinkled in
others, and dumped by the bucketload elsewhere, often
thousands of kilometres from where it evaporated. Some of
these moist currents are bigger than others, and it's these
larger tracks that have been dubbed atmospheric rivers.

The frozen or condensed water we see in the atmosphere
takes a variety of forms, including ice crystals, snowflakes, hail,
sleet and liquid droplets. These grains, pellets and blobs are
known collectively as 'hydrometeors', and they range in size
from a few microns to more than 20cm in the case of
occasional freak hailstones. Where water falls on land, it might
evaporate again within minutes (plants make particularly
effective surfaces for evaporation because of the large area of

their leaves). Or it might be frozen, it might percolate away into soil or infiltrate porous or fractured rock, it might be taken up by a living organism, or it might continue its free journey, combining with other flows to form rivers.

The total mass of water falling as precipitation on land every year is estimated at around 119 trillion tonnes (119,000,000,000,000 tonnes, or 119 teratonnes): one of those numbers too big to easily imagine. But it might help to know that the total mass of living material, plus *all* the stuff that humankind has ever made (values which are at present broadly equivalent, with anthropogenic mass estimated to have exceeded biomass for the first time in 2020) is just more than one teratonne. That's a lot of water, and it all has to go somewhere.

It has been raining on Earth for around 4.5 billion years. When the planetary surface cooled enough to allow water falling onto it to remain in liquid form, the rain would have begun to flow and pool. One trickle joined another, following grooves and wrinkles as dictated by gravity. Because of its unrivalled nature as a solvent, water seeping into and around rocks dissolved some of their mineral content. As rivulets combined, they became a force in their own right, and their trickling, scouring, scrubbing and pummelling was occasionally enough to work fragments of rock away from the geological matrix. Every such erosion was an affirmation – channels formed that carried more water, which in turn exerted more erosive force. Big particles and small ones, from boulders, pebbles and gravels to sands, silts and clays were all caught in the flow, where they jostled and tumbled and collided, and continue to do so. The smaller the particles, the further and faster they can be carried, and where the flow eases, they settle for a while. The shifting balance between erosion and deposition means that rivers are dynamic entities. Over time, their courses flex and sidewind like the bodies of serpents.

Only some precipitation that falls on the ground runs directly into rivers. Most of it soaks into soil and deeper still into bedrock. This is groundwater. Rock varies in porosity (the amount of void space in its structure) and permeability (the accessibility of that space), and thus in its ability to conduct and store water. A rock formation that can contain water is an aquifer, and the surface level of water in the aquifer is known as the water table. Where the water table is close to or above the ground level, we get springs and wetlands. Where the beds of aquiferous rock are tilted, water in the lower lying portion is under hydrostatic pressure, and given a way out via a natural fault or a well, it can rise through overlying rock layers. Groundwater might stay in the ground for anything from a few hours (in fact soil water can be swiped by plants in a matter of minutes) to more than a million years in the case of very deep aquifers.

All this makes it hard to know where a river begins and ends – we may draw lines on maps for convenience but no such lines exist in nature, and as the much-quoted words of the much-quoted conservationist John Muir have it, 'When we try to pick out anything by itself, we find it hitched to everything else in the Universe.' The vast majority of water in the hydrological system of Earth is not river water, but it was, and it will be again. Rivers are simply the places where water is most visible and alive. Most drinkable, most generous, most ferocious. As a kayaker I have been carried by them and I have seen some of their wonders. Gorges, cascades and canyons; places where rivers spurt from cliff faces, others where they disappear under the ground; ephemeral winter palaces with icicles thicker than my waist, rotating ice pancakes, glaciers that groan and boom and spew rivers from their nostrils. I've paddled some you can only reach by helicopter with kayaks strapped to the skis. I have known some riverscapes to change over years, others to reinvent themselves overnight. I've seen water of almost every colour, a million sunlit rainbows, and just one lit only by the moon. I've heard rivers trickle and lilt, thunder and roar. I've tasted them sweet and salty. I've seen them free, and I've seen them dammed and straightened. I've seen them flood and run dry. But do I know them? No, not really. Not at all.

Snow dome

Watershed *A theoretical line on relatively high ground, dividing catchments or basins from which water drains into a particular watercourse or river system. Can also be used to refer to the entire catchment.*

Continental divide *A line between drainage basins from which water flows to oceans on different sides of a continent.*

In 1996, two-thirds through a doctorate tracing the neural development of sea urchin larvae, I attended the ninth International Echinoderm Congress, hosted by San Francisco State University and the California Academy of Sciences. It was a chance to meet the world's scholars of urchins, starfish, brittlestars, sea cucumbers and feather stars, but also a free ride to the other side of the world. Having delivered my presentation I begged a lift to Yosemite Valley, and from there travelled north, mainly by bus. I had a tiny tent and no stove, so cooked in a steel mug, or directly on a fire, mainly beans and incinerated potatoes.

I was clueless about many things. One morning on Vancouver Island I almost stood in a heap of gleaming purple bear poop on the beach near my tent. It looked like a double helping of porridge with berry compote. Two fishermen I met told me I was lucky to be alive, having failed to separate my stash of snacks from my sleeping space in bear territory. I took a small boat with a group of strangers to try and see orcas on a day when three large pods were travelling together. We bobbed in choppy water while more than 100 whales surged past, so close I could smell their breath. I got profoundly pissed in remote and unfamiliar places with total strangers. In Jasper National Park I climbed a small mountain without a map, and somehow lost my drink bottle along the way. On the way down, more dehydrated than I have ever been, I made it to a tea house above Lake Louise where they refused to give me water – they had to portage it up, it had to be boiled, and they only had enough for making tea, not for supplying cold to idiot tourists. I ordered tea, cried (tearlessly) for the ten minutes it took to come, then scalded my mouth and throat trying to drink it before it had cooled. I admit to all this foolishness because it puts into context the story I heard a few days later. Risk is something we can be taught to manage, but there's no better instructor than experience.

While in Banff, I took a tour of the Columbia Icefield. It's a major tourist attraction – snow coaches on giant tyres grind up and over the moraines and on to the grubby glacier that spills off the flank of a mountain known as Snow Dome. Our guide explained that while the summit is not particularly high by Rocky Mountain standards, it holds another claim to significance as a triple continental divide – one that separates water not two ways, but three, into separate oceans. Here, he said, it was possible for three drops of rain or flakes of snow falling together from the same cloud to find separate ways into the Arctic, the Pacific or the Atlantic Ocean.

Once on the glacier, passengers were allowed off the coach to wander. For the most part they slipped and shuffled in trainers and street shoes, or lined up along ropes on stakes hammered into the ice to mark safe distances from the moulins – cavernous blue holes into which rivulets of meltwater running over the surface gushed and disappeared. I maybe explored further than most because the guide came to get me, and as we walked back, told me the tale of a young mountaineer who tried to take a shortcut off a neighbouring glacier and was swept into a moulin. A nightmarish fate, but one that in this case became an extraordinary story of survival. Somehow, the guide told me, this lad survived the fall into the crevasse, and a ride all the way into the river that ran under the ice and out at the snout of the glacier hundreds of metres below. The young protagonist became one of my survival-against-the-odds notables; though I've thought of him every time I've peered into the mesmerising blue depths of a glacier since, I also suspected the story might be at least partly a tourist myth.

That was until 25 years later, when I found myself watching Canadian writer Lynn Martell interview the man himself. Robert (Bob) Sandford, now in his seventies, told how in 1970, he attempted a solo crossing of the Saskatchewan arm of the Columbia Icefield. 'I was cold and wet and worn out, and all I wanted to do was get down. So I took a shortcut … One moment I was looking at the sun-sparkle of splashing water, a moment later I was in the centre of a waterfall, plunging into complete darkness beneath the ice.' He describes sliding down a series of icy sills and into the river that ran beneath, scraping along in darkness under the belly of the glacier, smashing into boulders and breathing the few inches of air between the water and the ice. Despite the terror, he also recalls a strange calm, and even wonder. 'I heard from everywhere around me so many of the different sounds that water makes. Here I was, inside a planetary artery, examining first-hand what water does to the world ... ' After a time being rattled along in the icy dark he realised the light was coming back. 'As the river swept me onward, the glow intensified. Green gradually merged into a pale blue. I noticed then that rocks were hanging out of a ceiling made entirely of light. Then I washed out of the glacier into sunshine and into the full flood of the North Saskatchewan River.'

It's sometimes hard for me to accept that one flow of water can deliver a naive and unprepared person cold and wet but very much alive from the guts of a glacier, while another holds an experienced and prepared individual helpless, mere inches from the reach of her friends. We're all snowflakes. It is however a comfort to learn that Sandford has devoted his entire working life to rivers since, becoming a specialist international advisor in water and climate security.

CHAPTER 2

Torrent

In Xanadu did Kubla Kahn
A stately pleasure dome decree
Where Alph, the sacred river ran
Through caverns measureless to man
Down to a sunless sea.

Samuel Taylor Coleridge, *Kubla Khan*

I don't remember a river until the Thames, which we visited on a holiday 'home' from Northern Ireland when I was five. We walked a stretch near my grandma's house in the Reading suburb of Tilehurst. It was the summer of 1976, the banks were drought-parched, the grass scratchy. Dead thistles prickled bare legs. The river was dark and sluggish, with a skim of dust.

In 1978 we moved to Germany, a land with its own broad, khaki arteries. We criss-crossed the Weser, took day trips on the Rhine, and stayed by the Mosel, in a caravan park surrounded by vineyards. But it never occurred to me to wonder where these flat, blank waterways came from or where they went, and the only time I remember considering them as anything other than scenery, transport link or obstacle was when we visited Hamelin and watched a re-enactment of rats and children being danced away into the Weser by a harlequin piper.

When I was ten, we moved back to England for good. My dad, an officer in the Royal Electrical and Mechanical Engineers, was stationed on the School of Infantry base in Warminster on the edge of Salisbury Plain, a landscape characterised by chalk and a singular scarcity of running water. My bedroom window overlooked the steep, thorny flank of Battlesbury Hill, and beyond that near horizon were 15 miles of tumuli and tank trails, barrows and bomb holes, all the way to Stonehenge. That place, and the careless freedom my sister and I had to explore it for three years, made me; setting chalk in my bones, a touch of chlorophyll in my veins and establishing the connections, drove roads and desire paths in my brain that still govern the way I think to this day.

I don't remember there being many rules beyond *don't go past red flags* and *come home for meals*. When we did come home, it was sometimes with flints and feathers, sometimes with brass cartridge cases collected from the rifle ranges. The occasional live round was an exciting find, though our ambition to one day 'set one off' with the aid of a large rock and a hammer was never fulfilled.

Being back in England meant that holidays were freed from the obligation to visit or receive relatives and old friends – we could now do that at weekends. We started going to new places – not to see people, but to explore. Our first forays were to North Devon, where we stayed in a tiny flat in a converted granary on the Torridge Estuary. It had cold linoleum floors, a living space with a Formica kitchenette and a knackered settee, and two tiny bedrooms with the ricketiest of beds. We adored the place. From it, we visited the stony beach at Westward Ho! (with its eccentric and fascinating exclamation mark) and the sandy ones at Woolacombe and Croyde. We walked miles of coastal path. But best of all was the wild expanse of Exmoor, full of rocks and ghosts, villains and heroes, ponies and deer, gorse-scented slopes and endless trails of springy turf. There were steep woodlands where the trees were bearded in lichen, ancient but wise enough not to grow too large, and there were rivers. Nothing like the sluggish Thames or the bloated Rhine. The French express this difference best. Where we use bland terms such as 'moving water' or 'white water', they have *l'eau vive* ('living water') and *l'eau sauvage* ('wild water'). I can think of no better way to describe those North Devon flows than to say they were alive and wild.

Something began there, I think. An inoculation of sorts, by water that delivered what Nan Shepherd called 'a sting of life'. And there was one flow whose effect on me was especially potent, not just because of its vivid beauty but because of its terrible strength. For almost four decades I've coveted the place in memory and a handful of square Kodacolor snaps. Going back might break the spell. But the more I think about rivers, and of re-engaging with their flow, the more this one dazzles and dances in my dreams. I've begun to think of it as my personal Ur-river. My own sacred Alph.

It's mid March, and well after dark when I drive through Porlock: closed, except for a steamed-up chippy. It's almost obligatory when referencing this quiet Somerset village to mention Samuel Taylor Coleridge, and the 'person on business from Porlock' whose visit interrupted him when he was feverishly committing his trippy epic *Kubla Khan* to paper, sometime around 1797. He later claimed that a complete poem of more than 300 lines came to him fully in a dream-state, induced by two grains of opium he'd taken for dysentery. It's set on a sacred, mazy river that runs five miles through cavern, wood and dale and which, in the frenzy of its creation, spouts from heaving earth and tosses rocks 'like rebounding hail, or chaffy grain'. It is very much an *axis mundi*, linking visions of heaven and hell, through a human, cultivated space. If you search the globe for a real River Alph, you'll find it in Antarctica. Like its poetic namesake it runs largely underground, but it was mapped and named long after *Kubla Khan* was published, by Thomas 'Grif' Taylor, a geologist on Robert Scott's Terra Nova Expedition. Coleridge's inspiration may have been the River Alpheus of Greek mythology. Or perhaps he named it for Alpha, as a place of beginning. He never finished the poem after that fateful interruption, but published it incomplete 20 years later, by which time it had acquired a mythology of its own, not least in the poet's own mind.

Rain begins again in earnest as I coax the car up the one-in-four hill out of Porlock and onto the moor. Shapes loom: huddled clumps of gorse; wind-clipped thorns; clusters of grim-looking sheep. The road is awash, and I'm tense with the effort of trying to focus beyond the windscreen, squinting against the headlight glare reflected in rain and fog. My plan to sleep in the woods has lost its appeal, but it's late to be searching for a hotel. I might have to bed down in the car. But then a light shows, fuzzy in the mist. It's a pub – one I recognise from a photo my dad must have taken of my mum, my sister and me, sat outside in August heat with coffee and cokes. Ten minutes later my bag is stowed in a comfortable first-floor room of the Blue Ball Inn and I'm contemplating the bar menu over a glass of wine.

It's not yet dawn as I creep from the pub, but a song thrush is already busy issuing proclamations, repeating headlines like a town crier. It seems we are both keen to make the most of a short break in the rain. The track uphill towards the moor is flanked by moss-covered drystone walls. The ground is saturated, swathed in mist, and the greyness is almost overwhelming. I'm adjusting to the idea that sunrise is not going to be much of an event when a skylark takes off from the moor above me. I don't see him rise, or perceive the brightening that perhaps persuaded him to do so. But when he begins to sing I automatically turn my face up, and it seems then that he is casting something so bright and fine it must be a spell. It snags the fabric of the sky and the snag becomes a tear and the tear becomes a thinning. The thinning is dark blue rather than grey and in the blue the moon appears, like a faint, floury fingerprint.

Gulls begin mewling and a grouse rouses, irritably, not far away. Ice on a gate near the top of the hill melts under my hands and on the other side the soundscape changes, bringing the hiss of rushing water and a blackbird singing. The turf track is downhill now and below me lies a wooded crease in the land packed with cloud, like gauze used to staunch a wound. The path takes me through a thicket of flowering gorse, where the chorus is joined by several emphatic wrens, then through another gate.

I can't see the river below, but it inhabits the wood as a sonic fog. To live here is to bathe in continuous white noise, through which every other sound has to be filtered. Birdsong is honed to penetrate the background rush, while other sounds, including footfalls and scuffles, wind noise and breathing, are subsumed by it. Good for predators, less so for prey.

The trees are green despite being leafless; so blotched with mosses and lichen that their skeletal forms seem almost to dissolve as they parallax-shift in my peripheral vision. I walk among the trees, the trees walk among and through each other. When I stop, so do they, like a game of Grandmother's Footsteps, or musical statues. Their twisting shapes are those of dancers, poised and ready for me to turn away or some secret music to begin.

'*Burrrg burrrrg burrrg.*'

'Good morning Raven, *burrrg burrrg.*' It's no worse than talking to myself, and it banishes the slight heebie-jeebies the trees have given me. A red deer hind drifts between the trunks, emerging on the path, then notices me and bounds away. I follow her tracks in the saturated ground, breathing the air that seems to have thickened and curdled slightly in her wake.

Under the trees there's a carpet of fox-coloured oak leaves, sprouting with bilberry and holly saplings, and a tide of moss creeping up trunks like saggy green legwarmers. Higher up there are other epiphytes – lichen in abundance, ferns and the round, dimpled, succulently edible leaves of pennywort. Dead bracken glows like embers in the clearings, but as the path begins to descend I pass into a new zone, with swathes of heather and strap-leaved woodrush. There are birches now among the oaks, and the latter are bigger and stouter than those at the top of the wood.

I'm brought up by the sound of running water, close by. It's coming from a big rock next to the path and it sounds like a spring, but after hunting around and cocking my head this way and that to pinpoint the sound, I realise it's an echo of the rapid below. It's a cruel trick of nature's, to make running water one of the most difficult sounds to locate. But in this case it helps me see something else. The echo is coming from a deep crevice, and when I lean closer to listen I see inside a lost world. It is both miniature and cavernous, with a floor carpeted in neat dark green moss – a different kind to the pale feathery one on the outside of the rock. A tiny red-leaved stonecrop is sprouting among the moss and a brown snail glides by it, eyestalks waggling. As I watch it is overtaken on the trail by a pinkish, bristly-tailed creature about half a centimetre long. A collembolan, or springtail – a sort of six-legged insect cousin. It steps delicately past the snail, ducks under an arch made by a dead oak leaf and then emerges cautiously on the other side. It hesitates and peers, antennae tilting this way and that, then it tiptoes to where a trickle of moisture has spread on bare rock. It pauses, then lowers its head to drink. Another appears and they dip and sip, side by side, antennae continuing to swivel like gazelle ears. If they are sensing me at all – my breath, or my shadow perhaps, it's probably the way I might notice a change in the weather. When I pull my gaze away, the sun has hitched itself higher, the greens are brighter, and daybreak has become morning.

The soundscape shifts as the trail zigzags down. There's a confluence below me and heading one way, I'm facing the combined flows – a steady rush like a washing machine draining. But switching back, I'm facing a smaller tributary, and its song is higher pitched, more urgent and splashy, but also more contained. It's amazing how much you can tell about a river by its voice. I realise the river I'm going to see today is not the one in my memory. It's not a summer tableau of tinkling cascades and sunlit pools. It is going to be a torrent.

Watersmeet House is smaller than I remember, but the pinkish stone and the woodwork in British racing green are otherwise achingly familiar. The tea lawn possibly has more tables and high-capacity litter bins than in my memory, but the zigzag fencework and circular stone seat around a raised flower bed haven't changed a bit. It's very much a garden, manicured and mown, despite being surrounded on all sides by woods and wild water, and the birds are garden-tame: blue and great tits, bold and expectant of cake and sandwich crumbs.

The house was built as a fishing lodge in the early 1830s at the behest of Walter Stevenson Halliday – a reverend by title, though he retired early on inheriting a significant fortune in 1829, and used it to establish himself as landowner and squire of the tiny parish of Countisbury. Walter was a philanthropist, a patron of the arts, an amateur historian, a naturalist, and a mischief maker. One of his particular delinquencies was to buy genuine Roman coins and bury them for future antiquarians to discover. Like much in his extravagant life, this house was a plaything. The inscription from Wordsworth that he chose to go over the door both resonates and dissonates.

The spot was made by nature for herself:
The travellers know it not, and t'will remain

Unknown to them; but it is beautiful:
And if a man should plant his cottage near,
Should sleep beneath the shelter of its trees,
And blend its waters with his daily meal,
He would so love it, that in his death-hour
Its image would survive among his thoughts.

Nature no longer has this spot to herself, because if 'travellers knew it not' in Halliday's time, they certainly do now it's in the hands of the National Trust. But had he not the wealth and hubris to claim and cultivate this wild place like a Devonshire Kubla Khan, I would probably have never come to know it myself.

I'm deep in reminiscence when I hear a familiar bright, clear sound above the roar of water, and see the whirring wings and direct flight of a brown-backed bird, flying fast and low upstream. It lands on a mossy boulder. I'm delighted and relieved, because I know I'm within a few metres of the place I first encountered this species.

The European dipper, *Cinclus cinclus,* is both smart and dumpy, with a deep body the size of a tennis ball, and wings that seem at least three sizes too small. It has a short tail, habitually cocked like that of a wren, and a strong but narrow beak. Its plumage is mostly chocolate brown, except for a neat white bib and a rufous cummerbund.

The name describes both the bird's characteristic bobbing movements while it perches on riverside rocks, and its hunting style, which involves repeated plunges into shallow, fast-flowing water. Down there, it walks upstream along the riverbed, turning gravels, probing crevices. The hard part of all this is staying submerged despite plumage that traps air. Dippers have relatively huge feet, with long, gripping toes, which help them cling to rocky riverbeds, and underwater those short, triangular wings, which have to work so hard in flight, can be angled in such a way that the flow helps to press them down. Rather than fighting the river, the dipper harnesses its energy.

The bird on the rock plunges in, and reappears after four or five seconds, flitting back to the same perch. It repeats the manoeuvre three times, then changes launch position. It'll be looking for almost any small aquatic prey: nymphs of a huge range of insects – river flies, dragonflies and damselflies, water beetles, worms and leeches, small fish and later in the spring, tadpoles. While dippers are widespread birds, present the length and breadth of the British Isles, their large appetites and hunting technique mean that they are closely associated with swift-flowing, shallow, rocky rivers with clean clear water and healthy populations of invertebrates – so they are not as common as they might be. Not seeing one today, though, would have been devastating.

I cross a bridge to a nub of rock that separates the East Lyn from the Hoaroak Water immediately above their confluence. The Hoaroak is a gorge with stair-like cascades and slides, whose flow kicks and thrashes against its confines. A wren singing close to the water seems to be doing so in a higher than usual pitch, which makes sense, in order to be heard. The songs and calls of many riverine birds – dippers, kingfishers, grey wagtails – have this quality, and great tits, whose variable songs have been the subject of intensive research, are known to sing higher in areas with continuous traffic noise, so it's not fanciful to imagine that a population of a highly sedentary species like the wren might evolve a local song variation in such a noisy habitat.

I make a detour up to the road because there is a layby I want to visit. There are two on the A39 above Watersmeet. One is a long parking bay hewn from the rock and the other, on the side of the road overhanging the valley, is much smaller and used for staff cars. In this inauspicious spot there is a thing of genuine wonder.

It is called the No Parking Tree. An idiosyncratic name for a most unusual being. Both its English and its scientific name, *Karpatiosorbus* (formerly *Sorbus*) *admonitor*, refer to a sign that was nailed to it at the time it was first noticed in the 1930s. A careful survey revealed around 100 further specimens in the Watersmeet valley, and that, ecologists have concluded, is the entire population of this ultra-local form. It's a whitebeam, part of a group that also includes rowans and service trees, with a well-known predisposition to mutation, hybridisation and speciation. In 2009 molecular genetic analysis confirmed it as a species in its own right, and instantly one of the rarest trees in the world. At the same time, a further six new whitebeam species and hybrids were discovered and named in Wales.

The No Parking Tree grows with no fanfare and no signage, close against a stone wall covered in ivy-leaved toadflax. I have to be honest: it's seen better days. The trunk has split, a huge piece has fallen away at the back, and there's an enormous cavity in the main trunk. Its outer bark is rough, cracked and split, lichen covered and peeling. Buds on a spray of branches at the top suggest it is still just about alive, but it is little more than a husk. I begin to step away, when two impish forms helter-skelter around the trunk, and alight just long enough for me to glimpse a lick of flame on each head, then off again in a dizzy, spiralling chase. Goldcrests. I interpret their brief hesitation as an indication I should look again, and from this new angle I see the gaping aperture in the trunk differently. It reminds me of a *sheela-na-gig* – one of the fantastically lewd female figures carved into some old churches: some fat, some skinny, but all displaying eye-wateringly enlarged vulvas. Whether they were intended as a warning against lustful thoughts or to embrace Pagan representations of birth and fertility, nobody really knows.

Slightly self-consciously I lean in and sniff the blackened inner wall of the trunk. It looks charred, but there's no smell to suggest it's been burned. There's a streak of white fungus, a small troop of woodlice and more of those brown snails. A braid of ivy stems, rooted in the base of the cavity is growing up through the place where the tree's heart once was. Some of the tarry lining of the cavity is peeling away. I press a finger to the pale timber underneath and it yields easily. It is saturated and spongy, and when I press harder, green water runs out over my fingers. This rarest of beings is in a parlous state, but water is going to be as much part of its decay as it has been part of its life. It's not dying, so much as transforming. When I withdraw my hand, the water drips from my fingertips onto ground that slopes steeply down. There it will mingle with the rain to run through the woodrush and the ferns, through leaf litter and humus into cracks in the rock, across footpaths, over the bedrock. I wonder how long until it makes the river? Perhaps it won't in this cycle – it might be drawn into roots, or cushions of mosses, or fungal hyphae. It might be sipped by a wood mouse or bristle-tailed collembolan. It might be evaporated and rain down again in another country altogether.

Back down by the river I meet four figures wearing red drysuits, helmets and buoyancy aids and carrying throwlines. Two of them, a man with short grey hair, blue eyes and smile lines, and a small dark-haired woman with pink cheeks, grin as I approach. They exude an air of health, competence and kindliness, and I ask if they are fire crew. Swift water rescues often fall to the fire service, and they train routinely. It turns out, though, that these are members of Exmoor Search and Rescue team: 'Though when it comes to water', says the man, 'it's mostly search and recovery. Two already this year.' It's an extraordinarily selfless thing they do, given that for all their verve and positivity, their call-outs don't always end happily. I ask if the fatalities were related to the recent heavy rain. The woman shakes her head. 'No. Just people who decided that they'd had enough and chose the river as a way out.'

I climb a short way up the side of the Hoaroak, finding a place to perch next to a rocky slide where I can watch water the same pale green as recycled Spanish glass sliding past. The sun has come out and clouds of gnats appear from nowhere. There's a slight upkick in the middle of the flow, where the water fins up like the back of a whale, and in another it spouts and splays like a rooster tail. The water goes through all this chaos and comes out perfectly clear.

Sunlight illuminates billowing clouds of vapour, and I dwell on what the search-and-rescue woman said. I recognise the tug of very deep, very clear or very powerful water. Those childhood years in Germany involved a lot of ferry crossings. We'd take a night boat from Ostend or Flushing, and some mornings I would climb on the stern rail, feel the shudder of the huge ship engines, and lean just a little further than felt safe over the dazzling white and aquamarine turmoil of the wake. It wasn't a death wish that I was experiencing, though – quite the opposite.

We never talked about death when I was growing up. That's not unusual – western culture generally fails hopelessly in this respect and Christian indoctrination with its promises of everlasting life did nothing to prepare me for bereavement. Death was something to be resisted so absolutely that when it happened, suddenly and at a good age, to my dad's mother, I imagined she must have been found with a dagger in her heart. The idea that dying could be natural or peaceful or part of a larger process was anathema. I rejected it utterly when I read it, so gently done, in E.H. White's *Charlotte's Web* and again in Richard Adams' less gentle *Watership Down*, both of which turned the authors into monsters in my young mind. Then we saw my other grandma fade away with Parkinson's disease. She knew she was dying and tried to talk about it once, when I was there, but Mum wasn't having that. And so when the inevitable happened I rejected that too, refusing to cry and putting my mind so firmly elsewhere that all I remember of the funeral is the

daisy chain I made while sitting in the crematorium. I
made myself impervious to tricksy contextualisations of
death. Steinbeck's *The Red Pony* added another name to
my list of murderous heretic authors, another layer to the
brittle armour I was building.

Something had to knock that shell off, and in the end, it
was mountains. It could have been rivers, or the sea, or
even fast cars, but mountains came first. Aged 17 I was
selected to join an expedition to the Pyrenees, for which
we were required to get very fit, and learn navigation and
campcraft, climbing, rescue and first aid. And I found
myself exposed repeatedly to places where the difference
between life and death was a slight shift in bodyweight.
Adventure recast mortality almost overnight. It was no
longer the shadow, but the light that made life golden,
precious and magical. In the wake of that revelation came
another: that wrapped in every loss is a parting gift. A
reminder to live.

A short distance downstream of Watersmeet the river
narrows, and a pair of stone footings stand either side of a
thunderous rapid. These are all that remains of a bridge that
once stood here. There's a newer one just downstream with
a span three times as wide and very high, designed to
accommodate a vast quantity of water. The stonework is
teeming with hundreds of those same flat-whorled brown
snails. On a bench on the riverside path close to the bridge
is a solitary sodden workboot, brown leather, left foot, and
in it a tightly knotted green bag of dog shit. It's so *placed*, I
wonder if it might actually be art.

Downstream the river jinks and gleams about a garden of
mossy boulders. It has an air of docility and permanence,
which is entirely misleading. I pass the place where a
stoneware ginger beer bottle is embedded as a memorial to
a small mineral water factory that stood here, drawing water
whose radioactivity was once believed to be efficacious in
the treatment of gout. There's barely a trace of the building

now. It was obliterated the same summer night as the old
bridge almost 70 years ago.

In mid August 1952 the holiday season on the North Devon
coast was in full swing and the population of Lynmouth had
trebled to around 1,200 with the annual influx of visitors
drawn to 'the prettiest seaside village in Britain'. The first
half of the month had been a washout. Fifteen centimetres
of rain in two weeks was disappointing even by famously
soggy British summer standards. But no one could have
predicted the apocalyptic rain of 15th August. In total
around 23cm (an estimated 90 million tonnes) of water fell
in a matter of hours on the edge of Exmoor. Witnesses
report a sky of purple, black and dirty yellow, and rain so
hard it was painful on the skin. It fell on land that was
already waterlogged, and thus swept straight into the
brimming tributaries of the East and West Lyn.

To give a little perspective, the entire Lyn catchment is
just 100 square kilometres, and yet the volume of flow
recorded that night had only twice been exceeded by
extreme high-water events in the Thames, which drains
an area almost 100 times larger. The resulting flood event
remains among the most intense recorded anywhere in
the world. The East and West Lyn passed through mainly
wooded valleys and under a total of 31 bridges before
converging a couple of hundred metres from the sea, in
the centre of Lynmouth itself. The West Lyn dropped
steeply in the last few hundred metres, then entered a
Victorian culvert designed to create more space in the
village for homes and businesses, including several
romantic villa hotels.

The torrents that poured off the moor that evening
contained not just water, but huge quantities of debris. As
water, soil, boulders, trees and dislodged masonry hurtled
downstream, the culvert was blocked, and water and flotsam
began to pour through Lynmouth's narrow streets. Upstream,

felled trees in full leaf became snagged in the many bridges, trapping further vegetation, boulders and soil and forming temporary dams. Between eight and ten o'clock in the evening, water behind some blockages on the West Lyn rose more than 18m, or six domestic storeys, above normal levels. When these obstructions gave way, the surges of water were powerful enough to turn 50-tonne boulders into gigantic waterborne wrecking balls. Survivors describe an avalanche of rock and water roaring down the valley in fading light. In Lynmouth the greengrocer's shop and the chapel took the full force of that surge. The greengrocer and his wife, their neighbour and her nephew were swept from the buildings and against the Lyndale Hotel where, miraculously, quick-thinking staff and guests were able to haul them in through windows, before fleeing upstairs. A few minutes later the shop and the chapel were gone, and the river was surging through the lower two storeys of the hotel, forcing 60 people into an upper corridor. It was now fully night, and the electricity had cut out. There was no chance of rescue until the water dropped or daylight came. They eked out a handful of Christmas candles, not knowing whether the structure below them would hold. At around two o'clock in the morning, the back of the hotel collapsed with another horrifying roar, but the main part stood firm.

Having seen the harbour overwhelmed and the entire village fleet swept from its moorings, fisherman Ken Oxenham raced uphill to find his wife and child, climbing through the woods because the road was washing away. The three of them then scrambled to higher ground and watched as an entire row of cottages below 'folded like a pack of playing cards', illuminated by flashes of lightning. Above the tumult they were able to hear the screams of people they knew well being swept out to sea. More houses were erased further up the West Lyn at Barbrook, where the water took four members of the postman's family, the two boys holidaying with them,

their neighbour and two young Australian tourists she had
offered to shelter – all carried away with the wreckage when
the West Lyn rose six metres in minutes. Cars descending
Countisbury Hill in the darkness plunged into seething water
where once there had been road.

By morning, the survivors emerged into a scene of
unimaginable devastation. A photo now displayed in the
flood memorial hall shows the guests of the Lyndale Hotel
on the veranda, waiting their turn to leave while Beryl Eyres,
the greengrocer's wife, a small figure in long skirts and a
shawl, a handbag over her shoulder, is helped down a ladder
because the ground in front of the hotel was gone, leaving a
chasm of rock and dirt.

Thirty-four people died in the disaster. The water was as
water is, indiscriminate, taking nine men, sixteen women
and nine children, souls aged three months to eighty years.
Twenty-three were locals, eleven were holiday makers.
Bodies washed up for days – some were never found.
Twenty-eight bridges and more than a hundred buildings
were destroyed, including roughly a quarter of properties in
Lynmouth. The homes of 420 people in the wider district
were lost.

Meteorologists, hydrologists and geologists have since
identified several factors that added to the scale of the
Lynmouth disaster. The moorland soils on the parts of
Exmoor where the East Lyn rises are shallow and were
already saturated before that fatally intense downpour. The
geomorphology of the catchment, and that ill-advised
Victorian culvert, undoubtedly exacerbated matters. And
questions about the nature of the rain cast a further cloud
over the whole appalling business. Between 1949 and 1952,
a project known as Cumulus was being carried out jointly
by the Royal Air Force and the Department of Meteorology
at Imperial College London. Project Cumulus was an
investigation into the possibility of weather manipulation,
and in particular whether rain might be created artificially.

Cloud seeding is a controversial technique that usually involves spraying salt, dry ice or silver iodide into clouds to serve as nuclei around which water might condense into droplets big enough to fall as rain. The last of the seeding flights carried out as part of Project Cumulus took place out of RAF Cranfield on 14th August 1952 – the day before the Lynmouth flood. Reports written prior to that day suggest things had been going well, and on 14th August itself after Pilot Alan Yates sprayed salt into clouds over Bedfordshire, he claims scientists congratulated him for triggering the heaviest rain for years in Staines, 50 miles away. But following news from Lynmouth, said Yates, jubilation turned to stony silence. A television documentary about the project, already recorded, was never aired.

Could it be that attempts to induce rainfall in the preceding weeks contributed to the saturated ground conditions on Exmoor? Or that flights the day before the flood concentrated that last devastating deluge? These questions were raised in a BBC Radio 4 documentary, *The Day they Made it Rain*, in 2001, along with a patchwork of anecdotes, oral testimony and circumstantial evidence. The timings are striking, as is the alleged disappearance of documents pertaining to the tests, noted by former North Devon MP Tony Speller when he attempted his own investigation. The alleged disappearance of the classified files is not proof of a causative link, but certainly suggests serious anxiety over the possibility. Meteorologist Philip Eden has since countered that Lynmouth had suffered at least two previous severe floods, in the seventeenth and eighteenth centuries, and highlighted similarities with the 2004 flooding of Boscastle in Cornwall, which occupies a similar, naturally vulnerable hydrological setting. Furthermore, the depression that brought the rain over Exmoor in 1952 was hundreds of miles across – altogether a different scale to the cloud-by-cloud treatment described by pilots flying for Project Cumulus, which took place 150 miles away. On the other hand, US weather scientists claimed as early as the 1950s that seeding with silver iodide could trigger rain up to 300 miles away.

The potential advantages of both rainmaking and cloud clearing are myriad. In the US, experiments with cloud seeding have been conducted since at least 1946, with the results always subject to some dispute. In China, cloud seeding, first trialled under the enthusiastic aegis of Mao Zedong, has been routine since the 1960s, and in 2008 the technology was credited with keeping the skies clear for the opening ceremony of the Beijing Olympics. In July 2021 the National Centre for Meteorology of the United Arab Emirates claimed success in generating artificial rain in Dubai during a heatwave using salt and drones programmed to deliver electrical charges into clouds. In 2022 Chinese authorities expect to activate Project Tianhe (Sky River), a scheme to carry billions of tonnes of water vapour north each year from the Yangtze Basin to the Yellow River Basin – an area regularly beset with drought. A judicious increase in rainfall, the thinking goes, could support a greatly increased human population in the Yellow River catchment. But weather modification on this scale may also have regional implications for the wetlands of the Qinghai–Tibet Plateau, and other major rivers including the Mekong, Brahmaputra and Salween, whose headwaters gather in the area.

In Britain, most forays into weather manipulation have been military. Among the experiments conducted at Orford Ness in 1916 were trials in cloud-making aimed at disrupting anticipated raids by German flying machines, but by the 1940s interest switched to clearing clouds to facilitate take-offs and landings, and enhancing visibility over target zones. By the early 1950s, rainmaking was on the agenda. At a meeting in the London War Office in 1953, visiting American meteorologist Irving P. Krick described the potential military advantages of rainmaking, including the encumbrance of enemy troops and darkest of all, the enhanced distribution of radioactive contamination following an atomic-bomb detonation.

The clear-up and rebuilding of Lynmouth took six years. More than 100,000 tonnes of debris were removed and the largest boulders had to be blown up, it being impossible to shift them by mechanical means. Several further buildings were demolished to make space for a new, massively enlarged channel, which looks out of all proportion to the river running through it, even after a wet winter. It's the kind of space and respect afforded to alpine rivers, and should be reassuring, but it sits uncannily here. A reminder, like the exhibition in the flood memorial hall, of events that are fading from living memory and of unanswered questions which lurk like the premonition of a nightmare in an otherwise sweet dream.

Hollowing

Siphon *A gap in a riverbed through which water flows, but in which flotsam of all kinds, including swimmers, can become wedged. Siphons most commonly form under or between boulders, but in limestone landscapes they might also connect with underground systems.*

We speak of geological time as if rock were the epitome of durability. It isn't. Where rock meets water, it is water that wins in time, every time, and there are few places in England where this is more obviously true than the Yorkshire Dales. Hollowness is ubiquitous here; a limestone landscape riddled with caves and pots and channels. You can even watch them forming in many rivers and becks, where below most drops, you can find circular dishings in the rock, some shallow, some deep, some containing pebbles conscripted to the river's work; swirling and scouring, day and night. These hollowings range from thimble-size to cathedral-scale and vary in form from saucers, thrones and toilet bowls, to caverns and canyons.

The first time I paddled the River Wharfe as a novice we finished up at Linton Falls – an impressive, tiered drop not far from the visitor hub village of Grassington. I was riding an endorphin high, relieved to be off the water and just watching a handful of the club's more experienced paddlers contemplate the final drop. The river was relatively low, its bones exposed, turning what can be a thunderous chasm into a more technical challenge – a kinked, restricted slot, hemmed in by angular blocks and walls. In the end, only Lyndon was up for it. I loved watching him paddle – as a slalomist his technique was so precise you seldom saw any effort; he moved like a dancer totally at ease with his partner, the river. Safety cover was set as a precaution, with no expectation that it would be needed – Lyndon was someone folk generally watched to learn from rather than to look after. When his boat jolted to a sudden stop halfway down the first drop, he looked so surprised, I laughed. But no one else found it funny. The mood had changed in an instant from goofy to dead sober.

Lyndon was in a classic 'pin' situation – his boat had found a space between jutting rocks that might have been made to measure. He was upright and stable, but partially blocking the flow with his body so that water colliding with his back fountained up over his shoulders.

The exposed rocky platform on both sides of the river was suddenly humming with activity. Everyone seemed to have something in their hands: throwlines, tapes, karabiners.

'Can't he just get out and swim?' I asked Roy.

'Not here, there might be siphons.'

I began to understand the danger. In higher flows it is highly unlikely that a swimmer would be drawn into one of these lethal features, but at this level, with so much of the rapid's geological anatomy close to the surface, no one wanted to take a chance. Low water brings its own dangers, and this rapid has claimed several lives.

I stepped away, feeling useless, weighted by ignorance. Signals and body language made clear that angles, plans and contingencies were being communicated over the rush of water. With the river pounding past his ears, Lyndon probably couldn't hear much. He waited, grim-faced, beginning to sag under the unrelenting pressure.

In the space of three minutes a line was set across the river and used to pass a karabiner with a second line to where Lyndon could reach it and clip it to the harness of his buoyancy aid. He was then able to release his spraydeck, tip sideways out of his boat and into the channel. He was whisked along, and swung into the next eddy, safe on the end of the line. Laughter was quick to return. But in those moments several things had happened: I had seen the hard-wired competence underlying the happy-go-lucky antics of my new friends; I had gained some inkling of the loneliness of a trapped paddler; and I had learned perhaps the most important lesson anyone putting themselves in a river can know – simply that it will keep coming.

It's not necessarily the speed, volume or power of a river that wins, but its relentlessness. It needs no breath, no sleep, no pause to stretch or shake. And in time, without fuss or ceremony, it will take heat from flesh, life from limb, tree from bank, rock from channel, mountain from continent. It will hollow the land. And it demands total respect.

CHAPTER 3

Oak-water

My trip to North Devon has left me spooked. The place was very much as I remembered, but going back has unpicked way too many threads. If that was a starting point, it wasn't at all clear where I should go next. So I came home.

A few mornings later I realise that there is another source I could try – one close enough that I can explore it right away, in wellies and pyjamas, mug of coffee in hand. Close enough that I will hear Lochy yell from the house if he needs me.

Home since 2009 has been a semi-detached cottage built into the side of an old quarry, 150m from the Yorkshire Derwent. Having scrutinised flood probability maps when we were house hunting, Roy insisted on elevation, and we settled on a place 20 metres above the level of the river, where it flows through a sinuous notch in the landscape known as Kirkham Gorge. He was willing to accept the less overt risk of a spring that rises just opposite the house.

The spring is marked on the map as a tiny blue circle, and when we first moved here I went in search of it right away, hoping to see water welling bright and clear. Instead, after wading, ducking, weaving and struggling to balance, I found an expanse of liquorice-coloured ooze, trapped between blocks of broken brickwork.

It's much the same today. At first I thought the masonry might have been dumped 50 years ago when our house and next door were converted from a row of tiny two-up-two-down quarry workers' cottages. There are half a dozen slabs of mortared brickwork, suggesting the remains of a very small building. A coal shed perhaps, or a privy. But later I read the first-hand account of a woman named Val, who lived in cottage number three as a child until 1951 and remembered her mother collecting water here. Perhaps this was a tiny well- or pump house.

Today, the bricks have gained a thick coverlet of moss and other woodland plants, including primroses in full flower, and there's a scattering of pale feathers that draws my eye to a space under one of the toppled walls – a low hovel – crammed with a couple of ripped plastic feed bags and the remains of a woodpigeon.

I follow the water as it seeps from the first black pool through a bank of spoil, from which a small channel flows. The water clears astonishingly fast, and within a few paces it runs bright and swift over sand. It passes a willow, which previously lived in a half barrel by the front door when we moved in. It was the rootstock to which a dainty ornamental pink-leaved variety, known I think as 'flamingo', had been grafted. The fact that this chimera never grew unsettled me, so one day I took some loppers and decapitated it, removing the graft entirely, and transplanted the stem out of the barrel and into the damp ground by the spring. I watched with glee as it shot skyward at the most astonishing rate. It won't grow huge because every two years the electricity company come and cut it back from the overhead cables, but its unshackled vigour makes me smile. From the willow, the spring runs past the place where we park our cars, past our fruit trees and Lochy's swing. In summer it is surrounded by dense beds of brooklime and knapweed, and shoulder-high meadowsweet, figwort, willowherb and wild raspberry where once there was lawn – I let that rip too. The flow continues over and under the ground for the next 100m, then disappears under the railway and into the swampy woodland alongside the river.

The Yorkshire Derwent is one of four English rivers of the same name, and is longer than the others, despite being less known than its Cumbrian and Derbyshire namesakes. Their

name is from the Celtic *dar* for oak – indeed some locals still
call it the Darwent. On a map of North Yorkshire, the county
outline is shaped like an ancient spreading oak, broader than
it is tall, with a stout trunk. The city of York lies at the top of
the trunk, the western bough is the Dales. The upper half of
the eastern bough is the Moors and the lower part is the
edge of the Wolds. The Derwent runs between them, then
down the side of the 'trunk' like ivy. It is a forgotten river – it
has no dale named for it (that honour goes instead to its
tributary, the Rye) and remains little visited despite its
proximity to the tourist hotspots of the coast, York and the
Moors. Yet despite its lack of celebrity, the Yorkshire Derwent
is remarkable in many ways. The strangest is that it rises in
sight of the sea, then turns almost immediately inland, taking
a detour of almost 240km before finally reaching an estuary
as part of the Humber. We live on a bend of the middle river,
where the water still flows resolutely away from the coast,
through a gorge incised into the land when water pooling
upstream after the Ice Age found a way out. Kirkham Gorge
is no longer the canyon it first was, but it is still a significant
feature in the landscape, 70m deep in places and forcing the
river and the adjacent railway into serpentine curves that
trains must take at a crawl.

There are dozens of springs like ours along the gorge.
None of their courses are more than 250m long, but their
slow work has softened the topography from chasm to
sweeping valley. Those that are less choked with organic
material than our home spring are not black, but white with
calcium carbonate dissolved from the limestone bedrock
and deposited as calcite almost as soon as the water emerges
into air. This crusty mineral coats everything in its path over
the woodland floor: twigs, shells and cones – even quite
delicate organic matter can be petrified faster than it decays.
I have peeled rotting leaves from delicate crusts of calcite,
leaving perfect but impossibly fragile casts that show every
blemish and vein, but shatter as they dry.

I've never known the springs to run dry, and they are surely among the conveniences that made this a good place to live long before any of the buildings we know were here, and before the quarry, which yielded both lime and the honey-beige stone that constitutes the local vernacular construction material. The slope behind our house, into which the quarry was hacked over hundreds of years, forms part of a promontory around which the river makes a slight deviation as it enters the gorge. On that promontory is a huge rectangular earthwork, thought to date to the Iron Age. The view from there is now largely obscured by trees, but in winter you can see the water sliding below and for the people that lived or worked here (we don't know if it was a settlement, a strategic location or a place of industry) two thousand years ago, the river must have been vital for transport and trade as well as a source of food.

On the other side of the quarry behind our house, archaeologists have identified the remains of six Roman age kilns, once used to produce no-frills, wheel-thrown platters, bowls and storage vessels, the fourth-century equivalent of IKEA basics. Crambeck ware, as it is now known, was available in three colours – grey, red and parchment – and was used as far north as Hadrian's Wall. The location of the pottery would have been dictated by the availability of suitable clays dumped by glacial meltwater and by the river, which served as a transit route, a supply line, a channel of communication, commerce and opportunity, and a link to the rest of the world.

In 2008 Roy and I travelled with a group of kayaking friends to India. Our destination was a remote and spectacular tributary of the Indus called the Zanskar, also known as the copper river. Getting there took a week. A long-haul flight to Delhi, and then a connecting flight to Leh – capital of the Himalayan region of Ladakh and the world's highest commercial airport. The runway is short, and surrounded by a cirque of immense peaks – I've never experienced a landing that felt more like being dropped. After a day provisioning in Leh, we boarded a bus with a smashed-out back window, which admitted fumes from the exhaust, meaning everyone on board was nauseous within an hour, and we wondered how we were going to endure three days of this. But soon we understood. This bus was a replacement for one stuck on the other side of a bridge after a section of road had washed away in a recent flood. To get to it we had to unload and cross an improvised bridge made from a couple of hastily felled trees, to which were lashed a dozen old doors. Thirty centimetres below was the ferocious little river – its waters thick and dark as mushroom soup. And yet across this bridge, with minimal fuss, were stepping youngsters in flipflops and smartly dressed seniors in polished brogues. We followed with our boats and our duffels and our drybags.

For three days we rode on, gaining altitude all the while, travelling more than three quarters of the way around a huge loop to the glacial source of the Zanskar. We passed one night in Kargil, and a second camped on a vast washout plain near Rangdum, where we slept badly, cold and lightheaded from altitude. The time it took us to reach this remote area served us usefully as an acclimatisation period, but this isolation is a fact of life for the local people and a major factor in the unique identity of the Zanskar region. The population is tiny and scattered. Most Zanskaris practise Tibetan Buddhism and subsistence farming, and for centuries the population has been maintained at a level the land, on the very limits of cultivability, can sustain, with growth curbed by a strong monastic tradition and polyandrous marriage. It felt a world away, even from Leh. And yet, given good water levels, crack teams of paddlers have been known to make the descent back down to Leh in a single day. This wasn't an option for the locals, but in winter, when metres of snow block the high passes and make even the lengthy road trip impossible, the river offers a way both in and out, used for everything from

medical emergencies to children returning from school for
the winter holiday. This extraordinary 100km ice road, known
as the Chadar, has also become an attraction for adventure
trekkers. But its days are numbered. On day four of our five-
day descent of the river, we came to the place where a new
road was being dynamited from the cliffs. If you go there
now – in real life or via Google Earth® – you will see this
road as the river's pale twin, matching it flex for flex, curve for
curve, only high and dry. Meanwhile climate change is
thinning winter ice and making the Chadar an increasingly
perilous undertaking.

Picking my way up and down my home slopes of the Derwent
Valley, following the springs as they come and go above
ground, it strikes me that this was the kind of exploring that I
did as a child, when any clump of scrub, any gap in a hedge,
any climbable tree was an invitation. I grew up believing that
exploring was in my blood because my great-grandfather,
Lichfield Henry Moseley, known as Lich, had been 'an explorer
in Africa'. I used to picture him in pith helmet, hacking
through jungles, canoeing great rivers, and sitting down to
smoke with tribal elders. All this was partly true. Lich did travel
extensively in West Africa, initially for the Royal Niger
Company and later for Lever Brothers, of which he ended up
a director. His 1899 map of the western tributaries of the
Benue River descending from the highlands of eastern Nigeria
and Cameroon is archived with the Royal Geographical
Society. In letters and reports since collated by my uncle, I read
how Lich claimed to have overcome the (justifiable) hostility
of the indigenous Benue people with firework displays, and to
have quested further upriver than locals were willing to go,
seemingly unconcerned as to their reasons. I wasn't sure that I
wanted to know more, and a little more research seemed to
justify my unease. It is now clear that Lever Brothers' much-
vaunted progressiveness at Port Sunlight in Merseyside did not
extend to Africa. As managing director of Huileries du Congo

Belge, a subsidiary of Lever Brothers set up in 1911 to establish palm oil plantations in the region, my great-grandfather objected to meaningful increases in local wages. HCB later became notorious for its use of forced labour. Lich died before any of his descendants living now were born, so I have no way of knowing what kind of man he might have been if he'd been born in different times, been taught different values, followed a different career, or just asked more questions. I will be sure to tell Lochy about him one day.

A century on, Lich's story is not easy reading. But his accounts emphasise one thing I can relate to. That to travel in a wild land – as everywhere once was – the easiest way is often to take to the water. The ice-bound Zanskaris did it. And since the Bronze Age my neighbours-through-time on the Derwent have been doing it too. A river is a highway.

On the oldest surviving chart of Britain, the fourteenth-century Gough Map, our local town of Malton is clearly visible, looking somewhat more significant than it does today at the confluence of the *Fl Derwent* (the Latin abbreviation *fl* is for *Flumen,* river) and the *Fl Rie* (the River Rye). The name of the Gough Map refers not to the chart's author, but to one of its owners. Richard Gough was an eighteenth-century antiquarian, but the map was already 400 years old when it came into his possession. The origins of the map and the manner of its making in the late 1300s or early 1400s are lost, but experts have surmised that it was created as an administrative resource rather than for display or decoration. Yorkshire and Lincolnshire are depicted with particular accuracy – perhaps, thinks Gough scholar Elizabeth Solopova, because English central government of the day employed a lot of men from the region. York, named as *Eborienc* on the map, was in effect the capital of the north, so its environs and those en route between York and London were well known.

The features of the map that stand out most are the rash of red-roofed settlements and the rivers. The latter are massively enlarged – like the probing shoots of some vigorous vine. Roads are marked in spidery red lines. Time has faded the original ink, but even if these lines were once more conspicuous than they now appear, they were finely drawn and insubstantial – fittingly so, because the road network of medieval times had changed little since the Roman occupation and it was to be a further 500 years before the canal and railway networks offered any kind of transport system to rival the rivers.

In 1891 the *Yorkshire Weekly Post* ran a series of articles on Yorkshire rivers by travel writer Tom Bradley. The series was later collected into a series of books accompanied by hand-drawn maps giving a 'birds-eye view of the river and the roads adjoining.' It is a reprint of one of these, *No. 6: The Derwent*, that my neighbour Anne thrusts into my hands one day, and I am immediately captivated. Bradley's text is of its time, with a strong focus on churches, fishing and social stereotyping – but the map is a wonder. I love a book with a good map, and this one is a beauty, unfolding vertically over six and a half concertinaed pages. I pore over tiny sketches showing the old station at the bottom of our lane where Anne and her husband Edmund now live, and familiar bridges and weirs, islands and meanders, grand houses and mills. Because the ribbon of water running from page to page compels it, I follow with my finger, up past the suspension footbridge at Huttons Ambo, which children love because it wobbles, past Malton and Norton, under a railway that no longer exists, and through a long section of convoluted meanders over the Vale of Pickering and then into higher ground, weaving between forests and riggs, the topography so cleverly rendered it's like a pen-and-ink version of Google Earth®. Eventually, at the very top of the topmost page you come to a place high on Fylingdales Moor called Derwent Head. Seeing it, I realise with some shame that I have never been there.

Finding the source of a river is not as simple as it seems. Most rivers have tributaries, and so each time you encounter a confluence on such a quest, you have to make a decision about which arm to follow. If the river is rain fed, the true source is likely to be close to a high point in the land, a watershed. But a spring can rise at almost any altitude. The 'true' source of a river is the one furthest from the mouth. The mouth can be either an estuary or a confluence with another river whose upstream distance is longer. It you take a strict approach, this means the source can't be identified until all other contenders have been measured. It's a bit unromantic but at least it's clear, right? Well, no. In some cases, tradition takes precedent – not least in the case of the Thames. The spot known as Thames Head, marked with a stone in Trewsbury Mead at Kemble near Cirencester in Gloucestershire and recognised by the Environment Agency and the Ordnance Survey, isn't the true source. A stronger claim is Seven Springs near Coberly, more than 22km further from Thamesmouth than Thames Head. Furthermore, these springs flow year round, while visitors to Trewsbury Mead often find no sign of water at all. If you visit Seven Springs, you'll see water issuing from several holes in the base of a rocky outcrop, and a stone plaque set into a wall and with the inscription *Hic tuus o Tamesine Pater septemgeminus fons* – 'Here, O Father Thames, is your sevenfold spring'. To me, this is a runaway winner over the mundane and officious inscription at Thames Head, reading thus: *THE CONSERVATORS OF THE RIVER THAMES/1857–1974/THIS STONE WAS PLACED HERE TO MARK THE SOURCE OF THE RIVER THAMES.*

The claims of both Thames Head and Seven Springs can be trumped by those of another tributary, which rises inconspicuously, further upstream still, in the grounds of a college for students with disabilities and special needs near Ullenwood. This site is close to the Thames-Severn watershed, and while it may be the truest source in textbook terms, Seven Springs is more romantic and reliable, and

Thames Head speaks for tradition. I guess you can take your pick.

We plan a family expedition to Derwent Head in early summer, driving up onto the Moors and hiking up the other side of the watershed alongside the dwindling flow of Eller Beck, which drains into the Yorkshire Esk. We track the perimeter fence of the Fylingdales Early Warning Station, a gigantic grey trapezoid hulk containing a solid-state phased array radar system that scans the heavens for incoming missiles and who knows what else. It's an incongruous landmark – both a symbol of Anglo-American cooperation and a brutal reminder that all is not well between humankind.

The moor is alarmingly dry. The areas that should be wet are marked by patches of bog cotton, flower heads shaking vigorously in the wind. The peaty soil is cracked, crumbling and charcoal-coloured from decades of heather burning, and the wind casts sand, dust and fragments of peat into our eyes – Lochy catches the worst of it, being closer to the ground. With his eyes scrunched tight he stumbles often and then pitches full length into a clump of bog cotton and just lies there, face down. Fearing a mutiny I pick my way over the tussocks, mentally auditing options for bribes and cajolery. But when I reach him, he is peering into the thatch of vegetation, in which, by dint of it being precisely in front of his nose when he fell, he has spotted a miniature botanical marvel, a tiny round-leaved sundew *Drosera rotundifolia*. Its half dozen lurid green leaves are no bigger than Lochy's fingernails, but they are perfectly formed, each with a bristling of red hairs and minute beads of sticky liquor. We've kept carnivorous plants as curiosities from time to time, but this is the first he's seen in the wild. Watching him lie there transfixed, I'm reminded of Charles Darwin's assertion in 1860 that 'at the present moment, I care more about *Drosera* than the origin of all the species in the world.' It was Darwin who first proved that the snaring and dissolution of insects by the leaves of this species and its relatives is not accidental, but active carnivory, allowing the plants to occupy low-nutrient habitats that exclude many other species.

The mucilage of sundews has extraordinary adhesive and elastic properties that draw the attention of biomaterials researchers, and in the past it was used as a cough medicine and a love potion. I begin enthusing some of this to the boy, but he's not listening. He's just looking. It's not even that he's obsessing over the carnivory – the potted pet versions have sated his appetite for botanical violence. This time, he's just taken with its tiny perfection and the unlikeliness of having spotted it in all the vastness of the moor.

After an hour's slow climb we arrive at Derwent Head. The water that gathers in this boggy depression, marked by a large clump of cotton grass, is rain. More than a metre a year falls up here, and from the watershed you can see its destination, the North Sea, about eight miles away. But this water has much further to travel than that. Prior to the recent glacial period, the Derwent ran out more or less directly to the coast. But as glaciers advanced, what is now the North Sea became a wall of ice. As the ice began to melt, the river found its way blocked. Water pooled to form a huge lake, which eventually overtopped at its southern end and cut an escape route to the south, incising a gorge now known as Forge Valley. The lake drained and left the wide valley of Hackness.

This delightful fertile vale was home for many years to William Smith, often called the father of geology, who arrived after a period of financial woe that saw him serve a stint in debtors' prison. He was taken on as land agent to a wealthy benefactor named John Johnstone. It was a good move on Johnstone's part – Smith was still at Hackness when his contribution to science became widely acknowledged, and he is celebrated to this day in the lovely Rotunda Museum in Scarborough, one of the oldest purpose-built museums in the country, which Smith designed and where his legacy rests among an astonishing collection of Jurassic and more recent treasures.

The Forge Valley is now managed as a woodland nature reserve, with a long riverside boardwalk that protects the ground flora and makes the saturated ground passable. Walking it is like playing a primitive, untuned xylophone – every plank echoing the same pitch. In summer, speckled wood butterflies loop and spiral. The tassels of woodrush tickle your legs. Dragonflies of many kinds flicker and hurtle. The river here is five metres wide and the colour of black tea, but very clear. It drops steadily over occasional little weirs formed by fallen trees in varying states of decay, and between them are pools where small trout leap and jackknife. There's a popular dipping spot, where working and defunct rope swings of varying colour and vintage hang from the trees like ragged prayer flags. There are springs here too – lustrously clear water emerges from the wooded sides of the gorge with a pleasing trickle-chuckle and runs through thick beds of moss and fern to reach the river. Like those at home, each spring dumps calcite and their early courses appear as pale grey streaks through the wood.

At the foot of Forge Valley is a castle, once home of William Ayton, who gave his name to the villages east and west of the river. It was an impressive building, judging by the area covered by earthworks and the remains of medieval fishponds by the river, but the only part still standing is now a cowshed.

Having escaped from Hackness, the waters of the post-glacial Derwent spilled into the vale below but were still unable to reach the sea, so they pooled again, merging with flows coming from the western Moors and forming an even larger body of water now known as Lake Pickering. Lake Pickering eventually drained in a similar manner to Hackness, when its waters topped a low point at Kirkham and carved another gorge, to spill into the Vale of York. With miles to go (the last 30 via the Yorkshire Ouse and the

Humber) to reach the sea, the river's journey from Derwent Head is now more than 10 times longer than its pre-glacial course. And with barely 30m of descent below Forge Valley, the middle and lower Derwent became a dillydallying lowland creature, sprawling frequently into fen and carr.

We can't come to Derwent Head without also visiting the stone monument of Lilla Cross, which stands close by on the high point of Lilla Rigg, on an ancient medieval road which can still be trodden today. Lilla, we know from the writings of Bede and Florence of Worcester, was a seventh century Anglo-Saxon thane and minister in the court of King Edwin of Northumbria, whose palace is thought to have been at Buttercrambe on the middle Derwent. History might have overlooked Lilla, were it not for the manner of his death. On Easter Day 626, an assassin commissioned by the prince of Wessex talked his way to an audience with the king by posing as a messenger. Mid-message, he drew a concealed blade and lunged. Lilla, standing close by, flung himself in front of his king, and took the dagger in his chest. Such was the force of the attack the blade passed right though his body and into Edwin – all very *Game of Thrones*. Lilla died, but the king survived, and the experience is said to have contributed to his decision to convert to Christianity.

This does seem a fitting place for Lilla to be commemorated. Perhaps he was interred here, though the two round barrows are much older and the stone cross that stands on one of them is about 300 years too recent – perhaps it is a replacement, or a later tribute based on Lilla's historic significance. Perhaps it was placed with no thought of Lilla at all, and the association came later. But pausing by it now, more than a thousand years after it was erected, nearly 1,400 years since a blade skewered a brave man's chest, it marks this place, made as much of sky as of land, as significant. Just as the barrows do. Just as the early warning station does. Just as our coming here does. Just as the water gathering among the dancing cotton grass and ribboning away downhill does.

Derwent Head is only one of the river's roots. There are many more – a few rain hollows on the highest ground and literally hundreds of tiny becks and springs. There is a meadow in a valley called Deepdale on the edge of Dalby Forest where I once spent a frosty full-moon night listening to the distinctive voices of the springs that rise out of the surrounding wood. One that chuckles, another with a higher pitched giggle, another has a deeper note like a glass bottle being filled, another faster, falling over itself in its hurry to be on its way. These are the sources of the White Beck, which joins the Derwent above Hackness. I remember a sense of urgency that night – it mattered that I listened to those young spring voices as they chattered and laughed in the moonlight, because that water would never speak in quite the same way again. I wondered then how long it had spent under the ground before rising at my feet, and I wonder now where the water that rose that night has gone to.

White Beck is aptly named. Its water sheds calcite where it drops over fallen trunks to form shifting staircases of tufa. I have watched small brown trout waiting to climb these staircases – wriggling up through tangles of twigs and branches, jumping low steps or waiting below larger ones for the springs to begin pushing harder in winter, making the ascent swimmable.

Many more becks run though clefts that notch the edge of the Moors plateau. These too were formed by glacial meltwaters that have now dwindled to tiny flows, inhabiting valleys so steep you have to lunge between trunks of small twisted, moss-clad oaks to descend under control. The water at the bottom runs through chasms that are green with mosses and crevice-rooted bilberry, and often crisscrossed with trees that have fallen from above over the years.

The easternmost tributary of the Yorkshire Derwent, the River Hertford, is perhaps the least interesting to look at, being canalised for most of its length. But it deserves a mention for its sheer contrariness – it rises just 1,750m from

the sea, dawdles a short way north, then having seemingly
forgotten its job, turns west, away from the coast, until it
encounters the Derwent. The Hertford is also the river that
drains Star Carr – once on the shores of another large post-
glacial lake and site of some of the most spectacular
Mesolithic archaeology anywhere in the world. Preserved in
peat were artifacts made from bone and wood, including a
large number of harpoon points, the earliest evidence of
carpentry anywhere in Europe, and also what is thought to
be the oldest known built dwelling in Britain. Most haunting
of all though are the antler headdresses made from red deer
skulls, thought to be shamanic in function. The finds are
evidence of centuries of occupation, of intense seasonal
hunting and processing of animal carcasses, and a complex
culture involving ritual activity – all in the immediate
aftermath of the Ice Age 9,000 years ago.

In the Vale of Pickering, the Derwent doubles in volume
where it is joined by the River Rye, which drains a huge
area of the south-western Moors. The Rye and several of
its tributaries are flashy and flood-prone – as was the
Upper Derwent until the early nineteenth century, when a
5km channel excavated through the glacial deposits that
blocked the original, pre-Ice Age course of the river,
provided a shortcut to the sea. A sluice at the top ensures
that in low flows water continues down the established
channel of the Derwent, but in high levels, water is diverted
into an artificial channel called the Sea Cut, built as an
extension to Scalby Beck in 1804 to reduce the risk of
flooding in Ayton and to power mills at Scalby. Lower
down the Derwent though, after heavy rain, the middle
river still routinely turns as brown and opaque as milky
coffee, and bursts its banks.

The regularity of flooding along the course of the
Derwent through the Vales of Pickering and York means the
land either side is highly fertile, but not conducive to the
development of large settlements. In fact there are only two

on the middle river – the modest twin towns of Malton and Norton and the large village of Stamford Bridge. Further downstream, the space given over to the river because of this natural flooding means that the Lower Derwent remains one of the most intact and functional lowland river ecosystems in Europe.

This improbable watercourse is a source of pride and exasperation, fertility and detriment, pleasure and argument to those who know it well. But for most of its length, such people are surprisingly few. The lower river certainly has its devotees – mainly ecologists and birdwatchers – but the middle Derwent, instrumental in the creation of a landscape and central to human lives and livelihoods for millennia, has become a hidden river, unassuming, unvisited, unexplored, and generally remarked upon only when it overspills.

Groundwater

Spring A place where groundwater held in an aquifer emerges at surface level.

The steeply sloping sides of Kirkham Gorge are a mixture of woodland and pasture – the latter steep and studded with the little hillocks made by generations of yellow meadow ants. Being warmer and better drained than the surrounding turf, each one of these knee-high tumps is a microhabitat – a miniature raised garden of tiny plants. The ants themselves are small, mustard-coloured and mild-mannered, too busy with their own business to swarm or attack. In recent years several of these hillocks have been mechanically scraped from the hillside; an act I struggle to understand, given that the slope is too steep and uneven to be mown or cultivated, and the anthills do no harm to the sheep that graze here intermittently. So when I spot two men in orange high vis with a green digger on the slope, I fear more needless destruction, and the dog and I make a detour on our run to see what is going on. The men have already dug a substantial hole, and I explain by way of greeting and introduction that I can't help wondering what it's for. They say they're working for the water company, trying to locate a leak in a pipe running somewhere under the field.

I wonder aloud how they knew where to start and the younger man told me they had a rough idea, but the quickest way was to use the metal rods poking out of a pocket in the older man's overalls.

'You're *dowsing*?'

I'm astonished, but they tell me they do it all the time and nod into the hole to prove their point.

There's water there, welling gently, but no sign of pipework. Of all the places they could have sunk a hole in this large and topographically complex field, they hit running water first time. Not the pipe they were looking for, but emphatically a flow.

A few years ago I'd have rolled my eyes and moved on. I know I would – in fact I did when I met a couple divining ley lines at Byland Abbey. But age is making me more curious, not less, and ever more hungry for experience. I ask if I can have a go.

The older man hands the rods over and his colleague takes the dog's lead. The rods are copper L-shapes with long arms of about 35cm, and shorter ones in loose brass sleeves. I grasp the sleeves, one in each hand, feeling self-conscious and slightly absurd – as if I'm taking the controls of an imaginary spaceship. They suggest I walk off a bit and start somewhere that seems dry, so I move away to a slight rise, then turn around to face them again and hold the rods so the long arms rest parallel, pointing ahead of me. I walk, not towards the hole, but across the slope above, as slowly and as smoothly as I can. The rods are cool and inert – it's easier than I imagined to keep them still – they rest in their sleeves, steadied by their own weight. But then, abruptly, both are moving, in opposite directions. The one in my right, uphill hand, swings left; the other swoops right, and they cross and come to rest like the bars of a turnstile in front of me.

I yelp and stop moving.

The men exchange glances, seeming neither pleased nor surprised. I might as well have demonstrated the magic by which a light switch turns on a bulb.

I back up a step and come forward again. The rods waggle.

I look where I am – a little way uphill of the hole. It makes sense that there might be a springline here – the faintest depression in the slope, and perhaps a slightly greater concentration of rushes. But it's far from obvious, and while I've noticed the rushes before, there are clumps of them all over the hillside.

I look more closely at the rods. They are incredibly simple. The older man tells me he bought them cheaply online because they looked smart, but that others make their own out of wire coat hangers.

I make several more passes. The rods swivel every time I cross a line above and below Pete and Jack's hole. I tilt them a little, thinking that I might be making it happen myself by failing to hold them level. I know the reasons to be sceptical. I know science has never been able to account for this, except as a subconscious effect based on the dowser's sensitivity to other cues, to their expectations, and to the relatively high chance of finding water in a given terrain. I know the evidence of our senses is fallible. But it would be hard to imagine less woo-woo individuals than these two, and yet here they are, routinely dowsing as the best and fastest way to get their job done. I ask how they think it works, and they just shrug.

I went back a few days later. The tracks of the digger were still evident, and there were two heaps of disturbed ground. It seems they dug one more hole after I left, not far from the first. Both had been roughly backfilled, and in amongst the disturbed clods of the second hole were several fragments of terracotta pipe.

I've walked there many times since, back and forth. Some days I take my own rods, made from galvanised wire. They swivel as I cross every spring, and stream, and rushy slough, and in some other places too. I'm not directing them on purpose, but I can't deny I like it – so perhaps I am making it happen. Water is an imperative, and evolution equipped life with ways of finding it millions of years before a lineage of reasoning, self-aware bipedal apes appeared on the scene. Is it possible that the rods are helping us reconnect to a sense that was displaced by our intellect? I have no idea, but it doesn't seem crazy anymore. What was once a familiar tussocky hillside now feels more like the integument of a beast, over which I wander like a prospecting flea, seeking the rush of veins beneath the skin.

CHAPTER 4

Fly while we may

On a narrow bridge in a forest, two men meet. Both are fighters. Both are proud. One is a seven-foot powerhouse, the other lithe and sharp-witted as a fox. They duel, first with words and then with quarterstaffs, and find one another's measure in more ways than one. Before long, both are in the water. The giant claims a win but emerges from the river with a new destiny and a new name.

The meeting of Robin Hood and Little John is my favourite baptism story. The river serves a dual role, as rivers have done in stories since forever, as a boundary that divides the two men and the means by which they become bonded. In the 1980s TV adaptation *Robin of Sherwood*, liberally and deliciously laced with magic by screenwriter Richard Carpenter, the dunking also releases John Little from an enchantment placed on him by a Satan-worshiping Norman baron. Despite my exposure to a good measure of military patriotism, my somewhat rootless childhood left me with a half-formed sense of indigeneity. That show made me feel English to my bones, and filled in some gaps with older gods than the one we went to church for. I forgot them all for a while in the years that followed, but they never really left, and the words spoken to Michael Praed's Robin by a mysterious forest shaman in the guise of Herne the Hunter still haunt, inspire and reassure me in equal measure. *Nothing's forgotten. Nothing is ever forgotten.*

Whether you regard a river as a connector or a barrier is very much a matter of perspective. To drivers in traffic backed up either side of the two road bridges in the centre of York, the River Ouse is an obstacle. But York wouldn't exist if not for the river, which was far more amenable to movement than the fen that once largely surrounded the

city, and which served a role in shifting cargo until at least
the 1990s. In London, the Thames is a cultural divide as well
as a physical one, but also the city's greatest and oldest
natural asset.

This duality of rivers as both boundary and portal is
refrained through history and mythology. When Julius
Caesar and his army crossed the Rubicon in 49 BC, it was an
irrevocable act of war. Crossing the mythical Styx was part
of the journey to the classical underworld.

Rivers are natural places for jurisdictional borders
between anything from backyards to nations. In Britain
they have long been used as parish and county boundaries.
I'm walking one such today, close to the village of Maxey
on the Cambridgeshire–Lincolnshire border. The river was
straightened in the first half of the twentieth century, but
the county line still faithfully follows the old wiggling
course so that the water now flickers like a barcode from
county to county, with tiny snippets of Cambridgeshire
marooned on the Lincolnshire bank and vice-versa. The
river is the Welland, which crosses part of a huge agricultural
plain north of Peterborough, much of which was once fen.
The area has seen more than its share of administrative
boundary changes. Maxey was once part of the medieval
soke of Peterborough and the Nassaburgh Hundred, then
incorporated into the short-lived amalgamated county of
Huntingdonshire and Peterborough (of which Peterborough
itself was not part), then reallocated again to Cambridgeshire
(of which Cambridge was no longer part). I wonder what
locals say now, when asked where they are from.

The waters of the Welland once sprawled over a vast area of
fen, and along with the Nene, it fed the huge expanse of
Whittlesey Mere. This was once the largest lake in England: six
miles long by three miles wide, though never more than a few
feet deep, but it was wholly drained in 1852 to create rich
agricultural land. The Welland has been heavily modified
upstream too, and now runs through a series of dykes, cuts and

channels you could lose your mind trying to understand – even with the aid of schematics. Meanwhile, abstraction (including to the 1970s reservoir at Rutland Water) means the whole system carries much less water now than it once did. To my outsider's perspective this cartographic, hydrological and administrative mayhem lends a sense of nowhereness to the place.

I walk from West Deeping towards Helpston, along part of the route of a Roman road now known as Kings Street. Traversing the Welland floodplain must have posed a significant challenge to the original engineers – this short section of road now crosses no fewer than nine bridges over various cuts and channels. Under one of them, now dry, there is a plethora of centuries-old incised graffiti, including the words *J Clare Helpston 1811* carved by the peasant poet John Clare at 18 years of age when he was training to be a stonemason. But the most startling thing about the place today is that someone appears to be living here. Arranged under the bridge arch are a bed, a carpet, a table and shelves, a drawer brimming with vintage kitchen implements, tins of food and ornaments, even a sheaf of decorative pampas grasses in a heavy vase. It is both homely and squalid, and I can't say if it is mad or sad or something else. It's rather like the kind of den I dreamed of having as a child – well equipped, decorative, ingenious.

My walk brings me across the Maxey Cut and into an area of flooded gravel workings that have replaced what was once one of the largest ritual landscapes in Bronze-Age Britain. The place has held an allure in my imagination for several years, since I read Francis Pryor's account of archaeological investigations here in the early 1980s. Pryor made his name with excavations across the Fens and East Anglia – at Fengate in Peterborough, here, and later with the excavation of the extraordinary timber monument of Holme I, better known as Seahenge, uncovered by the tides at Holme-next-the-Sea in Norfolk.

The full extent of the henges, causeways and cursuses in the Maxey landscape was only realised when the drought of 1976 revealed cropmarks – the result of slight differences in plant growth caused by underlying features. Pryor and his colleagues spent several years making as much sense as they could of what was there before most of the site was given over to gravel extraction. It isn't immediately obvious what might have made this flat, featureless landscape significant to Neolithic people, but Pryor suggests it might be the same thing that made the landscape of Holme I special: at the time of their making, these monuments were in landscapes close to or surrounded by water. Such places are biologically productive and may have been favoured for ritual activity because they were close to the edge of the habitable world of the time. They were, to use what has become a somewhat overused term, liminal spaces: natural, physical expressions of metaphysical boundaries, and were perhaps, as rivers, springs and lakes often are, seen as potential crossing places from one world to the next.

To my untutored eye there is nothing now to show for the earthworks, enclosures and henges that once stood here. I've pored over aerial photographs of cropmarks and compared them to modern maps and satellite images, and I know more or less where a 2km-long ditch-lined track known as the Maxey Cursus crosses the modern road and meets the main channel of the Welland. Do I imagine the hairs on the back of my neck standing up as I cross it? There's a strange thrill in my bones – a sensation I associate more with acupuncture than exercise. I'm sure not, because it happens twice, once on the lane and again on the path by the riverside. When did I become so suggestible?

From this point I follow the Welland towards Market Deeping. On a bridge across a tiny tributary watercourse I cross from Cambridgeshire into Lincolnshire. There, hovering between counties, I find mayflies – the first of the year. They remind me that today is 6th June – the anniversary of my dad's funeral. He died on 24th May 2005, just short of his 69th birthday. And ever since, that strange transforming fortnight has been marked for me by the appearance of mayflies on the wing. Mayflies are unusual in having two winged life stages, in addition to many aquatic larval stages. They break free from the watery nursery that has been home for months or years as non-breeding 'duns', which then moult again almost immediately into the final adult form, the 'spinner', or imago, whose only biological purpose is procreation. It is this short, glorious, sexual phase that has passed into aphorism. It may last hours, or very few days, but what days they are. Mayflies are not wholly associated with May – different species emerge right through the summer, but in England, most years, this seems to be the peak emergence time.

The small cloud here contains maybe 50 spinners, and they are performing an ancient ritual of their own, oscillating up and down on the spot. It's a mesmerising display – they rise about a metre on rapidly fluttering wings, bodies held vertically so they resemble ascending angels, trailing threadlike tails (cerci) folded together. At the zenith of each rise they lock their wings open like a parachute, and splay their cerci – the change in tail position lifts the body to the horizontal and they drop in a skydiver posture so effective at slowing the descent that coming back down to the point where they began, level with the tops of the reeds, is no faster than going up. It takes them about a second to rise, a second to fall, over and over. Occasionally I notice two dropping together and separating at the low point in the display but I have to watch for several minutes before the dance resolves. It's the males doing the rising and falling, and every now and then a female flies up into the throng, where she is clasped briefly and mated – a consummation that lasts no longer than the second of the fall, after which she flies down and away. This happens maybe a dozen times and then, in a matter of moments the whole crowd disperses.

The twin themes of transformation and the ascension were not lost on the renaissance artist Albrecht Dürer, who created an engraving known as *The Holy Family with the Mayfly*, around 1495. The mayfly in the image is said to be representative of the infant Jesus Christ as an embodied link between heaven and Earth. Uncharacteristically for Dürer, it's not a very *good* mayfly. Necessarily represented very small alongside the human subjects, it appears to have a wormy body, clubbed antennae, a curly proboscis and rather rounded wings. As a result the piece is sometimes referred to as The Holy Family and the Butterfly, or Dragonfly. Butterflies and dragonflies also undergo miraculous transformations, but neither performs such angelic dances of ascension – I feel sure it must have been something like this that Dürer had seen.

Mayfly mass emergences can be jaw-dropping spectacles – a biological strategy to overwhelm predators with abundance and thereby ensure at least some survive long enough to reproduce. The emergence on the Yorkshire Derwent in 2017 was astonishing. Lochy and I were on one of our regular walks to Kirkham Abbey when we noticed something unusual. His sharper eyes spotted it first.

'Look at all those birds! What are they doing?'

It was a flock of gulls, very high, swirling in a kind of elongated maelstrom. As we got nearer we saw more, and by the time we reached the river we were walking beneath a column of birds 200m high, loosely stacked by species – flycatchers and wagtails feeding close to the water, above them martins and swallows, then swifts, and finally thousands of gulls. Over the next hour the spectacle developed. The stack of birds became a curtain, running along the curve of the river. Thousands of duns clung to riverside vegetation and the leaves of trees in the wood. The bodies of thousands more floated on the surface of my neighbour's ponds.

Not every summer brings such an emergence. The most I saw together at one time in 2019 were four that drifted in close formation over a car bonnet outside the community hall in Farndale, where we'd driven to watch a gig by acclaimed father and daughter folk artists, Martin and Eliza Carthy.

Farndale is the valley of the little River Dove, another tributary of the Derwent. It's best known for the carpet of wild daffodils that spreads either side of the river in April. Wild daffs are smaller than most garden varieties, and paler yellow, and to my eye they have a slightly urchin scruffiness. Their trumpets and petals are less rigid than those of pumped-up cultivars, making them more inclined to bob and flutter. En masse they are breathtaking. For the few weeks of this annual spectacle, fields in the Farndale hamlets of Low Mill and Church Houses are converted to temporary car parks and the tiny Daffy Café and tea garden does a roaring trade in bacon sandwiches, cake and local jam. The dale has a strong community vibe, not least perhaps because it survived a plan in the 1960s to dam its upper section with a colossal earth bank to create a reservoir. On the evening of the Carthy gig, the daffodils were over, but the ramshackle corrugated community hall at Low Mill was packed out. You could tell the regulars because they brought cushions to make the folding chairs less of a bone-ache to sit on.

I remember the night well because it was 24th May, the 14th anniversary of the phone call from my sister. She'd choked out words I fretted at for years. She didn't say 'Dad has died', but 'Dad is dead'. For some reason the adjective was worse than the verb. I wanted words that recognised my father as a participant. The verb would have kept him active, somehow. Someone can't be dead and still alive. But they can die and still be present. My dad is still my dad. It was an absurd and unreasonable objection – my sister is a greatly more considerate human than me, she was in a state of deep shock herself and the news was never going to be anything other than devastating – but it took many years to shake it off. I can only rationalise it by assuming that a sense of wrongness that exploded at the moment of loss attached itself to the first thing it could find – the manner of the announcement. When I finally confessed this to her, she wondered if she'd chosen the most bald statement she could to shock us both into believing something that seemed impossible.

Martin Carthy was struggling that night. He seemed tired, blamed hay fever and apologised that he could only play while leaving the vocals solely to Eliza. When he briefly forgot the chords, she gave him time, and the audience did likewise. The second time he faltered, she chided him gently.

'Come on, Martin.'

Martin was my dad's name, too. I slipped out of the hall and wandered down through the cow parsley to the bridge over the Dove. Dusk was approaching and I thought I might see a few more late mayflies. I've crossed this bridge many times – it's an easy, child-friendly walk up the valley and the first time I came here was with Kate. It was daffodil time, Lochy was three months old and Hannah a sturdy toddler. I remember leaning on that same wooden rail, watching the water and talking about how much I wished my dad was around to get to know his grandson. I don't remember what Kate said. Maybe nothing. It was the listening that mattered.

In the gathering twilight outside the gig, bats were hurtling and jittering above the water, occasionally dipping to the surface and opening silvery circles. There were a few gnats, but no more mayflies, in fact no large insects at all. I found I couldn't leave until something came, and eventually it did, a small, pale, dithering moth, which a bat homed in on like a guided missile. It looked like an obliteration, but it was more a transition – moth energy had become bat energy. I walked back to the hall and leaned against a wall near the back to listen to the end of the gig. Eliza was setting the scene for the next song.

'A song or an album needs a point,' she said. 'A point, or a story, like, like um ... ' she groped for an example ' ... like the life cycle of a mayfly.'

What made her say it, I don't know – perhaps she'd been looking for mayflies too – but I felt a jolt as though her words had completed an electrical circuit. Tears welled up and wouldn't stop.

Dark water

A section of the River Kent below Kendal in Cumbria was a particular favourite with just about everyone I paddled with, partly for its ease of access and reliability in different levels, but mainly for the number and variety of features in the last couple of kilometres. First off, there's a gorge with an entrance rapid that delivers you into a little Tolkienesque canyon with overhanging walls clad in mosses and ferns. In winter, the innumerable rivulets and seeps that maintain the greenery develop rapidly into fantastical ice formations. The decadence of them, often created in a single night and thawing away in the course of the following day, always had me spellbound.

Beyond the gorge there are further drops and weirs and the grand finale of Force Falls – a belter of a drop, hard to get badly wrong as long as you paddle with gusto and stay upright, but intimidating, because from the river you can't see much at all on the approach. From the brink, past the point of no return, the last thing you see is a maw of white water. Wide-eyed novices flop into it and might part company with their boat, but the hole flushes and there's a huge quiet pool in which swimmers and kit can be reunited. And that's the end of the trip – dry clothes and hot drinks await.

The sheer fun of paddling the Kent never paled. Sometimes as a small group of confident paddlers we'd go round three times in a day. It was the first river I ran after Lochy was born – ten weeks after a C-section, knowing I could do so without strain.

The lure of 'one more go' once led to us running the final drops in almost complete darkness. When you're out at dusk your eyes adjust, and maybe we didn't realise quite how late it was. Maybe we'd misjudged how long it would take to shuttle the cars for a final run. Either way, we ended up setting off in twilight and within a few minutes found ourselves paddling in the dark. A dark river is hard to read. By the time we reached the approach to Force Falls the water was either featureless black or dim, noisy white. We were paddling by feel and familiarity. I wouldn't, couldn't possibly, recommend it. But at the same time, I was never so aware of the musculature of the river – not so much its power, but its anatomy – the way each little bump and lift and shove represented a component of the flow, like the myriad small muscles in a body that allow it to maintain posture or perform intricate or nuanced movement. We pay attention to biceps and quads, abs and deltoids – but it takes thousands of small contractions and flexures to use a keyboard, say, or balance barefoot on a wobbly log, or speak a simple sentence. And just as it pays to be aware of those smaller muscles and how we use them, it benefits a paddler to recognise them in a river. They are easy to overlook, but that night, in the dark, I felt their invisible tugs and nudges and the extent to which they held, pushed or pulled the boat. I was paddling alongside my friend Sarah – close enough to confer a little over what we could see and remember of the route and far apart enough to give each other space to manoeuvre. I remember her face in the gloom, the whites of her wide eyes, and her teeth showing the same half-grin, half-grimace I wore myself in the guilty thrill of something we knew we shouldn't be doing.

CHAPTER 5

Lines upon the land

We're told the seas are rising
But this stretch of land I will defend
The wetlands are flooding, fading is the lapwing
But these small creatures I'll curl my body round.

Kitty Macfarlane, *Man, Friendship*

The Somerset Levels and Moors swallow you pretty much as soon as you swing east of the M5 at Bridgwater. This is a place of straight lines and deceptive horizons, the land crisscrossed by reed-lined ditches and broader drainage channels, known as the rhynes (pronounced *reens*). The roadside hedges are high, their inner flanks trimmed to bus height by passing traffic, creating rectangular tunnels. In July the verges are vivid with the pinks of campion and loosestrife, among which sprout signs advertising willow crafts and cider farms.

To an eye accustomed to undulating landscapes, the levelness takes some adjusting to. There is higher, wooded ground in the distance; like the dark green rim of a flat saucer, I think that might be a good place to get my bearings. Then I notice what looks like a significant hill some miles away, towering over the landscape, topped with a most impressive ruin, and decide to head for that instead. But it's a trick. The hill, which I will discover is called Burrow Mump, is neither large, nor far away. I'm there in no time and close up, it is both conically perfect and comically tiny. Climbing the 24 vertical metres to the equally diddy ruined church at its summit takes all of a minute. But 24 metres around here buys a lot of view.

The scene below is like something from a Charles Tunnicliffe children's book illustration. White marquees are being erected for a village fete or show. There are small green and gold fields, the latter already with hay in combed rows, and a little red tractor is stacking old-fashioned cuboid bales of hay. Field sizes here are constrained by an intricate system of ditches, which drain into the curving line of the River Parrett. Roads and waterways are demarcated by trees – bushy alders, shimmering aspen, gracious ash and plumose poplars – some so evenly tapered you could mistake them at a distance for church spires. But most abundant of all are the willows: dabs of rippling grey-green as far as the eye can see.

Geologically, much of the Levels and Moors landscape of Somerset is new – the Moors were created as peatland after the last Ice Age when the main rivers of the region, the Parrett to the south and the Axe and the Brue further north, occupied huge wetlands. Their waters spread and percolated, rather than flowing. These wetlands, like Star Carr in Yorkshire, were places of biological abundance that made the effort required to access them well worthwhile. Early settlements grew up on islands of higher ground, and communities addressed the difficulty in moving about by constructing networks of timber walkways. Of these, two running close by each other in the Brue Valley are among the oldest such structures known anywhere in the world. The Sweet Track and the slightly older Post Track, dating to 3807 and 3838 BC respectively, were narrow boardwalks made of single-width oak and ash planks resting on crossed posts of hazel and lime. They were in use for a relatively short time – perhaps only ten years in the case of the Sweet Track, after which it seems a rising water table may have made permanent settlement untenable. Water has always been a mixed blessing here, and seasonal flooding is the characteristic that gave the principal settlement of Roman and Anglo-Saxon times its name, Somerton, meaning summer-town. Somerset was a land for summer. In winter it was, and sometimes still is, a realm of water.

Efforts to control inundations here have been going on for most of recorded history and drainage was well underway by time of the *Domesday Book*. From the twelfth century, the monasteries at Glastonbury, Athelney and Muchelney took a lead, enclosing and draining thousands of acres, then reaping dividends by renting the new land out. The work has continued for 900 years – rivers walled in, redirected, diverted, and created (among others, the Kings Sedgemoor Drain in 1795, the Hunstpill in 1940, and the Sowy River as recently as 1972). Collectively these natural and artificial channels amount to thousands of kilometres of ditches, rivers, drains and rhynes.

According to the National Trust interpretation board, Burrow Mump is 'a great place for a picnic'. A couple of families are doing just that. Someone has edited the sign in permanent marker, overwriting *picnic* with *joint*, and I expect they are right. If it wasn't so hot I could while away an afternoon here, watching the shadow of the diminutive church grow from its midday minimum and sweep around like the gnomon of a sundial. But the sun is fierce; I know there must be cool green water nearby, and after the long drive from Yorkshire there is nothing I want more.

I drive on a little aimlessly, until a heron drifts across the road between the osier stands and out over the reeds and shows me a parking place where the road crosses a rhyne in the shade of several willows. There's a campervan parked up and a smaller car with two dozing senior citizens. I change quickly, using the open car door as a partial screen, hoping they don't open their eyes at the wrong moment. But the car engine starts seconds after I've pulled up my swimsuit, and the old couple putter away, whether in disapproval, discretion, or giggling their heads off, I'll never know.

The banks are thick with flowering mallow and comfrey, nettles and burdock. There are meadow brown butterflies and bumblebees. The air is pressingly still, and if it wasn't for the unmistakeable cadences of Test Match cricket commentary from the campervan radio, it would be incredibly quiet. Small birds flit high in the willows, warblers I think, but through with song and bluster for the summer, adopting wise quiescence as they moult and regrow flight feathers before migration. Little white moths puff up from the grass as I move. The water is about four feet deep according to a depth gauge, green and weedy, with drifts of yellow-flowered waterlily. There's also a busy half-metre of airspace over the surface, in which clouds of gnats bounce and dragonflies and damselflies manoeuvre expertly past each other. They are all some shade of blue, coordinated like members of a dance troupe: stout chasers and slimmer black-tailed skimmers, common blue damsels and banded demoiselles in more strident enamel hues. The fish are long, slim-bodied cyprinids with pinkish fins, bronzy above. Dace, I think. They rise here and there, every few seconds, and the water surface is hatched with their overlapping circular ripples.

There is something dead floating in the water near the first place I plan to get in – a furry dome showing just above the water, with an avid congregation of shiny bluebottles. I cross the bridge to enter upstream instead.

I can't feel any current, though the weeds indicate the direction of flow, and out of habit I swim upstream first, through patches of warm and cool. The dragons and damsels buzz overhead. Collared doves coo. The buds of the waterlilies look like Roman amphorae – those terracotta wine jugs with a narrow neck. In the shade beneath each leaf are multitudes of tiny fish.

I swim back downstream and venture as close as I dare to the dead thing under the bridge. It is a very bloated mole, lodged in a mat of weed and swollen to a balloon twice its original size. Mindful of the carcass, I swim carefully, splashing as little as a I can to avoid getting water in my mouth, but I can't help but cause disturbance. Water rises in a sky-coloured bow wave before my steady breaststroke – small amplitude ripples looking bigger from my frogs-eye viewpoint. I see bubbles rising from the bottom – the shockwave of my passing must be dislodging them from the weeds and detritus where gas is released by the processes of photosynthesis and decay. The bubbles grow, shimmy and flip as they rise, gleaming gold – like coins tumbling in a wishing well, but in reverse. Seeing them makes me realise how conspicuous even my most careful strokes must be to the fish – my movements generate ripples that go down as well as out. These vibrations have frequencies far too low to be audible as sound, but in addition to ears, most fish are equipped to pick up exactly this kind of low-frequency mechanical 'noise'. The lateral line organ of fish is a row of tiny pores running along each flank. The pores are linked under the skin by a waterfilled canal, and the canal is lined with cells called neuromasts, each of which thrusts a bundle of tiny hairs into the canal fluid. The hairs, which come in a range of sizes and sensitivities, detect pressure changes in the water and mainline the information direct to the central nervous system. It's broadly similar to the mechanism by which our ears detect sound, but sensitive to much longer wavelengths and lower frequencies, allowing fish to sense changes in pressure caused by water moving at different speeds. They can literally hear flow, and interpret tell-tale wrinkles, insinuating currents and chattering vortices that tell of who is close by, who might be approaching and who was here, even after they are out of sight.

I float for a while on my back and watch foliage rippling on the whiplike branches of a pollarded willow. Green to grey, grey to green, the movement is almost like swirls of water. Willows are the *genius loci* of this place. Second only to oaks in the abundance and biodiversity they support in Britain, these beautiful, exuberant trees were once a significant crop, grown over thousands of acres to supply a range of useful products.

Willow can be coppiced (cut close to ground level) or pollarded (cut above head height) to encourage regrowth.

Which technique is used will depend on whether the growth needs to be accessible to livestock (for which it makes excellent fodder), or kept out of their reach. The cutting interval is varied to provide regrowth of different thickness, which can be put to an incredible variety of uses. The thinnest shoots, known as whips, are long and unbranched in their first year, ideal for weaving. For the first months of his life, Lochy slept in a four-legged, wickerwork bassinette Kate loaned us – one in which Hannah and Kate herself had slept as babies. Wicker shares a root with the Norse *vika*, and *vikker*, meaning willow. The druid, naturalist and experimental archaeologist Chris Park, who keeps bees the old way, in handwoven skep hives, told me of an old Irish saying probably dating back to the oral tradition, that 'willows are the strength of bees', owing to their being among the first trees to flower in March, when their catkins produce prodigious quantities of pollen and nectar. But there's a less-known second part to that wisdom, says Chris, that 'willows *have* the strength of bees' – a collective strength whereby many small stems, when worked together, create immensely strong and functional structures – baskets, hives, fish traps, fences, even buildings. Willow wood is resistant to rot, and thus especially valuable for structures that will remain outside. Left a little longer, the whips thicken to withies, then sturdier rods – both still weavable – then stakes or posts and finally chunky stems that can be used in construction or chopped up for firewood or charcoal. Willow charcoal is soft with a low ash content, and was thus especially valued for making gunpowder, though these days it is more likely to be used by artists for drawing. The medicinal properties of willow have been known for millennia. The leaves, bark and the sappy new wood laid down in the outer part of stems and branches contain salicin, which has anti-inflammatory properties and is a precursor of aspirin.

Willows are also a dominant arboreal feature of riversides all over Britain, and in fact many riverbanks are effectively made of willow roots, which form a dense fibrous mat that holds the soil together. This stabilising role is hugely important here in the Levels. Not only are willows extraordinarily useful, but as a crop they could not be much easier – they grow fast, yielding useful materials in a year and require no watering or artificial fertiliser.

I hang my swimsuit in the willows to dry and I lean over the bridge while my hair dries into post-swim crinkles. A man arrives in a work van. He grins as he strips off to his shorts, revealing impressive tattoos, executes a bounding dive into the waterlilies then climbs straight back out, casts me another conspiratorial smile and jumps back into the van and drives off, renewed after a visit of no more than 90 seconds.

I'm heading for the wooded high ground again, hoping for a more expansive view, when I see a sign for the Bere Cider Company, and can't resist. In a blessedly cool barn a blue-shirted, white-haired man is filling bottles from a row of wooden barrels with chalked labels.

'Wan' a drink?' he drawls, by way of greeting. I thank him and when he waves a half-pint glass enquiringly at the barrels, I point to the one labelled *DRY*.

'Hmm,' he says, and pulls two glasses, passes me one and we chink and sip. The cider is the kind of dry you taste with your teeth and cheek-linings as well as your tongue. He tells me his name is Jim.

'Where's you come from then?'

I tell him.

'You don' sound like you'se from Yorkshire.' His own dragged vowels are unmistakeably, deliciously Somerset.

'No. I'm not really *from* anywhere. Army brat.'

He notices my damp hair and I explain I've freshened up with a dip.

'People must've thought you was mad.'

I tell him that no, there was someone else swimming too, and after a moment's consideration he asks how deep it was.

'Not deep.' I indicate chest height.

'Not deep now maybe. You should've seen it in the floods.'

He pulls up a stool with the air of someone with a story to tell, and gestures me to another. 'Took two years to get people back into the houses. But least now the Envir'nment Agency's dredgin' again – they stopped, see, for ten years. All my life, they been doin' it. Then they just stopped, an' sold off all that equipment. And then came the floods. Never seen anythin' like it – whole place just a great lake. Down at Moorland, the houses are below river level but never flooded in a hundred years – but then they did. Two years homeless some was. So they started dredgin' again. Stands to reason they got to, else there's nowhere for the water to go, there just ain't room for it all.'

He asks what has brought me south and when I say I'm a naturalist he asks if I've come for the festival. I say I don't know about any festival.

'Oh, we got a big one coming up – four 'undred of 'em naturalists. Don't know what it is they'll be doin' exactly. They look better with their clothes on if y'ask me.'

The following day I rent a sit-on-top kayak in Langport and paddle up the River Parrett, towards Muchelney. The water is clear – I can see to the bottom, through swaying ribbons of weed. Swifts and swallows scribe arcs overhead. I came here to experience rivers different to those I have known – the antithesis of steep white water – and this is the flattest I could think of. The water just about knows its way, but it doesn't take much to paddle against it, and I have heard that the ease with which the flow is overruled has become a problem for eels, which use flow as a directional cue to find the sea on their downstream migration. Here, where natural flow is so sluggish, the draw created by large offtakes – such as for electricity generation, irrigation or drinking water – can fool them, and these days, with populations in critical decline, every individual lost this way is a tragedy.

Round a bend, I paddle into an airborne troupe of about 20 banded demoiselle damselflies. I'm so busy watching them I don't notice a thread emerging from the bank, entering the water at an acute angle, until I almost drift into it. Fishing line. I make a quick evasive manoeuvre, notice two black rods protruding from the reeds, and tense instinctively as two fisherman stand up.

'Hi!' says one of them, smiling.

'Oh, hi. Sorry I nearly caught your line. I don't suppose it's kayaks you're fishing for.'

'Ha, no, but I fancy a go in one. Is that from Langport? How much are they?'

I'm so relieved they are friendly. We chat for a few minutes, about kayaks and the demoiselles, more than a hundred of which are now dancing above and around me. I ask about the fish I saw yesterday and they agree they were probably dace.

'Twenty-five centimetres though – that's big,' the second guy chips in after I've given him a clichéd 'this big' indication with my hands. 'Specimen size. Where was they exactly?' And I laugh and say I can't remember the name of the village or even which rhyne I'd been on.

I paddle for a couple of hours, but from my low perspective the view changes little. Since the floods of 2012 to 2014, the Parrett has been hemmed in by earthen bunds, and the land beyond is completely hidden. The banks are thick with stands of purple loosestrife and billowy drifts of chamomile, and a family walking along the top is disturbing hundreds of butterflies as they walk – to the delight of the children. They must also be crushing the chamomile underfoot, because the smell is heavenly.

I pay a visit to an old acquaintance, Kate Merry. Kate and I both worked with the same wildlife charity, the People's Trust for Endangered Species, a decade ago – me as editor of their magazine, she as education officer. She now coordinates outreach for another small charity, Butterfly Conservation, and lives in a converted stable barn in

Muchelney with her husband, Nigel Bunce, a master thatcher. They have their own land, where they grow the long-stemmed wheat Nigel uses as thatching reed, and an old willow bed that he has pressed back into production for the long straight withies used to bind the tops of thatches.

'There used to be thousands of acres of withy beds in the Levels, but reduced demand and cheaper imports killed off the industry. Now they are really grown only to stabilise ditches,' Nigel tells me. 'I can only use so much, and while there are still people working with willow for basket work, hurdles and the like, those things have become a bit of a luxury. Maybe that will change in a post-plastic future. It would be great to see it properly commercial again. It's an amazing tree.'

There's a rule of thumb in flood-prone areas that settlements with ancient churches are a safer bet as they tend to be on higher ground. They don't get much more ancient than Muchelney Abbey. A monastery was first founded here in the late seventh century. Another encouraging sign is in the name – Muchelney means 'great island'. As a general rule, while the village has been routinely islanded by winter floods, the homes here have tended to stay high and dry.

But not in November 2012. At the time Kate and Nigel's first child Elliot was eight months old. At two-thirty in the morning, Kate was in Elliot's room, feeding him.

'I realised I could hear trickling – like the sound radiators sometimes make – only we don't have radiators. Then I noticed my feet were wet and in my sleep-deprived state had a vague thought that I should probably wipe up whatever had been spilt – then I realised it was everywhere, coming up through the floors, which are made of poured concrete, as well as under the doors. We had a lodger and a visitor at the time and so the four of us spent the next few hours moving everything we could – most of the house is on the ground floor, so we used bricks and blocks to raise furniture: one brick, two, then three. But by morning it was knee deep.'

The water lay for weeks. Muchelney was cut off for two months, during which time the only way to get out was by boat or Unimog, or by tractor-trailer rides laid on by a local farmer twice a day.

Kate and her family were able to move over the road to some holiday cottages that had stayed dry. 'It became a bit of a commune for flooded-out neighbours. It was strange to have the luxury of a jacuzzi bath, then have to wade in mucky knee-deep water into our own house to find a pair of pants, or whatever.'

Eventually Muchelney dried out. Life settled down and the residents took comfort in the description of the flooding as a once-in-a-hundred-year event.

'But then it happened again. Just over a year later. This time we could see it coming. November and December 2013 were just absurdly wet. Then in January water started rising around us again. We called the Environment Agency and they said, "Don't worry, you're too far from the river." It seemed strange that we had to explain to them how the water table works. Even the firefighter who came to the door to see if we were OK kept asking where the river was. But river water and groundwater are all the same thing around here, and that poor baffled fireman and I just stood there watching it rise in the kitchen. I was pregnant again, with Elliot on my hip. It was weird, but at least that time we were more prepared. Everyone was.'

She makes it sound almost as though periodic flooding isn't a disaster. She laughs. 'Well, we're happy here. In the past people lived with this kind of thing. These days it's about insurance, ripping things out, starting again. But there is another way. An older, more resilient way. We're lucky in that our house is old, with hard floors, lime render and unplastered stone – even the kitchen units survived both floods because they are wooden: Nigel took them apart, sanded them down and rebuilt them. You can still see flood marks on them but that's part of the house's story.

'I guess we're so much more in tune with the real nature of this place now. We notice details – exactly where water is lying and how long for. Almost a sixth sense.'

There have been changes. The earthen bunds put in since the floods took some of Kate and Nigel's land and made it unsuitable for ploughing, and for the hundred-year-old reaper binder machine they use for bundling the stems. They have planted it instead with fruit trees. The other major change has been the raising of the road. 'I have mixed feelings about that, really,' Kate says. 'I mean, we can now always get to Tesco for bog roll when we need it, but Muchelney will never be a great island again and it's sort of lost something of itself in that. It reminds me that as a society we need to relearn how to work within the limits of what the land gives us.'

I finally make it to the wooded high ground just before I start the drive home. It's still fiercely hot, but there's cool in the shade of ivy-clad oaks and a swathe of open grassland thick with orchids and grasshoppers. The view is enormous, and it is only too easy to imagine the lake of floodwater Jim described over a glass of cider, stretching all the way to the Quantocks and the sea, with Muchelney and Burrow Mump islanded. This whole area is on the front line of climate change, and in some ways the future feels as precarious as the ancient timber walkway of the Sweet Track. But the people here have been managing water for a long time. There is tension between acceptance and resistance, but also an old bargain between human and nature, give and take. It's comforting, in a strange way.

Bath toys

Whirlpool *A rotating mass of water created where opposing flows meet.*

The volume and silt load of the Zanskar gives a heaving, burly character to its flow. It brawls around bends and boulders, pounds over ledges, but is at its least predictable when forced through constrictions with no discernible gradient. In such places, reflections off the canyon walls combine to create vortices, which appear and disappear unpredictably, lasting anything from a second to several minutes. Some are very large, and if they form as a kayak passes over, both boat and paddler are sucked straight down. We encountered dozens of these 'swirly alleys' — startling at first, then hugely amusing. Typically we'd be paddling steadily, or sometimes just floating in a relaxed formation, chatting or occupied with our own thoughts, when someone would just disappear. The dunking never lasted more than a second or two before our bulk disrupted the whirl and we'd bob back to the surface like bath toys, huffing or whooping with the shock of cold water, to move on, wondering who'd be next.

CHAPTER 6

The meanings of water

The summer before the world falls silent under COVID-19 restrictions I find myself in pitch darkness with a woman I've known barely an hour. The only light I can see is the red LED of a tracking device clipped to her rucksack. Coco (Colombine) Neal is on a long journey on foot across some of the most remote and exposed landscapes in England, following water. The tracker is there so that her loved ones can see where she is, even if there is no phone signal. I wonder if they can see her now, under the ground. The red glow reminds me she still has far to go and that the last thing she needs is to pick up an injury. The next thought is that I'm easily old enough to be her mother and that perhaps I ought to be the responsible one. I speak to the dark. 'OK. Here's the deal. You're not allowed to break any bones. Please say if you're not comfortable.'

The reply is a chuckle. 'This is mad. But I'm loving it so much!'

I sense her pausing for a moment and we're obviously having the same thought because she laughs again, the sound bouncing off the invisible surfaces around us, and says, '*What are we doing here? How did this happen?*'

It does have a feeling of unreality to it. Ten days ago we'd never heard of each other. Two hours ago we'd never met. Now we're inching through blackness together, completely unequipped, no idea where we're going. And yet I already know Coco is one of the best and most interesting people I've ever met.

It happened via Twitter, an introduction out of the blue by the writer Robert Macfarlane, shortening unlikely odds to forge a connection just where it needed to be. Coco is a trilingual landscape archaeologist, anthropologist and poet, who grew up in the south of France and later Belgium. Perhaps unsurprisingly, she has a wandering soul. She now lives in Sheffield, and at the time we met was walking solo to Scotland, following a route of her own devising along rivers and trackways, threading together the deliberately flooded landscapes of reservoirs – places where water has risen and changed the shape of lives and vistas, as it soon will almost everywhere. She was also using the walk to promote and fundraise for the Snowdrop Project – a small charity that provides practical and emotional support for survivors of human trafficking.

We met at the campsite where Coco was staying. As I pulled up I realised my water bottle had leaked onto the passenger seat of the car and hastily covered the wet patch with a towel. Coco noticed and paused as she was getting in, so I started to explain – she exploded with laughter. 'God, I thought you'd decided I was far too filthy and stinking to sit on the upholstery!' The tone was set. This was not going to be an ordinary walk. It would become a journey of words rather than paces. Over the next few hours we would walk almost no distance but cover thousands of miles and many millennia.

The day was living up to its Met Office billing as the hottest of the year so far, and Coco was supposed to be resting, so I drove us to Upper Nidderdale – where the River Nidd passes through a deep gorge. It's not somewhere I know well, but I imagined we'd find shade and cool water and a short walk, perhaps a teashop or a pub.

We'd barely set out when a gap in a wall opened to a small path, and we followed it past a strange contraption in green-painted iron. An old turnstile, partially dismantled and welded immobile; an odd thing, we thought, to find on a riverside path. We paused a little further along, probably because there was a small junction where an adjoining path led to a cleft in the rock, and the decision about whether to take it kept getting deferred by the conversation. I'd just asked Coco how she came to archaeology – one of the few things I knew about her was that she was working towards a doctorate in the subject.

'Oh, I'm not really an archaeologist. Well, I am, but my work doesn't fit neatly into any particular field of research.' The usual subject matter of archeology, she tells me, is solid, not liquid, but there is a move to bring rivers into sharper focus in the discipline, and she cites the work of landscape archaeologist Matthew Edgeworth as an example. 'He calls rivers "the dark matter of landscape" because we see the effect, not the agent.'

Coco explained that her thesis is a collaborative process of map-making from memory and experience – her own, and those of people in communities through which she is walking. The landscapes and places she's mapping are buried not underground, but under the water of reservoirs. 'It's not melancholic though,' she was keen to point out. 'Rising water is something we are going to have to come to terms with in all kinds of ways, and I'm interested in what survives, what has become and even what might be, rather than what has been lost.' She is a fan of Swedish archaeologist Cornelius Holtorf, who argues, somewhat controversially in a field where preservation is so important, that accepting loss and change can be important in fostering resilience.

'Holtorf believes that seeing things fall apart helps us recognise process, and I wonder if it might also help us avoid falling into the trap – which is common in nationalist thinking, for example – of imagining past situations as if they were something fixed, when they were never anything of the kind. Melancholy can be part of that trap if we're not alert to it.'

When we paused to properly look around us, we found ourselves in the entrance to not just a cleft, but a cave. A tall entrance, with steep steps leading downwards, into the dark. We exchanged surprised, gleeful glances and descended the steps onto a floor strewn with boulders. It was blissfully cool. The cave appeared to continue some way into the cliff and we ventured in, over a worn but uneven floor. Soon the only illumination was a faint glow of daylight reflected on walls of slicked calcite, then that too disappeared and darkness engulfed us. We moved with arms constantly searching for space, sizing it, trying to feel in all directions for the unpredictable disappearance of wall or floor or the sudden appearance of ceiling where our unprotected heads might meet it. Four points of contact are a woeful substitute for the broad scan of vision, but our voices provided a little bit of guidance – I could sense there were walls close by but space above – a strange airiness when I waved my arms over my head, a feeling of being both outside and indoors. I will learn later that the cave is indeed very narrow and very high and be surprised at how accurate my rudimentary echolocation was.

We crept on. The cave narrowed until rock pressed in on either side, but the path continued. This was the moment when I saw the little red light on Coco's shoulder strap and I remembered another strand of the Twitter thread she had been writing about her walk. 'As always before setting off as a woman alone,' she wrote, 'I am learning to trust not just my own strength and resilience but the kindness and intentions of those around me.'

Is this OK? Am I betraying that trust? But her laugh at my enquiry and the delight in her voice matches my own. We fumble on – shuffling rather than stepping. I had been half joking about the broken bones – this place is so accessible I reason that it's unlikely to be truly dangerous, but in the dark, even a small step can be an ankle-turner and my imagination is filling the void to my left with a bottomless drop. I'm not sure which of us is Alice, and which the white rabbit, but today has already veered off the rails and it feels very much as if anything could happen.

Light appears ahead, a way out or just a crack, we're not sure at first, but we round a final bend and see a dazzling window of green and gold. And as my eyes adjust I make out twisted branches and light, shifting foliage. A very large tree seems to be straddling the opening. The dazzle resolves further into familiar pinnate leaves. I stop.

'Whoa! "The way into the Underland is through the riven trunk of an old ash tree."'

It's the first line of Rob Macfarlane's magnificent *Underland: A Deep Time Journey*, which I've recently finished and Coco is carrying on her walk. She clutches my arm and we laugh in delight. We emerge more fully into the light, finding ourselves in a small, steep-sided hollow with some steps leading upwards.

We climb up and into a field in a campsite, and cross to where the entrance track traverses a bridge over How Stean Gorge. Twentieth-century tourist blurbs called this 'Little Switzerland', but it is much more like Middle Earth.

We lean on the bridge railings, looking down, and talk about walking: long distances and short, the gift of going slow and the fears and challenges of being alone. 'Nan Shepherd wrote about walking into the mountain and out of her body, but I feel the opposite,' says Coco. 'I'm walking *into* my body. I've not been good at looking after myself, and there is still a lot of fear to overcome, but now I'm actually doing this, I am so *proud* of it, and so happy. Even with the aches and the tiredness.' We talk about the climate activist Mary Annaïse Heglar's magnificent recent essay 'But the Greatest of These is Love', singling out love as the most powerful weapon in the environmentalist's arsenal. Coco will later tell me that her entire walk was to become an act of love and of kin-making. 'I was so full of fear but people showed such kindness. I fell in love with them and the things they taught me, and I fell in love with the landscape because I was learning to know that too.'

Next to the bridge over the gorge, curiouser and curiouser, there is a wardrobe. An ordinary bedroom wardrobe. We open it, and find not a cupboard, but a path, leading down. In a moment it becomes clear: this is part of a tourist experience. Behind us is a ticket office where visitors are issued with hard hats and torches, and in some cases with abseiling harnesses and buoyancy aids. We grin again in unspoken agreement, and with a quick glance around to ensure the coast is clear, slip through.

Away from the fierce sunlight, the grey, emerald, bronze and jade hues of the gorge are balm to the eye. The river is running very low, with all its bones showing. The cliffs are blocky and undercut where bedding planes have fractured and chunks of rock have dropped away over thousands of years. In the bottom where peaty water runs, edges and ledges have been smoothed by time and flow, painted with algae and upholstered by moss. It's nearly noon and shafts of sunlight filtered by trees growing on the lip of the gorge create areas of intense contrast on the water. A grey wagtail flits from rock to rock, pumping not only its tail but its whole body and occasionally flourishing into the air to collect gnats. Once or twice it flies into one of the shafts of light and its wings appear translucent and incandescent, as though it must surely burn up. On one such foray I see, for a split second, the speck of life it is hunting – a mote of dancing gold – before it is engulfed, its energy transferred to another life.

We stand there a very long time, talking about water, and the myriad reasons it means so much. I tell her about Kate. And about Lochy – whose given name, *Lochlan*, meaning 'warrior of the lake', was chosen for its watery connotations. Had he been a girl, he would have been Selkie, after the seal-people of Celtic and Norse folklore, for similar reasons. This kind of entanglement of nature and culture, the give and take, says Coco, is why she studies rivers. 'Running water isn't just a resource or a setting against which human stories take place – it is part of our story – we are part of water's story. We control it, divert it, harness it, but it always has the ability to act back towards or against us. There are of course issues with ascribing agency to water, especially divine agency, but I do find myself thinking that way.'

She tells me about Veronica Strang, a cultural and environmental anthropologist at Durham University with a special interest in water and rivers, and the idea of a hydrotheological cycle as a shared phenomenon whereby human cultures over the ages have made sense of the world, physically and imaginatively. 'Strang suggests that the traits that different cultures share most consistently are those associated with how we experience, feel and think about water. For example, she describes the belief of an Aboriginal community in Queensland, that particular rivers contain spirit babies or children that jump into a person's body when they are born and must return to the water when they die. Strang compares that with practices in Dorset where people hoping for children still visit wishing wells.'

Hydrolatry, or the idea of water as sacred, is ubiquitous in world religions, featuring in rituals of immersion, libation, communion, celebration, promise, thanksgiving, healing, pilgrimage and purification as well as funerary farewells: we dip, pour, sip, raise a toast, deposit offerings, bathe, dose, follow, wash, and commit to water from the beginning of life to the end. The idea that we come from water was intuited long before it was understood in any evolutionary sense. We all emerge from a small, warm, private sea at the beginning of our lives, a sea that substitutes physiologically and phylogenetically for the water in which life on Earth originally began. Archaeologists often find concentrations of what appear to be votive offerings (objects of value placed ritually beyond reach – perhaps as a sign of good faith or in thanks for divine intervention) in rivers, marshes and peat bogs, and such places feature strongly in mythological scenes of transition: for example they must often be crossed en route to an afterlife or otherworld.

The fact that our survival depends on water is deeply embedded in every human culture. Springs and wells and watercourses are places where life is given. The dawn of agriculture only served to emphasize this dependency and alluvial floodwaters, which both irrigated and fertilised the land, were seen as gifts from benevolent and fecund gods. Often rivers are named for deities – in Britain the Dee is from *deva*, meaning 'river of the goddess', the Don is named for the Celtic mother goddess Danu (who also gave her name to the Danube), the Clyde is for the Romano-Celtic Clota, Clut, or Clutoida: a goddess of purification. In some tellings the spirit of the River Severn, Sabrina (also known as Sabren, Sabre, Hafren and other variants) is a goddess, in others an unjustly drowned princess. Some deities seem to have been reverse engineered. The name of the Thames shares a root in a Brythonic term meaning 'dark' (as do the Tamar, Tame, Thame, Teme, Tavy, Teifi and others). It was formerly latinised as *Tamesis*, from which has subsequently been drawn a male deity, Thame (Old Father Thames), who bears a strong similarity to the Roman Tiberinus, and a female one, Isis, adopted from the Egyptian pantheon.

As well as emphasising a link between water and fertility, some mythologies also seem to pre-empt scientific understanding of plate tectonics and continental drift, telling how the oceans surrounding the known world were a sort of circular river. The idea of a single encompassing body of water so neatly fits reconstructions of continental drift that geologists named the prehistoric ocean that once surrounded the ancient single landmass known as Pangea after the female Titan deity, Tethys. According to the myths, the divine aquatic offspring of Tethys and Oceanus were the sea-dwelling Oceanids and the freshwater Potamoi, and their grandchildren were a plethora of water nymphs or naiads. Those associated with freshwater included the Potamides of rivers and streams; the Limnades of lakes; the Crinaeae of fountains; the Eleionomae of marshes; the Pegaeae of springs; the Avernales inhabiting the swamps of Hades; the Pegasides of wells and the Camenae, also of wells but with additional jurisdiction over birth waters. Chief among them was Carmenta, whose name, from *carmen* meaning 'spell/song/oracle' is also the root of 'charm' – what greater, more everyday charm can there be than the life-giving magic of water? The naiads carried water and poured it from pitchers – a way of explaining the seemingly magic issuing of water from the Earth before scientific ideas of hydrology made it a little more complicated than that.

Water symbolises rebirth as well as birth. My early childhood was churchy, and I had a fondness for the story of baby Moses: born from water, then borne on water, and later commanding it to part. Moses appears as a prophet in Judaism, Christianity and Islam, and while I was never convinced about pronouncements from burning bushes, or geriatric mountaineering exploits (some tellings have Moses scaling Mount Nebo at 120 years of age to view the Promised Land, and expiring at the top), I always found the bit at the beginning irresistible. I happened upon it anew while pregnant and searching for Moses baskets online and was surprised to find not only the part I remembered – where water offered safety – but also a story of compassionate complicity between women on opposite sides of a social, cultural and racial divide.

Moses was born at a time when an insecure pharaoh had decreed that boy babies born to the expanding Hebrew population should be killed. His mother Jochebed fashions a waterproof cradle of woven reeds, caulked with pitch and tar, lays him in it and sets him afloat, safe in the reedbeds alongside the Nile, with his sister Miriam keeping watch from a distance. The pharaoh's daughter spies the basket and recognises the infant as a Hebrew child. When it is clear that the princess intends not only to show mercy, but to raise the baby as her own, young Miriam reveals herself and offers to locate a wetnurse. She brings Jochebed, who is thus able to continue caring for her son, while he is raised with royal status.

The motif of a baby cast adrift is a recurring one in mythologies. The Sumerian King Sargon I was set in a caulked basket in the Euphrates, and Romulus and Remus, the twin founders of Rome, were also left in or by a river, the Tiber, where they were protected by Tiberinus (one of the Potamoi sons of Tethys and Oceanus). In Celtic Britain there is the shapeshifting Taliesin, chief of bards, to whom we shall return in due course. All are symbolically reborn from water in order to achieve their destinies.

An account of all the world's water deities would fill a library. Suffice to say they exist in cultures around the globe, and many bear striking similarities to one another. As well as gods, there are innumerable other spirits and magical beings associated with rivers, and while many of these share common traits, they are by no means all benevolent. Some are downright nasty, but most are ambiguous. Often they are halflings or shapeshifters, alluring and monstrous in equal measure, offering both beauty and horror, sex and death.

In Norse and Germanic and Old English mythology the water spirits known as nix, näkki, nek, nixie, nøkk, nicor, knucker and nykur (among other variations) appear as animals or riverine merfolk. Etymologically, their names stem from the same proto-Indo-European root verb meaning 'to wash', which also gives us naked and nude. The English nicor and knucker often appear as wyrms or dragons, and seem therefore to tie with the French–Celtic legend of Mélusine – a daughter of the fae queen Pressyne and King Elinas of Albany (Scotland). Both mother and daughter are shapeshifters with the lower bodies of serpents. They elicit promises from their menfolk to never see them bathe or give birth – promises that are inevitably broken, causing them to desert, in some versions by growing wings and taking flight literally, in wyrm form.

In Slavic traditions the rusalki are mermaid-like creatures – in their earliest Pagan iterations they are benign spirits of fertility who irrigate crops, but in later folklore they become more threatening – the restless spirits of drowned women, with beautiful bodies and voices that lure young men below the surface to fatal entanglement in their long, red hair.

A similar siren-like allure is attributed to river hags of English folklore: Jenny Greenteeth, and Peg Powler, associated with northern rivers. When not appearing as beautiful young women they are grindylows – green-skinned, shark-toothed, exceptionally strong demons, related etymologically to Grendel, the monster slain by Beowulf in the oldest of written English stories. Grendel is male, but a greater threat comes from his lurking aquatic mother.

In Scotland there are kelpies, and in Wales *ceffyl dŵr* (water horses). In Central America there is the wihwin, and in Australia the bunyip. All will take you down, keep you there. Similar creatures appear in the folklore of China and the Philippines, where they are known as shui gui and siyokoi. In Japan, your green-skinned humanoid river assailant is more likely to be a kappa – turtle-shelled, child-sized but stronger than a man, and known for everything from mischievous upskirting to rape, murder or the removal of the victim's soul through their anus. Kappas are sometimes said to have three bumholes of their own, and are thus producers of prodigious farts. On land, a kappa is vulnerable, and its wellbeing is dependent on a small quantity of water carried in a dish-shaped depression on its head. If the water is spilled, it will die. They are associated with cucumbers, which either deter or encourage them – it seems hard to know which. It's trippy stuff, amusing even, but perhaps the primary purpose of all these fickle aquatic demons is to promote caution around water, especially in children.

Coco encourages me to read Veronica Strang's book, *The Meaning of Water*, which I will later do, and it helps me understand that all the shapeshifting and the dualisms of aquatic mythology are not surprising. 'The most constant "quality" of water', writes Veronica Strang, 'is that it is not constant, but is characterised by transmutability and sensitivity to changes in the environment.'

The transmutability of water allows it to take the form of any containing shape and lends an extraordinary ability to metamorphose between states – liquid, solid, vapour – endlessly and always reversibly. It retains a potential to move between extremes. The sensitivity to change Strang describes includes the way water transmits and reflects light. There's a reason we can't look away. Psychologists call it 'soft fascination': the sight and sound of moving water is sufficiently stimulating to occupy the brain, but irregular enough that it doesn't become hypnotic or monotonous. It holds attention without dominating thought, freeing the mind to swim elsewhere. It is highly conducive to reflective thought, and a powerful pull to what Strang calls 'secular hydrolatry: the sanctification of water without the burden of religious dogma'.

I'm fascinated by Coco's take on reservoirs. In my paddling years I spent many weekends at the National White Water Centre for Wales, located on the Afon Tryweryn, into which water is released from a dam just above. The controlled releases make for highly predictable and reliable paddling conditions all the way down to Bala, swift water with a mixture of natural and modified features on which paddlers of most abilities can hone skills, learn rescue techniques, play to their hearts' content, and where visitors can pay to descend in inflatable rafts steered by experienced guides. It's a place of life and energy in stark contrast to what lies just a few hundred metres upstream.

In the early 1960s the village of Capel Celyn was one of the last wholly Welsh-speaking communities in Wales. It was named for its river, a small tributary of the Tryweryn, which rises between the bosomy summits of Arenig Fawr and Arenig Fach, drops steeply and makes an easterly turn to wind across a flat-bottomed valley of woods and fields, farms and homesteads, a chapel, cemetery and a Quaker meeting house. It broadens out but remains shallow enough to be crossed by fords and stepping stones. At least it did.

Now if you drive the A4212 from Trawsfynydd towards Bala, you round a bend and find a changeling landscape. It's hard to imagine the gut lurch the sheet of wrinkled grey water must cause anyone who knew the place when it was a green valley with a village in its heart.

My own childhood was almost as rootless as Coco's, but in spite of that – or perhaps because of it – my memory for place is very strong. It comforts me to remember details and to know somewhere still exists after I have left. I'm very seldom lost and can usually find a place I've been before again, even after many years. But take me to a place that has changed and I feel a profound unease – a literal dis-location. My teenage hometown and university campus have both undergone drastic development since I knew them, and I find going back deeply unsettling. The coordinates may be right, but so much else is wrong.

Capel Celyn is changed in a wholly more emphatic way. The entire valley has been erased, flooded to create a reservoir to supply drinking water to the English city of Liverpool. Construction was authorised by an Act of UK Parliament, entirely bypassing any Welsh permissions process and a nine-year campaign failed to prevent the inundation of the valley in 1965. Wales has never forgotten the betrayal, not least because the slogan *Cofiwch Dryweryn* ('Remember Tryweryn') graffitied in large white capitals on a red background has become a political and a cultural icon. The original, credited to the journalist, poet and literary scholar Meic Stephens, appeared on a ruined cottage wall near Llanrhystud in Ceredigion. It has been vandalised and repainted dozens of times and recreated in scores of other locations in Wales and around the world.

If you park by the dam now and walk along it, the wind there strikes you with the force of something more than air. Even on a warm day with the sun glinting on it, I wonder if it can ever be beautiful, when you know. In his poem *Reservoirs*, R.S. Thomas described the serenity of such places as revolting, and it doesn't seem too strong a word. With this in mind I wonder out loud how a map of such a place can ever be anything but melancholic. Coco takes a deep breath.

'So… water has always been a big part of my life,' she says. 'As a child I lived for some years with my mother and stepdad on a Dutch barge on a canal outside Bruges where we'd illegally tap into the local electricity supply… I never really had a fixed sense of home, and my family was very dispersed.

My mother's mother was Danish and told stories of growing up playing on big ships and how her father was a sailor who drowned himself at sea. My dad was back in England so all through my childhood I would visit him several times a year, crossing back and forth over the Channel. Water was what connected us, even when it divided us.'

We compare experiences of moving often as children. Both of us are curious about what it's like to live in one place your whole life. 'It must be amazing to have friends you've always known', says Coco. 'But I also wonder if that sense of rootedness and belonging also cultivates a fear of change.

'So I guess I come to this idea of very rooted people losing a home or land they know intimately to water with the perspective of someone who has only ever known change. For them the water is this agent of massive disruption, whereas for me it has been both a constant and a connector.'

She introduces me to the ideas of cultural geographer Caitlin DeSilvey, whose work explores the cultural significance of change processes, in particular of heritage sites, including the concept of 'palliative curation', in which curators document and interpret loss and decay rather than attempting to prevent it. 'There's meaning and memory to be found in changing places,' says Coco. 'Sites of destruction are also the beginning of something new.'

This way of thinking reminds me powerfully of something another archaeologist told me some years ago. Jim Leary's work also deals with movement, from walking to migration. Jim and I first spoke in the run-up to the Brexit referendum, when I called him to talk about Doggerland – the area of low-lying land that once connected Britain to the mainland of Europe before being inundated by rising sea levels eight thousand years ago. Archaeological evidence suggests Doggerland was very much a peopled landscape, and with our modern preoccupation with controlling water it's easy to assume that the gradual loss of land to the sea was a traumatic process. But Jim scotched that idea right away. 'I don't see it like that at all,' he told me. 'To those people the water was an opportunity – full of food, and easier to travel and trade over than the wetland that existed previously. There's every reason to think the creation of the North Sea united people rather than divided them.'

The Tryweryn protest brought a unity too. That vast volume of grey water and the hurt it represents (which I'm very aware is not mine to try and rationalise) remains physically and politically conspicuous, but the rising water was not the end of the story. The number of people whose homes were drowned, 48, was tiny compared with those displaced by reservoir and hydropower schemes elsewhere – millions in India, for example – but for Wales it was a political tipping point. The Parliamentary Act that led to the construction was opposed by all 35 Welsh MPs who voted on it (one abstained), and subsequent events are credited with urgent and ongoing efforts to restore and secure Welsh identity and language, and with contributing to the narrow vote in favour of devolution from the Westminster government in 1997.

The river Coco knows best is another Derwent – the Derbyshire one, on which Ladybower reservoir was built, drowning another village, between 1935 and 1943, with progress slowed by the Second World War but not halted, such was the importance of securing water supplies to the East Midlands cities of Derby, Nottingham and Leicester. Coco has walked to the source several times. 'When you walk a river over and over you come to recognise it as a distinct personality,' she says. 'It's a multi-faceted character. Some of its traits are natural, like the particular hue of green, the smell, and the type of trees on the banks, but others are human – the accents of the people you meet, the ruins of former industry, the mixture of old brick and masonry sticking out of the ground making the paths uneven. And it retains all those flavours even when it flows through the city, where there has been so much development and its banks are littered with bottles and cans and needles.'

We end the day in Pateley Bridge, eating takeaway pizza on the banks of the Nidd and still talking, talking. We don't know it yet but Coco will be a mother soon too. Her daughter will be a true selkie baby, born *en caul* with her amniotic membrane intact. Coco will carry her on her walks, making more memories for the map.

Otter

It's no good – I've looked in all the usual places: coat pockets, my desk, the kitchen dresser, the cupboard by the front door, the windowsill in the loo. I can't find my phone anywhere. Exasperated, I recruit Roy and Lochy to the search. Roy opens the friend finder app on his own device.

'Ah. There you are,' he says, showing me his phone screen where a little icon that is usually me is in the woods, half a mile away. We mount a swift expedition. It's well after dark and the path is steep in places and slick with mud and wet leaves. Even the little stepping-stone hop across a tiny stream draining into the main beck is enough to make me think twice by bobbing torchlight. My phone is lying by the path, where it presumably dropped from my pocket on the afternoon dog walk. We turn happily for home, but just as we hop back over the stepping stone, Roy's torch beam picks out something in the main beck, just ahead.

'Ooooo-tter!' he half-gasps, half-yelps, and I have the fleetingest glimpse: a wink of amber eyeshine and then a long shadow, an insinuation, darker on dark, wraithing upstream like a drop of ink dispersing in gently swirling water. I'm reminded of the otters conjured in monochrome from the brush of the fierce, wise illustrator, Jackie Morris, and of my favourite Ted Hughes poem, *Visitation*, which expresses the otherness of otterness to perfection, never mentioning them by name and thus leaving them half-seen, half-imagined as they so often are in life. We scramble down the brambly bank, hoping to glimpse it again, but there is only water, flowing under the lightest of mists. No matter. This is by far the closest I've seen an otter to the house and it's cast a spell over the day. I dream it still, sometimes, always waking with a sense I'm being not so much invited, as summoned, upstream, and back in time.

CHAPTER 7

The Bell Guy and the Gypsey

Cette terre ardente, où se lamente auprès des sources l'oubli des morts.
This ardent earth, near whose springs voices lament the forgetting of the dead.

Rainer Maria Rilke, *Seen by Angels*,
translated by Merlin Sheldrake

I can't shake the idea that there is more for me to learn from springs, if I can find the right ones. So I start asking around, poring over maps and exploring unfamiliar corners of the internet – the realms not so much of naturalists and paddlers, but of hydrologists, geologists, historians, mythologists, witches and druids. And begin to realise just how leaky the land is.

I set out on my first explicit spring-quest in November while recuperating from a bout of flu that has left me struggling to walk even a slight incline. It's the first clear day after weeks of record-breaking rain and the sun has drawn me out like Mole in *The Wind in the Willows*, blinking into the light.

Following a combination of hunch and hearsay I take the car, cross the bloated Derwent and drive up onto the chalk of the Yorkshire Wolds. I park in a layby formed from a meander of road cut off by the A614, zip my jacket against the chill and walk. The footpath is blocked by a couple of sections of temporary fencing with warning signs in strident red, yellow and black: *Tree felling in progress*. And indeed, what appears on the map and satellite image as 37 acres of patchy woodland is now less than half that. The rest is brash and a few neat timber stacks. The work is still going on – I sidestep the fence and approach a small group of men gathered around a caterpillar-tracked forestry vehicle.

This isn't what I had in mind. I know the spring I've seen on the map is some way off the public footpath, and had hoped to find an unobtrusive route in through the trees. Not only are the trees mostly gone, but there will also be at least four pairs of eyes to witness my trespass and come at me with health and safety regulations. I opt for a direct approach.

'Hi! It looks like you've been busy.'

I can see now the trees they've taken down are a monoculture, only one row still standing before more natural looking growth beyond. I gesture to the timber stacks.

'What are they?

'Poplars, mostly,' replies the older of the men. He has the look of a landowner, but a friendly one. 'Planted in the seventies. They should have come out long ago.'

'What were they planted for?'

The younger man, wearing a fleece emblazoned with a logo saying *TreeWorx*, explains they were intended for matchwood, but then that started coming more cheaply from the Czech Republic, and it wasn't worth harvesting them.

'Now they're no good for anything but chipping,' he says. 'But even that isn't easy. The wood's so wet – these'll have to be dried out before we can do anything with 'em.'

I decide to come clean.

'I was hoping to go and look at the springs over there. Do you know them?'

The older man's eyes light up. 'Oh aye. Bell Guy. It's started pushing early this year' – he nods towards the tree man – 'made his job a whole lot harder.'

Tree man grins. 'Yeah, we thought we'd be in and out by now, but it's saturated everything.'

I say I'm interested in chalk streams and the older man, whose name I learn later is Alan Mullinger, explains it's for the beck that he's taking the trees down. 'Poplars drink a lot. So we're going to replace them with a native mix.'

We chat a while longer and Alan gives me directions to the spring from the far side of the wood, advising against trying to walk through. Five minutes later I'm skirting the other side, past fields of sprouting winter wheat. At the edge of the trees is a clear, fast-flowing stream a metre wide, running over pale gravel between heaps of dead leaves. Three roe deer erupt from the trees ahead of me, and bound across the fields, white bums glowing in the already lowering sun, and a minute later, two more. A shrew runs across my path. And while I'm distracted, the stream just ... disappears. I'm still walking alongside the channel, but now it's a ditch full of yellow leaves, and no running water at all. Puzzled, I retrace my steps a couple of dozen paces, and there it is again, in full flow. I step down into the water and turn upstream again. After a few metres I find a spring – a hole in the bank from which the whole volume of the stream wells gin clear, under enough pressure to pillow gently before riffling off in the direction I've come. It's fascinating, but not the spring I've come to see.

I check the map and walk on, still following the woodland edge. It was good advice to go around rather than through – I'm still a touch weak and wobbly, breathless with the exertion of just walking on uneven ground. I can see standing water in amongst the trees – puddles of bright sky, reflecting the mostly bare branches of alder, birch and sycamore. A little further on, an opening in the trees suggests a way in, and I can hear running water again. This stream is much larger – easily 3m wide, and just upstream is what I'm looking for. I had thought it would be harder to find, more subtle somehow, but it's almost laughably conspicuous. A circular pool, with an emphatic bulge at its centre. Bell Guy Spring. At times, I'm told, it rises under such pressure it looks almost like a small geyser and the penny drops that maybe that's what *Bell Guy* describes – a bell-shaped geyser. Today it's a low dome, the size of a hubcap. I pick my way around the squelchy woodland above the pool – it's definitely a source, because where upstream should be, there is nothing. It's a fully formed river, out of nowhere. It's what I expected, I suppose, but even so, it seems audacious.

This instantaneousness of chalk rivers has always fascinated people. The lack of visible gathering. The obscurity of their origins. Even when it's not pushing a fountain, Bell Guy seems to mark itself out with its self-cleaning ring of white gravel – giving the impression of a tended shrine. The quality of the water is a further miracle. Its dazzling clarity is the result of its passing through nature's finest filter. Its constant temperature is a promise that down there, through the portal of the spring, is a world unaffected through eternity by the vagaries of season and weather, unassailed by storms, never parched nor frozen, untroubled by human conflicts, follies and woes.

I gaze from the bank. The pool is about 4m across, with the spring at its centre. It's hard to tell how deep the water is, so I step in cautiously. I move slowly – partly because the air temperature is 4°C and I have no desire to overtop my wellies or topple in, but also because the plumes of silt and organic detritus stirred up by my boots seem like an insult. I don't want to besmirch the clarity of this water. The dome of the spring is glassy and taut, the only smooth part of the pool surface – everywhere else there are wrinkles and ripples. From the bank I thought it looked like a crystal ball, but now I have the unsettling impression of a great eye, like that of a whale, rolling in its white surround, with a dark pupil and glassy lens, bulging with vitreous humour.

We dissected the eye of a bullock once, at school, and when clear goo squirted from the tip of the scalpel, I fainted – mortifying for a wannabe biologist. I feel a ripple of nausea at the memory and tell myself that this is only water. But I can't unsee the eye – it bulges and rolls. I look away to where the low sun, now brilliantly orange, is illuminating the bare trees and gilding the branches, making the moss on their trunks glow. When I look again at the spring it is no longer an eye. I can see tiny granules of chalk rising in it, rising and falling like the little plastic grains in a snow globe. I'm close enough to bend down and touch it, but I watch first. The water is so animated it's hard to make out what I'm looking at – in places where the surface is convex and taut I can see the bottom with complete clarity, but there are so many currents and gyres, creases and ripples that these windows of clarity oscillate, jostle and flare in and out of existence. Broken reflections of sky and bare branches overhead interfere, confusing the picture further, and I peer for a good minute before it starts to resolve, and my stomach lurches again. It's a concentric arrangement – the leaf-laden stream bed, a circle of clean white gravel, and in the centre, what I now perceive to be a hole – unevenly shaped, but with a defined lip and totally dark inside. The hole isn't large – there's no danger of me falling in – but the sudden sense of a void beneath my feet gives me vertigo, as though the silty stream bed I had waded across so carelessly might suddenly give way, casting me down into an underworld where, for all the whiteness of the chalk and the clarity of the water, there would be only dark.

This is no eye. It is a mouth. It is a mouth of the Earth, and she is speaking water.

I'm transfixed, and a bit anxious. I imagine reaching into that void, but am seized with a feeling that doing so would be, not wrong exactly, but unwelcome, intrusive ... inappropriate. I remember the scene in *Flash Gordon* when Peter Duncan reaches his arm into a hollow log only to be stung by some indescribable horror that makes him beg for death. It gave me night terrors for months when I was about nine. Besides, the water is too deep to reach into without getting soaked. So I settle for looking.

The shattered reflections that make the image so confusing prompt me to wish I'd brought goggles, or at least polarising sunglasses. I wonder if it might be clearer without direct light, and shift my position, shuffling around until I'm standing between the low sun and the spring, then bend to look again.

The image is different. I can see my own reflection against the sky, but it's a startling one. My face is completely in shadow, and there are bright orange flames shooting out of my head. I realise it's the sun lighting up my frizzy unbrushed hair, which does a good job of diffusing the fiery light, and the constant motion of the water makes the reflections roll outwards. I can account for it all in terms of physics. But it's not every day you see yourself as a flaming effigy framed in a flickering black and white portal to the underworld. I take a few deep breaths.

Right now, I'm not who I usually imagine myself to be.

Right now, I am what? A seer? A witch, perhaps. I feel I have been offered some kind of permission, and change my mind about reaching in to the water. I push up my sleeves as far as they'll go and use both hands. It's cool but not cold – all chalk springs well up at a constant temperature close to 10°C: they feel icy in summer, and warm in winter, and on very cold mornings they are often cloaked in low-lying fog. Today the water is warmer than the air, but is flowing so fast it chills my skin rapidly. There's way more force in the water than I expected – pressing my palms down I feel real resistance and I understand why Alan referred to springs as pushing, rather than flowing or running. There'd be no staunching this flow, no silencing this song.

The chill begins to make the bones of my hands and forearms ache. I scoop up water from the centre of the dome, sip some, rinse my face, and stand upright again.

My feet must have been slowly sinking into the leaf muck because, I realise, water is beginning to seep into my jeans. It's probably not conducive to convalescence, but I'm not ready to leave just yet. I stay, watching the light play on trees and branches, hearing leaves fall, rooks call, while the water dries and bonds with my skin, forming a cool patina on my cheeks and forehead. I begin then to shiver in earnest, and with some difficulty haul my boots from the sticky bottom and wade to the bank.

Along with the Gough Map on my study wall is another – a special edition published to commemorate the bicentenary of William Smith's 1815 *Geological Map of Britain*. One of the most striking features of both Smith's original and this reproduction is a bright green swoosh the shape of a crooked number 2, or a swan looking up. It runs from the gannet- and auk-stacked cliffs of Bempton and Flamborough Head on the coast of Yorkshire, down through Lincolnshire and the bulge of East Anglia, then south-west via the North Downs to Salisbury Plain, and back east via the Wessex and South Downs, where it meets the coasts of Sussex and Kent. This is all chalk: Wolds, Downs, Cliffs. I've never lived anywhere in the UK that wasn't on it or near it, and though it covers only around 20 per cent of the map, it seems, culturally, the rock of England. Grit and slate and granite have an appealing Celtic wildness to them, limestone a holesome wholesomeness, but nothing quite compares with the crumbling grandiosity and benign liveability of chalk. The dense archaeology of chalk landscapes suggests this has long been understood. And for the biologist there is the added appeal that this soft, pale geology is, or was, alive. Chalk is made from the calcite skeletons of microscopic marine organisms – mainly foraminiferans and coccolithophores, deposited on ancient ocean floors. They are beautiful, these tiny forms, and their variability and delicacy means that compared to most other rocks, the microscopic structure of chalk is higgledy-piggledy – riddled with minute holes, and thus highly porous – between a third and half of its volume is space. Porosity isn't unusual – clay is also highly porous.

But while clay is often impermeable, the voids in chalk are accessible – they are joined up – so that it can both store and release water.

The same chalky area shows up clearly on another map of Great Britain I like – a digital one with a single GIS overlay showing the network of rivers and streams. The density is astonishing. Rivers are often described as the veins of the landscape, and the analogy is striking on this map – it really does look like an anatomical diagram of a circulatory system. If you zoom out to view the whole of England on one screen, the chalk stands out as areas of bony white where rivers are scarce. This is because water tends to infiltrate down into chalk rather than running over it. But where chalk water does emerge above ground, it is something special. Eked through nature's finest filter, it flows pure, clear and sweet from the Earth. Its constant temperature provides refuge from summer heat and chalk springs provide free running water even in the coldest of winters.

English chalk rivers like the Waveney, the Granta, the Itchen, the Blackwater, the Avon and the Test are celebrated both ecologically and culturally. They weave and sparkle through literature, from the works of Thomas Hardy to Richard Adams' *Watership Down*. They surface to glitter in the poetry of Keats, Wordsworth, Tennyson and Brooke, and of course in the aquatic odyssey of *Waterlog* – Roger Deakin's amphibious journey through Britain and the plethora of wild swimming books, blogs and essays it has inspired. Even the Thames, with many chalk stream tributaries, can claim some of the magic – its depiction in Kenneth Grahame's *The Wind in the Willows* strongly evokes the character of a chalk river. For fly fishermen, the chalk rivers of south-eastern England are places of pilgrimage.

Oddly, the chalk streams that rise in the Yorkshire Wolds barely get a look-in in all this celebrity. The Wolds landscape could be variously mistaken for the Chilterns, the Sussex or Wessex Downs or Salisbury Plain, but with few major roads, and a very quiet stretch of coastline on one side, they are more remote than any of those.

Not all of the springs here are as obvious or predictable as Bell Guy. There's another I want to see, but I'm not sure I'll be able to find it. Its course is marked on modern maps, and if you consider that rivers-only GIS overlay, it stands out as the only watercourse running west-east in the otherwise dry northern Wolds. My doubts about finding it aren't cartographical or navigational – they are hydrological.

This lonely ribbon of water is the Gypsey Race, the most northerly chalk stream in England, and thus, I believe, the world. Unlike the others that rise in the Wolds, it does not *appear* to drain into the River Hull, but makes its solitary way directly into the North Sea at Bridlington. I'm picking my words carefully, because the Gypsey seems capable of defying most things said about it. It is one of the strangest watercourses I've ever encountered.

The folklore surrounding the Gypsey Race stems mainly from the extraordinary unpredictability of its flow. The water comes and goes, not just with rainfall or season, and most bizarrely, not with any consistency along its length. It hardly ever achieves full flow, and when it does, unsettling events are reputed to follow. It is said to have appeared just before the Great Plague in 1664. It flowed again as William of Orange deposed King James in 1689 and in 1795, shortly before a huge meteorite landed close to its course at Wold Newton (the meteorite now resides in the Natural History Museum, while the impact site is marked with an obelisk near to an immaculate caravan park whose owner is happy to direct visitors to it). It ran again, allegedly, at the start of the two world wars. Yesterday, I got a message from my friend Jon Traill, living landscapes manager at the Yorkshire Wildlife Trust, to say the top spring is running hard, now.

The itinerancy and romance evoked by the name of this miniature river feels wonderfully apt for a flow that comes and goes, but while the etymology of gypsy travellers is from Egyptian, reflecting the Middle Eastern heritage of the Roma, the river's name shares a linguistic root with gypsum – from the Greek word *gypsos* for plaster and for chalk. The Gypsey Race is a chalk stream in both nature and name.

A hard frost has burned off and it is turning into a spectacular blue dome day. The sky is deep azure at its zenith, white at the horizon, with a light mist amplifying the light in such a way it is almost painful to look at. It's been a strange, unchill winter until this extended January clear spell – the result of a huge pressure system, the highest recorded since records began in the 1950s. These days have been strange in other ways. Science corners of Twitter are full of speculation about the fading of Betelgeuse, the red star at Orion's shoulder: specifically whether its dramatic decline over recent months might presage its imminent demise (or rather our imminent witnessing of a demise that might have happened more than 700 years ago). Some say it may be about to explode into a supernova, and last night between bouts of insomnia, I dreamt over and over of an explosion blooming like a white carnation in Orion's lapel. In my dream, it pulsed steadily, each pulse brighter and bigger, bathing the galaxy in icy white radiation, while the air around the Earth swelled and receded in a rhythm I recognised after I woke as the throbbing engines of Doctor Who's TARDIS. The dream looped maddeningly and so at three o'clock I got up and pulled a down jacket over my dressing gown. I was shoving bare feet into wellies when the dog appeared, ears pricked. We went out together and walked up the frosted lane to my farmer neighbour's driveway, where there's a clear view of the northern sky. Orion sat low on the horizon, and at his shoulder was an orange glow. Definitely faint, but definitely there*. I wondered if the Gypsey would be.

It's gone eleven a.m. when I reach Duggleby – the first settlement on the Gypsey Race and one that predates recorded history, being marked with an impressive round barrow. The first things that surprise me about the stream that flows though the village are how tiny it is, and how close it runs to the houses. The channel would be crossable in one stride, but to facilitate access to the adjacent cottages, each has its own little footbridge leading to the front door. Upstream of Duggleby, the stream runs alongside the road for a short distance, and you could easily mistake it for a field drain. Only the clarity of the water gives a clue that this is no ditch. It's flowing well today and chuckling quietly to itself.

I follow the channel upstream to where it diverges from the road, then along a field boundary. There's a decent 6m margin between the sprouting winter wheat and the channel, which looks as if it was sown last year with a seed-rich weed mixture for wild birds. The stream channel is thick with dead stems of great willowherb and meadowsweet and there is no chuckle here, just a silent flow evident only as a slight disturbance in the reflections. I pass a thicket of hawthorn and willow. The hawthorn branches are thickly clad in yellow and grey lichen; the willow is sprouting vigorously from a hard trim, its stems aortic blood red, with buds like filthy hooked fingernails. There are maroon shoots of briar too – an intense tangle of bloody colour under the strong sun. As I pass the densest part of the thicket there's a slight creak and something large moves within. I imagine it first to be a resting deer and whisper an apology – then it stands up and my heart

*A study published in 2021 suggested that the temporary dimming of Betelgeuse observed in 2020 was more likely to be a result of dust and other debris shed by the red giant than a sign of impending stellar death.

jumps. It's a hare. I don't think I've ever seen a live adult this close up before. And I'm astonished by its stature. It holds its ground a long time, facing obliquely away from me so I can see just one huge, fierce topaz eye, then it is gone – whipping over the new wheat so fast it has crossed the field in the time it takes me to exhale, leaving me tingling, goosebumpy.

The source is marked by a couple of large multi-trunked sentinel willows in which rooks rattle their beaks to create a soft, percussive clatter – a gentle drumroll. At the bases of the trees is a sunken pool, above which clouds of winter gnats are dancing in the midday sun. The pool is full of fleshy stemmed, bright green weed – I scramble down the bank and haul a strand out. It's fool's watercress – celery-stemmed and much tougher than real watercress, with leaves in opposite pairs and hairy roots sprouting from every leaf base. I'm not really in any doubt, but break a stem and sniff all the same – it smells strongly of carrots. The undersides of the leaves are covered in tiny leeches.

The water in the pool is several degrees warmer than the air. The light plays on the silt and flint gravel and bends in the meniscal curves associated with every leaf and stem at the surface – even the tiny leaves of duckweed each lie in their own little dimple. These, and the ripples eddying around individual surface features create a mesmerising lava-lamp effect on the stream-bed – each shadow has shimmering, spectral coloured edges. The longer I watch this play of light the more I realise how complex the flow is. Water is coming from more than one direction – there are several upwellings in the pool, but also, I see now, there are additional flows trickling in from the other side. I climb back up the bank and skirt around a slight dip in the adjacent field, where an area roughly the size of a tennis court is gleaming with reflected sky. It's been tilled and planted like the rest but the winter wheat isn't doing so well. The furrows between crop rows have clear water in them, and washed gravel and mats of bright green blanket weed. When I stop moving I can hear something – a rapid, irregular *blib-blib-blib-blib*. The ground is bubbling. A slight disturbance in the furrow nearest my feet catches my eye – water welling from a tiny hole. And once I've tuned in to the sight and sound, I realise there are scores of these little spring mouths – probably more than a hundred, from which water is muttering and guttering along the furrows, puddling at the field edge then finding its way through the leggy vegetation of the banks above the main spring head and into the pool.

How long has this water been underground? Where is it being pushed from? And why now? It's been a wet winter, but the dry spell has been going on for several days – puddles have evaporated, rain-fed streams are low. But this uncanny spring has a schedule all of its own. The fact that this area of the field is cultivated suggests that it's very unusual for this uppermost part to run. I can't help wondering what this rising might presage for the year that has just begun.

I retrace my steps to Duggleby and beyond, to where the Gypsey sweeps in lively curves through a grassy field in which regular shaped humps and bumps show the layout of the abandoned village of Mowthorpe. My arrival spooks a flock of 150 greylag geese into a chuntering take-off, but they settle again in the lush grass 100m away. At the bottom of the field the stream gurgles through a terracotta pipe under the lane and gushes out the other side with a sound like a huge ancient bathtub filling. A woman walking a spaniel stops to look with me and says she's never seen it running so high or fast.

I drive to Kirby Grindalythe, the next village down the valley, and meet the Race slewing around the first house in the settlement and overtopping its banks into a heavily trampled field, from the corner of which someone has dug a short ditch to return water to the channel. The excavated

mud and stones are still heaped nearby and the shovel has
been left handy in case of further need. Without this small
intervention the flow would be rushing into the house
below. This tricksy stream may be small, but its potential for
mischief is evident.

The next village down the valley is West Lutton and I
drive, intending to pick up the Gypsey there. Its course is
easy to find – more neat canalisation, more little bridges,
but, when I peer in, I'm nonplussed. The channel is
completely empty. I ask another dogwalker if she knows
anything about it. She says she moved here in 2017. 'It was
flowing then. But it dried up in the summer of 2018 and
didn't come back until this week when it ran for a few
days – that's why there's ice in there now,' she points to a
frosted puddle no bigger than a tea tray, 'Then it dropped
away again to nothing.' I tell her about the near-flooding
I've just seen a mile upstream in Kirby Grindalythe and
what the woman with the spaniel said in Duggleby, and I
ask where she thinks that water is going, if not here. 'Nobody
seems to know. There's talk in the village about it – some
people want the parish council to commission an
investigation, but the old folk say just to leave it, it'll sort
itself out. I don't know what to think really, it's very strange.'
We stand and look at the patch of ice as though it might
have an answer. It really is very strange indeed.

The old folk in West Lutton were right. I go back to the
Gypsey Race a year and a half later during a dry spell in July
2021, with archaeologist Jim Leary. It is running low at
Duggleby, with a mere half inch at Kirby Grindalythe. I
know better now than to assume this will mean no water at
West Lutton, and indeed, there is more flow there than at
either village upstream. Jim's explanation is that the Race is
not a single watercourse but a system of springs whose
inconsistent flows just happen to use the same channel. This
fits loosely with what Jon Traill told me: that the water

appearing from the aquifer at Duggleby is not necessarily continuous with that flowing further down. 'It seems that the top flow goes into a fault line somewhere above the Luttons. From there, who knows – it might appear in the catchment of the Hull. The other thing is the Gypsey always comes late – even with a good winter rainfall – sometimes in April. Sometimes not at all. Then in 2012 it flooded the larger downstream village of Burton Fleming – folk newer to the area couldn't get their head around where it was coming from and how it kept coming, not down the channel, but up out of the ground.'

Jim and I head to Rudston, a village claiming to be one of the oldest continuously inhabited settlements in England. It lies in the long scoop of the Great Wold Valley, with its Norman church on a slight rise around which the Gypsey Race performs a ninety-degree left turn. If you stand on this corner, and peek over the roof of a nearby house, you can see the top of the tower of All Saints, an attractive church dating to the fourteenth century. But the spiritual significance of this place predates the church by a very long way. What you can't see now from the bend in the Race until you walk up the hill and around the church, is a gigantic standing stone that would once have dominated the scene. The Rudston monolith is the tallest of its kind in the country at just under 8m – twice as high as the sarsen stones of Stonehenge, and with perhaps as much again embedded in the ground.

This immense menhir was somehow set into place in the late Neolithic or early Bronze Age and may predate the birth of Christ by as much as 2,500 years. The name Rudston is Old English, probably derived from *Rood-stane*, suggesting that Christianity had appropriated the monolith long before the church was built. This, says Jim, was entirely deliberate – it was generally easier to engulf Pagan religions than to shut them down. I wonder how many gods the stone has seen come and go? Celtic, Roman, Saxon and Norse religions may all have found it a useful focus before the Normans came – and all invaders have at least respected it enough not to go to the trouble of bringing it down. I've been here a few times now and what bothers me most about the location of the church, just a few paces away, is that it's no longer possible to stand here and see the sky all around, or to watch the sun dip. If its landscape context were not eclipsed by the church, this place would surely be as famous as Stonehenge or Avebury.

The stone is not local. Rudston is on chalk, but this great shard, shaped like a giant ironing board, is gritstone. The nearest gritstone outcrops are ten miles away, at Cayton near Scarborough – but the best geological matches to this one are further still, in formations on the North York Moors inland of Whitby, fully 30 miles north. Transporting the stone here, over undulating country, would be a massive logistical exercise even today. That it was achieved more than four thousand years ago almost defies belief.

In the intervening millennia, rain has scored deep runnels down the narrower edges of the monolith, which is also deeply pockmarked where conglomerated pebbles, once embedded like cherries in a cake, have weathered out. In 1773 a local worthy, Mrs Bosville, noticed weathering at the top of the stone and decided to address the issue by adding a cap made of lead. Some say she had an ulterior motive – to prevent the escape of the Pagan energy that seems to thrum here. The surrounding landscape is thick with ancient earthworks, including four cursus monuments: linear features demarcated by ditches thought to represent actual or symbolic processionary routes. Three of those converging at Rudston intersect with the Gypsey Race. There are dozens of burial structures, henges, enclosures and ditches up and down the Great Wold Valley. Jim and I spend a long day visiting some of them, including the round barrows of Duggleby Howe, Wold Newton and Willy Howe. Between these, almost every field we walk seems to have intriguing hummocks suggestive of former buildings, including several whole abandoned villages, and depressions that might have been quarries and holloways. The whole landscape is begging for archaeological investigation, and Jim is under no doubt about the significance of the intermittent thread of chalk water that links them all.

After we part company in Rudston I drive the last few miles of the Gypsey Race's course – it runs inconspicuously alongside the road most of the way to Bridlington Harbour, and there, still tiny, it trickles meekly from under a car park though a huge culvert, big enough to accommodate the next surprise flood delivered by this mysterious and capricious little flow. What no one can say is when that might be.

CHAPTER 8

A willow grows aslant a brook

There is a willow grows aslant a brook,
That shows his hoar leaves in the glassy stream;
There with fantastic garlands did she come
Of crow-flowers, nettles, daisies, and long purples
That liberal shepherds give a grosser name,
But our cold maids do dead men's fingers call them:
There, on the pendent boughs her coronet weeds
Clambering to hang, an envious sliver broke;
When down her weedy trophies and herself
Fell in the weeping brook. Her clothes spread wide;
And, mermaid-like, awhile they bore her up:
Which time she chanted snatches of old tunes;
As one incapable of her own distress,
Or like a creature native and indued
Unto that element: but long it could not be
Till that her garments, heavy with their drink,
Pull'd the poor wretch from her melodious lay
To muddy death.

William Shakespeare, *Hamlet* (Act 4, Scene 7)

As the bus crawls along the dual carriageway out of Kingston upon Thames, a woman in the next seat says she'll show me where to get off 'in the village'. I look out at the retail outlets, cranes, multilane traffic, dreary in February drizzle and her use of the word seems odd. But as we turn off the A240, quite abruptly, we're on a tree-lined road passing distinctly rustic-looking buildings. Ewell clings to its rural identity, despite having been engulfed by urban sprawl. I get off at Bourne Hall Park, where traffic noise is mingled with a pandemonium of avian woodwind and brass from at least 150 Canada and greylag geese, mallards, mute swans and coots, packed onto a murky half-acre pond like the world's least disciplined orchestra.

The river I've come to see, the Hogsmill, rises from a series of springs around Ewell, including one somewhere beneath that chaotic feathered throng. There's also a two-inch-deep trickle running past the park in a walled channel. Its bottom is covered in black silt and dead leaves, but its flow bears the signature clarity of chalk water.

I cross a sloping lawn smeared with goose droppings to the late-1960s rotunda that contains the civic offices of Epsom and Ewell and, on the first floor, the local museum. Curator Jeremy Harte meets me in the records room, which doubles as a shared office. It is a space packed with shelves and filing cabinets and mismatched furniture, and there's a grubby sink full of tannin-stained mugs. Jeremy shows me to a table where he has already laid files with information about the river. He makes me the first of several mugs of strong tea and tells me a story about a huge trout that lived for years under the bridge adjacent to the park, greatly admired by the Victorian naturalist and essayist Richard Jefferies. This fish evaded all attempts to catch it with hook and line but became trapped in a small pool when the river was temporarily diverted to permit the laying of a pipe. Four men attacked the pool, churning it to mud as they groped around, spears at the ready. Jefferies couldn't bear to watch, preferring to hold on to a vain hope that the great fish might somehow escape, but he never saw it again. Perhaps, I think, it disappeared, like the Moon in Lisel Mueller's potent poem *Moon Fishing*, where men (I'm afraid I always assume they are men) hunt the Moon's reflection with pitchforks, nets of hair, hooks baited with their hearts and eventually try to drink it, draining the pool until only mud remains. I ask if trout are ever seen here now and Jeremy's colleague Dave says I'm more likely to see fancy carp.

I scan several decades worth of leaflets, magazine features, gazetteers, newsletters and archaeological, historical and ecological reports featuring the Hogsmill, while a steady current of curator chat eddies around me, mingling football results, recent *University Challenge* questions, and gossipy speculation on the lovers of Elizabeth I.

I see the pond with new eyes on the way out. Hydrologically and historically, it is deeper and more connected than it looks. I've just learned that an opportunistic excavation that took place when the spring ran dry in 1990 revealed coins dating back to the Roman occupation; Iron Age and Saxon pottery; and an abundance of small spherical flints likely to have been used as slingshot for hunting wildfowl. If the density of birds was anything like it is now you could hardly miss.

Evidence of such ancient history makes me wonder when this story should start. I grope mentally and arrive a thousand years ago, with a Norse prince, who might be more myth than man. It flows from then to now through England's most famous playwright; an imaginary drowned heroine; a visionary young artist and a Victorian supermodel; a retired biology teacher, a semiaquatic rodent and a group of ardent young conservationists.

Yesterday I took a trip to Tate Britain. Walking there from the Underground at Pimlico you meet an artist in bronze on the border of John Islip Street and Atterbury Street. He is John Everett Millais, who was 22 when he came to Ewell in 1851 with William Holman Hunt for a summer of creativity and companionship. Millais was a prodigy – enrolled at a Royal Academy school of art at the age of eleven, he co-founded the Pre-Raphaelite Brotherhood with Holman Hunt and five others in 1848. The Pre-Raphaelites defied convention by devoting themselves to art that gave a true account of nature as well as certain favoured human ideals, resulting in works that were rich in detail and, in the championing words of the critic John Ruskin 'rejecting nothing, selecting nothing, and scorning nothing'. Inside the gallery, the most famous of Millais' works remains a crowd-puller. It's relatively small, presented in a heavy gold frame, mounted low down on the wall. I took a seat opposite. The gallery was busy – it contains dozens of astonishing works including other Pre-Raphaelite masterpieces. But this is the one that draws people in and holds them. The woman next to me on the bench had come from the Netherlands especially to see it, having done so regularly for years. 'I think this virus means we will soon be unable to travel, so I came now while I still could,' she told me.

The subject, Shakespeare's Ophelia drowning, is many things: tragic; compelling; beautiful – but most irresistibly for me, it is heartachingly familiar. I don't yet know this river, but I do know that mingling of verdancy and decay; the fuggy rot-fertile scent. I know how the water sounds as it trickles around the iris stems and how the air just above it is cool enough to raise goosebumps on sunny day. I know how the tresses of water crowfoot and starwort move in sinusoidal waves. I know how the bottom looks from high angles and low ones, and how it feels under the feet. I know how breezes shift willow boughs, and how the leaves scatter sunlight into whispers. Immersed in this painting I sense all the things the oblivious, imaginary girl in the river cannot.

The river Millais painted is the Hogsmill, as it was one summer 170 years ago. But it could be almost any English chalk stream. Lovely, lush, and just a bit mucky around the edges. Holman Hunt later wrote about Millais' discovery of the location: 'We pursued the crystal driven weeds with reawakening faith, then suddenly the "Millais luck" presented him with the exact composition of arboreal and floral richness he had dreamed of, so that he pointed exultantly, saying, "Look! Could anything be more perfect?"'

It won't look like that today, of course. February is the wrong time of year, and the intervening decades have not been kind to our rivers. But several of the leaflets and magazine articles I read in the museum suggested the Hogsmill remains a rare urban corridor of connected green space, though the Environment Agency reports tell a less encouraging tale of declining water quality and dwindling flow.

The river made this valley. It was the reason for settlement, and for a thousand years it was the principal source of power. Flour mills like the big white weatherboarded one just downstream of Ewell Bridge became less viable in the twentieth century – not only because other forms of energy were available, but because with ever-increasing abstraction from the aquifer for domestic and agricultural use, there simply wasn't enough flow to turn the stones. Some years the upper Hogsmill dried up completely. It's running now, though. A swift, clear stream, knee-deep over gravel through a wooded area with a network of paths and channels. The banks are lined with rushes and flag iris among which a moorhen is floating. In the water is a green galaxy of starwort, and close to where a huge fallen willow sprawls across the channel is what looks at first glance to be a Sainsbury's® Bag for Life, but turns out to be a gigantic, bright orange ornamental carp. One point to curator Dave.

Another fallen tree presents what could be a useful crossing option, except that on the other side is a substantial building site. A huge pit has been excavated and the river below is clouded with runoff. It passes under a railway and is briefly culverted through an Environment Agency gauging station. No sooner does the culvert end than the river leaps to life, slewing left to right like a snake released from a box. I want to clap. A set of stepping stones are slightly underwater – I splosh my way across.

In Chamber Wood there are catkins on the hazels, and the mature oaks and ash are thick with ivy. There's a woodland soundscape too – rooks, robin and wren, and great tits belting out their two-note song. But these familiar vocalisations are drowned abruptly by a brawling cacophony as several jade monsters hurtle overhead. Ring-necked parakeets have become a completely unremarkable component of home counties avifauna since I moved north. They are the greenest thing in this green place, but for all the sumptuousness of their plumage, the sound is hideous. I almost fall over my own feet watching them, but neither the couple walking up ahead nor their two dogs turn a hair.

Where the river disappears into darkness under Ruxley Road the rushes are clogged with a miserable debris of cans and plastic. And yet – something bright and white catches my eye and my breath. A little egret, close enough that I can see the barbs of its feathers, is wading in the stream, dazzling in the dark mouth of the culvert. As I watch, it spreads its umbrella-like arms and half-jumps, half-flies into an overhanging tree, yellow feet dangling for a moment, and balances ludicrously on a branch too spindly to carry its weight. From a slightly greater distance – perhaps from the road – one might easily mistake it for a snagged white plastic bag. Oddly, this thought cheers me – I've seen an orange Carp For Life and a plain unbranded egret, but very few actual plastic bags, for which there has been a charge in supermarkets since 2015. Before that they were an almost inescapable blight in rivers and the wider landscape, and while they were only one component of a much bigger problem, with political will, getting rid of them has been relatively easy.

Like the parakeets and the carp, little egrets have become everyday here, but to my eye they are exotic, and reminiscent of the improbable assemblages of wildlife adorning religious paintings and trendy wallpaper: placed together for symbolic or aesthetic reasons rather than ecological ones. I'm not sure Millais would have been able to resist the angelic white, the furnace orange or the embroidery-silk greens of these three. I can imagine them all in the scene of *Ophelia* – an egret on the bank, an orange carp hovering just below the waterline, and a pair of parakeets bending a willow bough above.

Crossing the road and the river I find an indistinct, grassy trail behind some garden fences. On the other bank is a tarmacked path, which explains the lack of use on this one. A thick border of thorn scrub has an almost instant damping effect on the traffic noise and within 25m all I can hear is the rustle of dead beech leaves under my feet and the scolding of a wren down near the water. I regret looking for the bird though – close to river level the vegetation is clotted with cartons, bottles and poo bags, interwoven with ivy and herb Robert.

I pass another huge fallen willow. This one has been cut into sections, laid along the bank and wired down, perhaps to prevent it washing away or being mischievously lobbed into the river. But it's ecological thinking too – left to rot here the wood will support life of many kinds. Willows are by far the most abundant tree along the river – the larger ones have all had drastic surgery, presumably for safety, but there is something fantastical and defiant about the vigour of their regrowth. Starbursts of new shoots erupting from the knobbly end of each truncated branch make them look like pugilistic old warlocks, blasting spells from raised fists.

In a small grove of ash set back from the river I find a kind of memorial. The leafless branches are weighed down with dozens of candle lanterns, Christmas tree decorations and other ornaments, teddy bears and a grey plush bunny hanging as though from a gamekeeper's gibbet, and on lengths of plastic ribbon, several small glass vinegar bottles – the kind you see in greasy spoon cafes. At the base of the tree is a disintegrating bouquet of artificial carnations, the frame of a funeral flower arrangement, and several plastic containers with dead plants in them.

There's a laminated birthday card with a poem: '*There is beauty all around us, in flowers, birds and trees, in streams and low topped mountains, in stars and deep blue seas.*' The intent is perhaps not so different from that behind the coins and the pottery excavated in Ewell, or the grave goods and votive offerings deposited in rivers the world over. But it makes me sad and conflicted to think all of this lovingly offered plastic will end up in the river.

A bounding grey squirrel accompanies me over the next road bridge and past a sign welcoming us to the Borough of Kingston, seeming far less perturbed by the six lanes of traffic than I am. An ironwork gate leads back to the river path, and the water hurries over a series of small stone sills. Its volume has swelled again and it is cloudy and khaki-coloured.

Two sounds register above the noise of traffic. Robin song and a hellish mechanical screeching. I expect to come across someone using an angle grinder to cut steel, but find instead a chain-link fence, beyond which two go-karts are fishtailing around a track with crash barriers made from stacks of painted tyres to keep the karts to the loops and bends of their artificial channel.

As if to ward off rose-tinted ideas of a more peaceful past, an interpretation board by the fence tells me that between 1720 and 1870 this section of the river was heavily industrialised, with more than a dozen mills churning out not flour, but gunpowder. This was the perfect location – with power from the river and abundant willows to provide suitable charcoal. The mills were notoriously dangerous. Whole operations were frequently blown up. Meanwhile their output wreaked wider devastation – exported for use in the American Civil War, and the Franco-Prussian War of 1870, where dubious powder quality is sometimes cited as a factor in the defeat of the French and the ensuing unification of Germany.

It was one of these mills that William Holman Hunt used as the setting for his painting *The Light of the World*. The image, which Holman Hunt painted at least three times, shows Christ carrying a lantern, knocking at an overgrown door. It symbolises hearts closed to salvation, but having learned about the dangerous business of gunpowder making I find myself inventing and performing for my own amusement a Monty

Python-esque scene in which ever more soot-blackened and scorched safety officials repeatedly fail to prevent mills being accidentally exploded by well-meaning sons of God carrying naked flames into restricted areas.

'You're not the Messiah…' I mutter to myself. 'You're a very n–"KA-BOOM!"'

The river has widened to almost 10m by the time it passes a bridge with curlicued metal railings and a heap of fly-tipped bin liners, spilling their contents of household junk. Nearby there's a faux-timbered pub with Georgian windows and dozens of deserted benches in the front garden, and a red sign identifying it as The Hogsmill. I go in, order soup, and find a large table where I can spread out the map. I reread a pamphlet on *Millais and the Hogsmill* I was given 20 years ago by Mervyn Newman, the then water vole officer of the Surrey Wildlife Trust with whom I collaborated on a pitch for a TV documentary that never happened. The pamphlet was written by a retired teacher and local historian called Barbara Webb, who devoted years to uncovering the precise location used by Millais to paint the backdrop for *Ophelia*. The artist's own letters gave only a loose indication, but he devoted far more detail to the discomforts and annoyances of working *en plein air*. He described a two-mile walk from his lodgings, his precarious seat on the bank, and lamented the size and ferocity of the Surrey flies. The heat and the wind were vexatious, as were two swans, which 'add to my misery by persisting in watching me from the exact spot I wish to paint.' He got himself in trouble with locals and livestock: 'I am threatened with notice to appear before a magistrate for trespassing in a field and destroying the hay, likewise by the admission of a bull in the same field after the said hay be cut.' None of this provided Barbara with a precise fix, but a breakthrough came in the discovery of contemporary notes by one Henry Chetwynd-Stapylton, held in the Surrey Records Office. Stapylton was newly appointed vicar of Malden in 1851, and he identified a willow 100 yards above a footbridge across the Hogsmill on the path towards Surbiton.

Barbara's pamphlet includes a suggested walk, describing the route I've already taken, but also recommending a diversion from the pub past the site of Worcester Park Farm, in which Millais and Holman Hunt lodged in 1851. When I get there I find the farm, the fields, and the avenue of elms are long gone. The area is residential, middle class looking – several properties are being developed, judging by the number of builders' vans parked outside. Two men taking down scaffolding are chatting cheerily in Polish. There is almost nothing the artists might have recognised, except perhaps the view over the valley from a small patch of recreation land at the top of the hill. I pick up a path flanked by garden fencing and a steep slope with dense scrub, pinging with blue and great tits. The path drops to Old Malden church, where there's a lychgate and wooden war memorial on which someone has placed a pot of fresh daffodils and someone else has daubed an inverted cross and the words GO AWAY over the names of the dead. Older than the memorial, and towering over it, is a huge holm oak, in full evergreen leaf. It's odd to hear the breeze rustling its broad-leaved canopy in winter. I pause to listen and as I stand there the clouds part and full strong sunlight penetrates the foliage. I'm transported out of season and century to summer 1851, a time this tree, I believe, might be just old enough to remember.

The path drops steeply again, past a great froth of white cherry plum blossom and a tree with a pair of trainers swinging by their tied laces from a branch, well out of reach. It rejoins the river just above a footbridge. In Millais' time this was a pretty, white-painted timber structure with a lattice design. Now it is a concrete slab with galvanised railings, and dwarfed by a brutalist railway flyover 100m downstream. The generous meanders of the Hogsmill clearly marked on older maps have long gone and the river is brown, too straight, and furnished with the orange traffic cone that seems now to be almost a requirement of the British urban watercourse. Downstream, another willow has dropped half its branches out over the water. I have seen hundreds of willows today. Some are vast, with huge branches growing out over the water and many are split, their hearts ripped open by the weight of their yearning towards the water. Recent high flows have decked this one with what looks like toilet flushings and other plastic debris.

I'm close to the spot the exuberant young Millais rhapsodised over, but I'm mentally preparing myself for disappointment, thinking that to give the place a better chance I should have waited to come in May or June, not February. But I'm here now, so I follow Barbara's notes, cross the bridge and turn upstream. The path opens out almost immediately into Six Acre Meadow, and the scene is suddenly and unexpectedly charming: soggy, tufted with rushes and grasses, with a bordering sweep of woodland. And there, 100m upstream of the bridge, just as the Reverend Stapylton and Barbara described, is the place.

Artistically, the painting Millais made here was revolutionary. The Pre-Raphaelites were already causing a stir, by rendering nature as it really was, including decay and imperfection. Millais took this to the next level by using a wholly natural setting, not a farmed or built or gardened one, and he began with the backdrop — it was at least as important as the figure of Ophelia, which was added afterwards in his studio. He broke with tradition in painting the flow of the river from right to left as it is in reality, spurning the convention that regarded leftward orientation as, literally, sinister. The flowers include some of those mentioned by Shakespeare — dog roses and loosestrife ('long purples') — and others that would have been naturally present on the bank and in the water, including irises, forget-me-nots and water crowfoot.

The broken willow is long gone of course, but others have taken its place, leaning slantwise over the water exactly as Shakespeare described. The bank is surprisingly steep – Millais must have perched on the slope, rather than on the top – and now, as then, it is densely vegetated. There are clumps of bright green woodrush and dabs of colour courtesy of some early-flowering herb Robert, a cluster of dainty dwarf narcissus escaped from cultivation, a strand of red and white warning tape snagged among brambles and a nestling Lucozade Sport® bottle. A small flock of parakeets clatter from tree to tree, shrieking over the repetitive bleeps of a vehicle reversing somewhere nearby.

I stand a while, staring at the brown water, trying to imagine how the scene might look in summer, when my breath catches. A kingfisher – a bloody KINGFISHER – zips upstream, a dart of supernatural blue fire. It's in my sight for the single gasp of a second and gone, but its electrifying passage has lit the day completely anew and I laugh in awe and disbelief. I know as I write that it's going to seem like invention – the poetic timing, the transformational effect. But truly, nothing could have been more perfect.

On my way back to the bridge I meet an oak I estimate to be two or three hundred years old. I slot my fingers into the grooves of its bark, and ask what it remembers. And a reply I take to be not only that of the oak, but also of the kingfisher and the willows and the river crackles my synapses:

Nothing is mundane. Nothing is forgotten. We remember what for you is history, and long before that too. All that was is held, a potential, like voltage. All it takes for current to flow is connection – for circuits to be made.

The notion of the spot in Six Acre Meadow as Ophelia's watery grave is several degrees removed from truth. *Hamlet* was based on the Norse legend of Prince Amleth, whose exploits were recorded in the thirteenth century by Danish historian Saxo Grammaticus, and appeared as Hamlet in

French and English histories and plays in the late sixteenth century; grist to the mill of Shakespeare's imagination. Ophelia was entirely his invention, but no less human for that. Into Millais' mind she slipped, through a further 250 years, to be translocated to a river in a Surrey meadow, where the face he painted was that of the luminous, twenty-two-year-old Elizabeth Siddall. Except Lizzie wasn't in the river but in a bathtub in the artist's chilly studio. Millais and Holman Hunt wrote letters and diaries and Barbara Webb made sense of them so that I could be here in the company of them all. It's a palimpsest of real and imagined lives responding to one another over 800 years. They jostle and swirl and run over each other, and they glow where they touch. Circuits are made.

By late October of 1851, Millais' rendition of the riverbank vegetation was complete. Working now at Worcester Park, he began another painting, *The Huguenot*, which he set against a garden wall, alternating between this and a new feature of Ophelia's setting – a water vole, swimming in the river. Water voles (or water rats as they were widely known) are chubby, blunt-faced rodents, which burrow into riverbanks and feed on a wide range of riparian vegetation. They were abundant in Millais' time, as evidenced by the ready supply of specimens procured by his assistant, Young. But if extracts from his letters are taken at face value, for all his prodigious talent, poor John Everett was rubbish at voles.

October 28th - My man Young brought me a rat after breakfast. Began painting it swimming, when the governor made his appearance, bringing money and sat with me whilst at work. After four hours rat looked exactly like a drowned kitten.

October 29th - Cleaned out the rat, which looked like a lion, and enlarged picture.

November 5th - My man Young, who brought another rat caught in the gin and a little disfigured, was employed by Hunt to

hold down a wretched sheep whose head was very unsatisfactorily
painted after a most tantalising display of obstinacy.

November 6th - Was advised by Hunt to paint the rat, but felt
disinclined.

November 7th - After breakfast examined the rat. From some
doubtful feeling as to its perfect portraiture determined to retouch it.
Young made his appearance apropos with another rat, and (for
Hunt) a new canvas from the carrier at Kingston. Worked very
carefully at the rat and finally succeeded to my own and everyone's
taste.

December 4th . . . Hunt's uncle and aunt came, both of whom
understood most gratifyingly every object except my water-rat, which
the male relation (when invited to guess at) eagerly pronounced to be a
hare. Perceiving by our smile that he had made a mistake, a rabbit was
next hazarded, after which I have a faint recollection of a dog or a cat
being mentioned by the spouse, who had brought with her a sponge-
cake and bottle of sherry, of which we partook at luncheon.

Perhaps aided by the cake and the sherry, Millais seemed
reconciled to failure over the vole, which was presumably
then scraped off the canvas once and for all. The following
day both artists returned to London, where Millais spent
the winter painting Ophelia herself. His was the first
portrayal to show the actual drowning (previous artists had
depicted her on the bough before it broke). At his
instruction Lizzie Siddall lay in a bath in his studio for
hours, wearing a second-hand gown embroidered with
sparkling threads, but filthy, and thus, again, perfect for his
vision. So absorbed in his work was he that he failed to
notice when the candles placed beneath the bath to warm
it burned out. Unwilling to complain, the stoic Lizzie
caught a chill that almost killed her. She survived to feature
in many more paintings, and became an accomplished artist
herself, though plagued with mental and physical ill health.
Her daughter with another Pre-Raphaelite brother, Dante
Gabriel Rossetti, was stillborn and she died from a laudanum

overdose in 1862, bringing a new pathos to the image of
the poppy drifting from Ophelia's posy.

The story of the missing water vole would be no more than a
footnote were it not for the fact that, by the late twentieth
century, the species had been eliminated from the Hogsmill
and almost every other river in England. By the time I began
studying biology in the 1990s, *Arvicola amphibius*, as it is now
known, had been for some time the fastest declining native
mammal in Britain. The crisis centred on habitat loss –
particularly the canalisation of rivers, which robbed them of
soft vegetated banks in which to burrow, feed and hide, and
on predation, most notably by feral American mink whose
population boomed after animals imported to fur farms
escaped or were deliberately released into the wild.

Water voles should be common. They eat all sorts of
things, and they breed fast. For a generalist, fecund rodent to
disappear from an ecosystem, something must be profoundly
wrong. For them to be threatened with extinction across an
entire country is an appalling indictment of our custodianship.
Back in 2001, Mervyn Newman had a vision for restoration
of the Hogsmill and the reintroduction of water voles, but
the condition of the river, and concerns about mink, made
this seem a distant dream.

Downstream of the footbridge the river path enters the
Hogsmill Local Nature Reserve, and I'm excited to see a
picture of a water vole on one of the interpretation boards,
but the text only says that the species was once common
here, and hints at plans underway to bring them back.
Nothing seems to have changed since Mervyn's time
though, and the board goes on to list the difficulties a
reintroduction would face: mink, scarcity of suitable habitat
and fluctuations in river levels and water quality resulting
from urban runoff. It doesn't mention dogs, but the mud on
the path is thick with canine paw prints. I want more reason
for hope than this.

I emerge onto another huge arterial road, lined with interwar housing. The map on my phone tells me this is Tolworth, which I know only as a traffic blackspot from radio travel bulletins. The river is culverted between huge concrete slabs and clogged with packaging debris, deflated foil balloons, fast food wrappers, cans, rags and hundreds of plastic bottles, many containing what is almost certainly urine, lobbed from the windows of gridlocked vehicles. Above the slabs there are willows, brambles, buddleia, the dead heads of last year's meadowsweet, and there is some greenery sprouting from between and above the blockwork. But below the waterline nothing is green, and dead vegetation and flotsam are uniformly covered in a fuzz of scummy brown algae. Could anything be less perfect?

I cross the eight lanes via a pedestrian underpass. Within a minute of picking up the riverside path again, I find I've joined a walking route called the London Loop. For the first time since leaving Ewell the path diverges from the river. I walk through a housing estate and emerge onto a busy main street with shops and takeaways. I pass Berrylands station, walk under the railway and follow a road tracking the perimeter of the Hogsmill Valley sewage works, a huge facility occupying an ellipse of land between the railway and the river. I glimpse the Hogsmill only briefly thereafter, on the outskirts of Kingston and then finally as a brick-lined channel joining the Thames. There's a railing there with signs on it instructing people not to feed the birds, and a man in a cagoule is leaning over it, tipping an entire bread bag of crusts, crumbs and vegetable peelings into an avid gathering of geese and gulls.

Several months after visiting the river, I receive a message on Twitter from an environmental campaigner in south-west London, asking if I can support a crowdfunding project. Approaches like this can be difficult. There are so

many worthy causes and being unable to donate to them
all can make me feel helpless. But this one has already
met its initial ask and is well on the way to making its
stretch target. And the money raised is going to be spent
reintroducing water voles to the Hogsmill. I retweet the
appeal and look up the organisers, a social enterprise
called Citizen Zoo, founded by a group of friends who
met on the Conservation Science MSc programme at
Imperial College London. They're a fresh-faced bunch,
and among them is Elliot Newton, whose day-job title is
Biodiversity Officer for Kingston Borough Council. I
watch a campaign video in which Elliot wades up the
river in a blue checked shirt with a knapsack on his
shoulders and a stout wooden staff in hand. He is slim
and red-haired, with a short beard, and looks strikingly
like Vincent van Gogh. For this reason as much as any,
he's the one I contact, and we meet by video call a couple
of days later.

Elliot is elated with the success of the fundraising, and the
extent of community engagement. Sixty volunteers have
been recruited to do habitat restoration work on the banks,
and to monitor for mink using floating platforms with
tunnels bedded with pressed sand or soft clay, that take
footprints easily. If mink footprints are seen, the tunnel can
be reset to trap mode. Non-target species will be released,
and mink will be removed for rehoming or humanely killed.
'Fortunately there's been no sign of them, which is good,'
says Elliot. 'We'll keep checking though, because mink can
disperse quite long distances, and if need be we're prepared
to trap them out.'

The project is collaborating with rewilding and
reintroductions specialist Derek Gow, who has bred animals
for dozens of previous successful schemes. 'We have to order
them a year in advance, so that the released animals will be
yearlings and not inexperienced juveniles' says Elliot. 'The
plan is to have them ready to go in the summer of 2022.'

I wonder where the release will take place, thinking of the quaggy footpaths, and myriad dog tracks in the nature reserve, and the self-evident popularity of the place with people and their pets.

'Well … people raise their eyebrows when we say this, but we're going to use the sewage works.' My eyebrows do rise, not because I'm incredulous, but because it is perfect – an extensive area with negligible human footfall, and no dogs.

'Dogs are a concern,' admits Elliot 'But it's really important that this remains a river for everyone. And with that in mind we're going to involve local dogwalkers to identify and designate "dog splash zones" away from the more sensitive areas.'

As if all this wasn't good news enough, Elliot tells me that Barbara Webb is still alive, and offers to see if she'd be willing to talk to me. He emails a few days later to put me in touch with her friend Alison Fure, who explains that at 90, Barbara is frail and housebound but keen to talk. We arrange a time for me to call. A carer answers the phone and puts Barbara on.

She's sparky, alert and informed. She tells me she's lived in Malden all her life. I ask about her earliest memories of the Hogsmill. 'Oh, I would have been three years old. It flooded quite frequently, so it dominated life sometimes. They changed it a lot over the years – straightened it and changed the banks. It was always somewhere you could walk, but there used to be a lot of bushes there and I don't remember being able to see much of it when I was young – we got it more accessible than it was. After I identified the plot where Millais painted they put in a seat, which a council officer who'd studied art donated when he retired. And some boards. I hope they haven't been graffiti-ed.'

I assure her the boards were looking smart when I was there. 'That's good. I used to lead walks there on Heritage Open Days and they were very popular. But I can't get there at all now. I can't even walk across the room. I can't get outside so I have to get outside in my mind. It's aggravating and very boring to talk about.' She laughs ruefully. 'I suppose lockdown means it's the same for everyone now.'

I ask if she can still read. 'Yes, I like to, but most books are too heavy to manage.'

I recount as much as I can about my visit – about the holm oak and the kingfisher and I tell her how close I felt to Millais and Holman Hunt, but stop short of sharing the other voices I imagined. She strikes me as a practical woman – talking trees might be a bit much. But she's with me on the charisma of those Pre-Raphaelite boys.

'Oh yes, the diaries bring them to life. I did start to feel I knew them and their world. I think they knew it was special. They wouldn't know Worcester Park now. But there's an effort to conserve the meadow and the river and to keep Old Malden distinct. And that's something, I suppose.'

'You definitely helped that happen!' I say.

'Oh there were a lot of people involved, and still are. There are some young people very keen to bring back water voles.' I say I've spoken to Elliot and ask about the vole that never made it into the painting of Ophelia.

'Oh yes! Millais tried and tried to paint one but people kept thinking it was something else – I think he got quite upset', she chuckles. 'He scraped it off and painted it over. But when I was doing my research they were doing something to the painting at the Tate, cleaning it I think, and they found a sketch under the frame, which they think was the water vole. So really it has been there all along.'

All that was is held: a potential, like voltage.

I say I would like to visit her when the pandemic is over. She's non-committal. 'We'll have to see how things turn out.' I post her a copy of *The Living Mountain* – not only a book I love deeply, but also a slim volume, and light. I hope she might manage it and that Nan Shepherd might help her 'get outside in her mind'.

A few months later, in early 2021, Alison emails to tell me Barbara has died. She says they are hoping to combine a memorial event with the release of water voles, and asks if I would like to come.

Minus seven

Stopper *A hydraulic feature forming below a drop – fast-moving water accelerating under gravity meets water below and is forced back on itself – creating a cylinder of rotating water moving down, up, back, and down again. At the surface this presents as a standing wave or a towback into what paddlers call a hole. Stoppers that flush at one end or both can be fun to play in, allowing a paddler to surf indefinitely, facing upstream, catching opposing flows to flip, spin or cartwheel the boat. Others are closed, ranging from inconvenient to deadly 'keepers'.*

One New Year's Eve we paddled the Upper Tees, a favourite and wonderfully scenic run. The temperature gauge on the car dropped steadily as we drove up Teesdale in freezing fog, until by the time we parked at the High Force Hotel it read -7°C. On days like that you get to see water do strange things. Familiar features take on new shapes, where ice layers on ice. We cracked plates of it to enter the river that morning, and after plunging through the first few rapids we all sported thick breastplates where splashes had frozen glassily on contact with our buoyancy aids. Drysuits and spraydecks crackled, our hair and eyelashes froze. In the eddies we encountered the peculiar phenomenon of slowly spinning discs of frozen foam. Foam in a river is often interpreted as a sign of pollution, but it also occurs naturally as a result of proteins in the water – the products of decaying leaves and other organic matter. It's completely normal on the Tees, and it doesn't usually last long, but in the fierce cold, foam in slow-moving eddies was freezing before the bubbles burst. Piles of it accumulated along the banks, but in eddies, the gentle circulation prevented it forming a continuous mass – instead, blobs of foam shaped themselves into pancakes. Over the years on this river I saw discs ranging in size from 5cm to about 45cm, with the texture of prawn crackers, and stable enough to be picked up and handled.

Paddling white water at very low temperatures takes a physical toll, and we dared not dally. Feeling her energy draining, my friend Sally opted to get off a little early and take a slightly longer walk back to the cars. On reaching them, she realised that the thick ice that had formed on her buoyancy aid and drysuit meant she couldn't undo the zips. The roadside recovery patrolman passing that afternoon probably didn't expect to be flagged down by a literal ice maiden asking for assistance undressing, but they don't call themselves the fourth emergency service for nothing.

Meanwhile on the river we ran the big drop of Low Force, that day a narrow tongue over a wedding cake of icicles, leaving just one more feature before the get-out. It has a bit of a reputation, this little drop. It's a double ledge with two stoppers. Usually I ran it on the left, but if too much speed was lost in the first hole and trajectory was not maintained, the second had a habit of whisking boats from left to right into a closed stopper and giving them a good tumbling. This 'typewritering' had never happened to me in scores of outings on this river. But today was my turn, and as I took my beating I distinctly remember thinking that, compared to the air, the water felt warm. I pulled my spraydeck, swam a little way downstream to the rocks, and felt the ice forming in my hair, eyebrows and drysuit even as I climbed out. My pigtails clattered against my shoulders all the way back to the car.

CHAPTER 9

The cry of the Dart

And I cried Dart, cruel River Dart
Every year you claim a heart
You've taken hers
You've broken mine
You cruel, cold river

Steve Knightley (Show of Hands), *Cruel River*

I'm at a loose end in Devon. A conference I was due to attend in Exeter has been cancelled at short notice. They didn't need to give a reason. We share the world now with a new and unwelcome entity, making itself at home in our cells, harnessing the molecular machinery that makes us for its own ends. Cases of COVID-19 are starting to spike in the UK, as they have, terrifyingly, elsewhere. I've rung the small hotel where I'd booked to stay, to cancel. The owner sounded resigned, and I found myself wishing him luck and telling him to keep the money. How businesses like that are going to survive if this goes on more than a few weeks, I can't imagine.

I have no immediate need for accommodation. The car is packed with camp gear and supplies for a week if need be, and I can steer entirely clear of people. And there is Dartmoor. More specifically there is the Dart – a fabled river I know only a little.

The Dart is a sister to the Yorkshire Derwent, both in name and in the nature of its upper catchment – both rise on moors and are named for the oak woods through which they descend. But the Dart gathers at more than twice the elevation of my home river and is fed by the much higher volume of rain that falls in the west of Britain. It swells faster, drops more steeply and is altogether feistier than its Yorkshire near-namesake. It also has a legendary voice. The sound is produced at certain flow levels by water pouring over granite ledges in a deep gorge downstream of Dartmeet, and echoes off the valley sides and the rocks of Mel Tor. It is heard rarely, and like the running of the Gypsey Race, it is regarded as an ill omen. Local legend has it that the Dart must periodically claim a heart, and the 'Cry of the Dart' is a portent of this hunger. Of the many lives lost on this river, that of a young farmhand has embedded especially deep in local lore. Jan Coo, the story goes, was apprenticed to the farmer at Rowbrook, a lonely house that still stands high above the gorge. One fierce night in the depths of winter Jan heard the river calling his name. He raised the alarm, thinking someone was in peril, and a search was carried out, but nobody was found. When spring came, the voice returned, and this time it appeared to respond to Jan when he called back. Wary of raising another false alarm, he set out alone and was never seen again.

I decide to go there. It's not an easy spot to reach, especially if you take the route I choose, dropping directly off Mel Tor through chest-height gorse and bramble and over granite boulders. But things get easier when I reach the trees that cover the steep lower flanks of the gorge. It's one of those abrupt vegetal transitions that propel you into an entirely different world. The woods are mostly oak, with a supporting cast of holly, birch, hazel and rowan. They are deeply, swimmingly green, thanks to mosses, lichens and ferns on every rock, trunk and branch. This is full-on rainforest: a world of intense, year-round, submarine verdancy. Having clambered down (an easier route, I discover later, would be to follow the descent of a stream called Simon's Lake), I find a place where the river drops over wide shelves between rounded granite bulges. In modest flows there are pools safe to dip in, and I swim to wash away the sweat and soothe the gorse and bramble scratches. In higher water this is a thunderous rapid. And under very particular conditions, the flow generates a deep resonating note, identified by some with a musical ear as an F. I hear no such thing but the river still fills the valley with its regular voice.

Back up on Mel Tor above the gorge, I'm reminded that the cry of the Dart was set in a different but no less chilling context by Arthur Conan Doyle in *The Hound of the Baskervilles*. In the story, Sherlock Holmes' long-suffering friend and narrator Watson hears a low moan that chills him to the core, and is informed by the superficially affable naturalist Jack Stapleton that the locals consider it to be the cry of a mythical hound, baying for blood; but that really it is nothing more sinister than 'the mud settling, or the water rising, or perhaps one of the last bitterns in England booming.' Watson considers it the 'weirdest, strangest thing that ever I heard in my life.'

Hayford Hall, one of the houses thought to have inspired Baskerville Hall, is only 5km away over the moor, and it seems to me that the baying of the hound and the cry of the Dart must surely be related. The hound is based partly on the myth of the Wisht Hounds, which are said to haunt Wistmans Wood on the West Dart, upstream of here, and the scene is certainly set somewhere very like Mel Tor. The map is peppered with marks for Neolithic architecture, including dozens of hut circles, which Stapleton also points out. 'Prehistoric man lived thickly on the moor' says he to Watson, 'We find all his little arrangements exactly as he left them.' I wonder about the motivations of those ancient people – more real and yet less reachable than Conan Doyle's fictional characters – in selecting such exposed locations in which to settle. I wonder what the voice of the river signified to them.

By the time I approach Newbridge, the river is gleaming in the late sunshine. It is wide enough here to feel generous, free-wheeling. From a paddler's perspective, after the section above, known as the 'Mad Mile', it offers breathing space between rapids of smooth, clean rock; slick tongues of water like polished glass and big, welcoming pools beneath. I never paddled the Dart – it's such a long way from home – but I can see why it's a classic and it makes me miss my boat.

From Newbridge I wander back up the other side of the river with no further destination in mind, just a vague intention to find somewhere to sleep under the stars. The evening chorus is striking up. The woodland here is mature and airy, the canopy still open but with an incipient green of leafbuds ready to burst. It makes a fine concert hall for a five-piece evening overture by great tit, robin, wren, blackbird and song thrush. There is no chiffchaff yet, but they can't be far now. Full throated spring is only days away. Male tawny owls strike up a call and response. There is no goading female *kewick*, just a series of querulous *huh-hoooos*, close by, but uncertain-sounding under the rush of the river.

I am here. Are… are you?

I am here.

Wh… ere?

Here.

Wh… where?

Here. I am here.

In my search for a sleeping place I almost settle for a mossy dell on a low islet easily reached in a stride, over a little backwater, but I remember the effect of trickling water on my bladder and the tendency of this river to rise fast. I'd not sleep easy here, and so I retrace my steps back to what looks a well-used spot close to the final rock sill above Newbridge, close to a cluster of hollies, dancing like elves or wise women. They remind me of *Ash Dome*, the living sculpture growing in a North Wales woodland where a group of ash trees planted and tended by artist David Nash grows in a perfect circle. Nash has trained the trees into complementary shapes that form a collective inward-leaning vortex. I read recently that he no longer expects the trees to outlive him – their death from the dieback disease caused by the fungus *Hymenoscyphus fraxineus* is almost inevitable. I'd love to see them before that. The dancing hollies are wilder and darker than Nash's coven of ash, their choreography unsynchronised. I feel I have caught them in an act of summoning, which perhaps they cannot complete while I intrude. It's not the right place to sleep. So I leave them to their secret, green business and find a platform under a larger tree, with a view of the water – it's dark enough now that only the white of the rapid shows clearly.

I unpack my bivvi bag and set up my stove, resisting using a torch to save my night vision – the furnace glow of the burner will give enough light to cook by. But before I ignite it, a beam of white light twinkles between the trees, a searchlight sweep, bobbing and swivelling, occasionally swelling like a supernova as the head or hand carrying it turns directly towards me. Someone is approaching from the direction of the road.

I freeze, glad I haven't shown a light myself. My eyes are dark adapted, I can still see enough to move around. I have the advantage that I know they are there, while they don't know about me. I don't turn my head – my face will show up much more than my woolly hat if the torchlight catches it – and the less I see of those dazzling LEDs as they approach, the better. I'm 15m off the path, so they might not notice me, but if there is a dog … dogs don't like to be surprised in the dark. If I hear it coming close I'll have to reveal myself carefully to avoid startling it. The light catches the trees on the other bank – dips, hovers, sweeps left and right, moves out of sight. I strain my ears for approaching footsteps or scuffling paws.

I hate this. It's not fear, but instant whole-body wariness and a kind of territorial, vulpine outrage: this is *my* piece of night – I don't want to share it. I wish I had whiskers to better feel tremors of air. I wish my nose would tell me what was coming. I wish my ears could swivel, away from the rushing river and towards the path. The irony of my suspicion of another human in the woods after dark is not lost on me, but instinct overrides rationality. Three minutes tick by. More than enough time for even a slow walker to have passed my lair, and slowly I turn around again. The light is gone. As the adrenaline subsides, I replay what I've seen, the bobbing descent from the road, the pause, the light swivelling side to side. And I begin to giggle. I've been that light-bearer a hundred times, caught short on a drive. And I'm glad for their sake I didn't show myself – no one wants to be startled in the woods at night with their pants down.

I've been ridiculous, but even so, it takes 15 minutes for my senses to dial down from full alert, and by then, it's night. I question my choice of sleeping place all over again. I'm too close to a road and the noise of the rapid makes it hard to pick out other sounds. Perhaps I should move somewhere quieter, where I might hear someone coming. I look for alternatives. A hollow behind a fallen tree blocks some of the sound, but also hides the view I'm so delighted by. There's also a colossal tree overhead leaning at a pronounced angle. If it chooses tonight to crash down like its neighbour, I'll be squished like a bug.

My stomach is grumbling so I finally light the stove and boil river water to make tea and reconstitute a meal in a bag. I wander about to eat, slowly. I can't hear anything but the rapid. But as I move, occasionally spooning hot potato mush into my mouth, I notice that the food pouch in my hand is fizzing. I hold it higher to my ear and realise that like the boulder near Watersmeet, it is echoing a narrow frequency band of river noise – a soft sound, but distinct from the background rush of the rapid. The foil has plucked one acoustic thread from the sonic fabric of this place. And having been shown it in isolation I can hear it clearly and separately even after I put the pouch down – like a familiar voice in a crowd. *Fizzzz*. It is the sound of air captured and dragged down deep, resurfacing. The sound of thousands of bubbles bursting every second.

There are other strands to the soundscape too, and I scramble out onto the rocks and try to isolate them one by one. Lapping of wavelets on rock; a sibilant *pssssshh* of fast and slow water colliding in the stopper; a deeper, more aggressive hiss that sounds like a freshwater crocodile I once met while swimming into a cave on a river in the Northern Territories of Australia. Its eye glowed faintly orange in the dark, like Betelgeuse. There's a clonk of loose stones in the channel; now and then a great glugging plop when water notices a temporary airspace between the rocks. And beneath it all is a deep bass of the central tongue of water burrowing into the channel it has carved over thousands of years.

The voices of this river were braided by the poet Alice Oswald in her mesmerising long-form poem, *Dart*, published 20 years ago. Many of the voices therein are real – those of people living, working or otherwise engaging with the river, whom Oswald interviewed over three years. Others are mythical or imagined: the uneasy spirit of Jan Coo, and the voice of the river itself. Oswald gathered these threads and echoes, and set them out, clarified, amplified, unforgettable. Unsurprisingly, it's the voice of an ill-fated canoeist that resonates powerfully with me. The Dart has claimed the lives of at least two more kayakers since the poem was published. The hugely experienced Chris Wheeler, something of a legend himself having once dislocated both knees escaping from a boat pinned on Conwy Falls in North Wales, died a few hundred metres downstream of Broadstone in 2009. Then in 2017, Toby Hamer was pinned by a tree near Bell Pool Island. I didn't know either, but they are both the canoeist in Oswald's poem and the voice she gives them is heartbreakingly familiar:

we come out of the river at twilight, wet, shouting
the river's been so beautiful we can't concentrate

Every white-water paddler I know has been that rewilded, re-childed, rain-dancing fool. Numb-fingered, pink-cheeked, river-giddy, the endorphin high is followed by exhaustion and profound content. We'd sleep like dead things, then get back into wet kit and do it all again, week after week, sometimes even fitting in classic sections after work in summer if it had rained all day and reachable rivers were in condition. But the poem also expresses the sense of self determination the sport requires. When you step into a solo kayak on a challenging river, you're on your own. You might be backed up by your buddies, you might be led and shown the optimum route by another paddler, but no one can do the paddling for you. Your senses, your reactions, your judgement, your actions, your life: all are your own responsibility. And as Chris Wheeler and Toby Hamer knew – as Jason knew, and Kate knew – if things go wrong there might not be anything anyone can do. Within an arm's reach of safety you can be entirely beyond help. You can be held an inch from air and birdsong and be denied either, ever again.

Oswald also gives a voice to the river as it claims the canoeist. It is soothing and smothering, familiar and strange, come-hither lethal.

> ... put your head,
> it looks a good one, full of kiss
> and known to those you love, come roll it on my stones
> come tongue-in-skull, come drinketh, come sleepeth

In the dark the words seem to twine around the thrust and rush of the flow. There is a tongue of water plunging into the throat of the rapid, too busy to be bothered with language, and yet ...

> come drinkethhhhh

I've already drunk it. Immersed the river in myself. I am water.

> ... breathe me please in whole inhale

I've seen water so clear it looks breathable. Am I in it now?

come sssssleepethhh

Sleep won't come.

breathe me

I did breathe it once. Following my friend Dan down a short gorge section on the River Clough in Cumbria, we knew there was a 'sticky' drop at the end. I didn't time my power strokes well, and my boat was instantly grabbed and flipped. Hydraulic suction and the lack of purchase to be had in aerated water made it impossible to roll, so I waited a while upside down, changing my shape, reaching down and hoping my paddle might catch some deeper flow that wasn't recirculating back into the stopper. When I realised I wasn't going to be flushed and that I couldn't hold on, I pulled the grab-loop on the neoprene spraydeck that sealed me into the cockpit. The water whipped me from the boat in an instant. Usually when wearing a buoyancy aid, a swimmer will bob straight to the surface, but not this time. This time, I went down. The reduced density of highly aerated water means that even with a buoyancy aid, physics was not on my side. The colour of the water dimmed from white to khaki and there was a simultaneous lessening and deepening of the sound, from sharp white noise to bass thundering. Far from being flung around, it seemed for a long moment that my body was hovering.

I'd heard about this place. The green room.

I'd also heard various theories on how to escape it. Make yourself big, so the current catches you and carries you clear. Make yourself small, so you go deeper to where the water is more dense and moving away from the drop instead of back towards it. And even, if all else fails, take off your floatation device to help you get deeper still. I made a few shapes. There seemed to be more space than you might expect. How deep could it be?

Then, like someone had turned a dial, the light and sound increased again, smoothly, and together. Something warm touched my face and I grabbed for it, seized by the irrational conviction that it was a hand and that someone, somehow, was reaching into this strange place to pluck me out. I took a hold and realised it was the neoprene of my spraydeck, flapping in front of me. I rose a little further and something large loomed above me. The hull of a boat. Someone *was* there. It was orange, and recognition dawned. It was my boat, empty and tumbling in the hole with me.

Another noise was growing in my head – not the pounding of water, but that of my blood. The light was strengthening again, almost to white. My face didn't quite break the surface but it was close and I tipped my head back and felt on my face the warmth of air trapped in bubbles. I snatched a frothy gasp before the flow started pulling me down again, and then for the first time I started to fight. Light and sound had become inseparable, sparkling in my ears, buzzing behind my eyes, when something swam into the periphery of my vision. Yellow and sinuous, whipping like an eel. A rope. I thrashed, caught it and hung on as it tautened. From above, Dan hauled me downstream of the hole. He allowed the flow to pendulum me into an eddy beyond the rocks he was standing on, and dragged me bodily onto a shelf. Textbook rescue. I lay, coughing but otherwise unable to move for several minutes.

The weird thing is, the memory of that whole episode isn't a bad one. It was intense, but not terrifying, and the fact that I wasn't afraid has been a source of comfort. Another friend who was once pulled from a river unconscious and unbreathing, and resuscitated on the bank said the same. There is helplessness, but also something akin to curiosity. Not about what will happen next – there is no sense of future, just a kind of avid wonder about what is unfolding.

I've never had nightmares about it, but now by the Dart, it replays and replays.

breathe me pleassssse

I take my sleeping bag back to the rock and wrap it around myself, watching the water in the dark. It's more familiar, less disturbing, when I can see it.

We could live a whole life unaware of our sensory potential. I read recently that human fingertips are able to detect the differences between surfaces resulting from a single atomic thickness of material – through changes in invisible texture and conductivity of heat and electrical charge. One atom. Our hearing is acute enough to separate sounds issued less than 30 millionths of a second apart, and minuscule differences in pitch and timbre that mean we know a familiar voice among thousands. These subtleties are the kind of thing I wanted to give my attention to. But now I wonder if it might be a good way to drive myself mad. This river has too many voices. I try to focus on something other than sound.

The night is black and blue. The sky strong French navy, with a black lace collar of meshing tree silhouettes; the water is inky black silk shot with crow blue. My brain tells me the foam is white but really it has only a narrow frequency-band of goblin light to play with, and the hue I'm seeing is in the realm of cobalt.

My jitters subside. Now full night has settled, and under a blanket of cloud the darkness is thick. I let it fill my eyes and the voice of the river flood my ears. The battery on my phone has died, and I'm glad to be free of its digital umbilicus, unmoored in the night.

come sleepeth

Cold wakes me, and looking up I realise I've lost a layer of insulation – the clouds have cleared and the stars are bright, but it's a mischievous glow, offering light but no heat. I pull my hood over my hat, toggle up my sleeping bag so only my eyes and nose show, and pull the bivvy bag close around. There's a diamond-bright planet overhead – Venus. Though named for a granddaughter of Gaia, Venus is more like Earth's naked sister in astronomical terms. Her slow turning days are longer than her years, her atmosphere comprises almost wholly carbon dioxide, creating pressure equivalent to a kilometre of ocean depth and runaway greenhouse heating means her surface is hotter even than that of Mercury, which lies so much closer to the Sun. The rocks of Venus are sterile and unabraded, and average more than 400°C in temperature. Yet from here, she has an icy whiteness, a stark brilliance containing all the colours and none.

I wonder if Venus would envy Gaia's cloak of swirling blue and tapestried green, and if she ever had such a thing? Or might she pity her giddily spinning sister, be revolted by the seething organic infestation of life and the water that scours and suppurates?

When I wake next, the faint glowing hands of my watch say it is ten to four, and I burrow deeper into the bag, determined to eke out a bit more sleep from the dwindling night. It feels like no time passes but suddenly it is light, the wood is once again full of birdsong, and I desperately need a wee.

I light the jet stove, but the flame from the near-empty gas canister is feeble and blue. I wrap my hands around the cylinder to warm it and coax the dregs to vaporise but eventually give up and make a brew with lukewarm water. I carry it back out onto the sloping plinth of rock by the rapid and sip the worst coffee ever. The instant granules haven't dissolved, and they stick to my teeth in gooey clumps. But with the grey light strengthening and the first tender blue seeping into the sky, it is somehow acceptable.

There is no rush. I have nowhere to be. The rock is cool grey and crosshatched with seams of white quartz. Philosophers of the classical world, including Pliny the Elder and Theophrastus, believed quartz to be a petrified form of ice so ancient it could no longer be thawed. The roots of the word 'crystal' and the prefix 'cryo-' in reference to freezing processes are the same, derived from the Ancient Greek *krystallos*, meaning ice.

The quartz was once liquid, running molten or in solution through weaknesses in the rock, between layers of ancient sediments, and leaving molecules of silicon dioxide behind in neat parallel deposits. There are fine, evenly spaced lines, like those in an exercise book, intersected by thicker seams at odd angles: faults and fractures infilled and healed, molecule by molecule.

I check my watch: still ten to four. Like the gas cylinder and the phone battery, the one in my watch has run out. It's poor expedition practice, and yet each little expiry leaves me better off. Without a tiny trickle of charge, the quartz in the watch mechanism – a cousin of the crystal in the rock I'm sitting on – no longer twitches away the seconds. Moments no longer form an orderly queue to tick by but pour past as free and uncounted as drops in a river, and I'm pleased by the idea that I've been gifted a dawn outside of time.

My dad's watch stopped when he died. The time its hands showed matched the estimated hour of his death from a massive heart attack, several hours before my mum came home from work that Tuesday in May. I suppose it's possible it had wound down the previous day, but Dad was a fixer, a completer, a polisher of shoes. He'd have noticed and replaced the battery from a pack in his neatly organised desk drawer. How or why it might have stopped I can't say. But he fought for those last moments. For our sakes, I know he would have done. He kicked off a slipper, disarrayed the furniture. He could easily have struck the watch hard enough to break the mechanism.

I curl on the rock, close my eyes and listen to the river, and I find the structure in the sound much faster than I did last night. It's no longer a white-noise hiss, but a song of many voices, many colours.

I walk upstream and bathe again before heading back to the car, where I dump my pack in the boot, change into clean shoes and slide into the driver's seat. The radio comes on with the ignition, and with it the morning news. They replay an announcement made by the Prime Minister last night. Time has not stopped after all. Somehow, while I floated apart, it has sped up. I listen to the end of the bulletin, the river still fresh on my skin, still damp in my hair, then turn off the radio, check the fuel gauge to be sure I can make the 330-odd miles to North Yorkshire in one go, and pull out onto the deserted road, bound for home, and lockdown.

Flow

Tongue *A section of surface flow that runs clear and smooth through a rapid or other feature.*

In 1975 the psychologist Mihaly Csikszentmihalyi published his Flow Theory, describing a state of mind exemplified by trained and motivated individuals performing complex, challenging tasks. In a flow state, body and mind are wholly absorbed, time appears to slow down, obstacles seem manageable, stress and anxiety are virtually non-existent. The best moments, he said, 'usually occur if a person's body or mind is stretched to its limits in a voluntary effort to accomplish something difficult and worthwhile ... There's this focus that, once it becomes intense, leads to a sense of ecstasy, a sense of clarity: you know exactly what you want to do from one moment to the other'. I've known flashes of this. Sometimes when running steep downhill trails where I know I'm going way too fast to stop; sometimes when writing – those rare days when four or five thousand words just seem to run out of my fingers; and for a while at least, when paddling. The first time was on the Zanskar.

The last major rapid before the Copper Canyon meets the Indus lies on a right-left chicane. We'd inspected it as best we could from the bank. The volume of the river made it hard to see much, but the line seemed clear enough – a long, asymmetric tongue of water cutting left to right, with heaving waves and holes on both sides, for 100m. We ran it in two groups. In mine, Pete went first, then Cat, then me, the weakest link, each of us separated by seven or eight boat-lengths – enough that we could see the one in front but avoid getting in one another's way. Pete seemed to be aiming for the tongue but then dropped left and disappeared. His boat resurfaced upside down on the crest of a wave and I saw him fighting to right it, bouncing like a kitten toy on a string. Cat followed, and I heard myself shouting.

'No! Go right!'

Perhaps she was too close behind Pete's lead and already in the wrong part of the flow. I'd never picked my own line on a rapid anything like this big before. But as Cat's boat was sucked left, and she began to be flipped and tossed just as Pete was, I felt a sudden detachment. *Just no.* I wasn't going there. I was going right – doing so even before the thought was formed. Three or four power strokes, and I knew I was where I needed to be. I couldn't see anyone anymore. Just me and the vast river, and a smooth, beautiful path, which I rode in slow motion, making only small corrections. We regrouped at the bottom – Pete and Cat dishevelled but laughing – and paddled together to where the others waited. The eddies were small and unstable, so they had got out to watch us. My boat was grabbed by Indy, a club-mate whose ability to read water – honed by obsessive practice – was truly enviable. He leaned out to speak in my ear above the rush of water. 'That,' he said, 'was sweet as a nut.' No paddling compliment had ever felt better, because I knew that this time, for sure, I'd earned it.

Csikszentmihalyi was right – Flow is well named – it is perhaps the closest we might ever get to *being* a river. For the next year or so, I was never scared. I could either run a feature, or I couldn't, and at last I trusted my ability to decide which. Our next trip to the Alps revealed it, finally, as the playground I'd always known was there but been too on edge to fully enjoy. Classic runs like the narrow cleft of Chateau Queyras gorge on the Guil, described in the guide book as like being flushed down a toilet, and previously far too committing for me to even consider, were opened up. There's a *via ferrata* fixed line climbing route above it, but down in the bottom there's no time to notice any of that. There is one eddy; the rest is a flume of continuous white water, fluffy, bouncy, beautiful and *fast*. Immediately below is the bouldery Guardian Angel gorge. I'd never paddled better and never will. Soon afterwards I became pregnant, slowed down several notches, then we lost Kate, and Jason, and in the years since I have had to accept that that particular wondrous feeling of certainty on the water now belongs to other people. I'm just grateful to have known it for a while.

CHAPTER 10

Trespassers will

Water is the ultimate element of trespass. Dam-buster, ditch-leveller and hydraulic digger, it has no respect for borders. It slips through cracks and gushes down hillsides; it falls from the sky and seeps up through the ground. As it reflects, it distorts, it dissolves definition, blurs distinction and spurns division. It is a nightmare for property lawyers.

Nick Hayes, *The Book of Trespass*

In lockdown, there is fear. Most of all for the children, immunologically resilient but threatened with being left behind, and the worst nights of insomnia I can ever remember. The days, however, are almost blissful. We are islanded, in the most glorious of springs. We do our own thing. My phone fills with pictures and videos of family walks, flowers, butterflies, birds, a slow worm, creative crafts and daft games. We eat strange meals made of ingredients found at the back of the larder. The world shrinks to the mile or so around home, but we are blessed by location, and the woods and fields and empty roads suddenly feel all ours.

The river is a godsend. In 15 minutes, we can walk to Kirkham Abbey, with its beautiful early nineteenth-century stone bridge and the ruins of the much older priory. There are no boats here now, but in the 1920s it was a popular mooring for pleasure cruisers and houseboats, with a tea garden and a fleet of rowing boats for hire. These were sideline enterprises established and run by the Lazenby family – Robert was also the signalman at Kirkham crossing and Charlie was the local postman.

The river at Kirkham was described by John Ogden in his 1974 book, *Yorkshire's River Derwent*, as so clear the colour of the bottom could be seen from the parapet of the bridge. The water I now know is usually green-gold, and heavily silted. But it is still beautiful and a favourite place to swim. The bottom is cowbelly soft, and the banks are slightly undercut, but the roots of a large alder provide a natural ladder on which to climb in and out. In summer you share the air here with swallows and martins, dragonflies and mayflies by day and bats in the evening, and the water with fish that leap or rise to kiss the surface from below. Once I came nose to nose with a newt, hanging with arms and legs dangling in a sort of blissful, sunsoaked trance.

Another place we visit often is a 10-minute walk upstream, near the small community of Crambeck. It's a little wilderness between the river and the railway that was once a coal yard from which fuel delivered by rail was distributed to the surrounding Castle Howard Estate. There's a square pit that once contained a weighbridge, and a small stone hut with a fireplace, and walls still lined with bookshelves, which served as the yard office.

In the 60 years since the coal yard closed, a skin of moss and tenacious pioneer vegetation has colonised the crushed stone and coaldust to form a layer of meagre, black soil. In high summer, this soil supports a giddy array of selfheal and clover, bugle and lady's mantle, scarlet pimpernel, bird's-foot trefoil and meadow cranesbill, a variety of orchids, and one extraordinary rarity: the tiny fringed rupturewort *Herniaria ciliolata*, otherwise found only on the Lizard peninsula in Cornwall.

Downstream of the coal yard is an area of wet carr woodland owned by the Crambeck village community, who manage it lightly and make valiant efforts to control the spread of invasive Himalayan balsam. Aside from a narrow path to a sitting place, the rest is wilderness that threatens to engulf you, literally. In spring the black mires are thigh deep, but splattered with the outrageous blaring yellow of marsh marigold. In summer it's marginally less wet, but the vegetation compensates with riotous thorny, stinging and ankle-snaring, face-scratching, hair-snagging growth. I love it.

During the exceptional winter of 2009–2010 we had a cold spell where temperatures stayed sub-zero for weeks and plunged lower than -10°C night after night. One morning, I ventured into the carr. It had transformed into a fretted wonderland of black trunks and branches, white snow, blue shadow, and for once, with the bog frozen solid, walking was easy. Everywhere there were the footprints of birds, foxes, squirrels, voles, and at intervals along the bank, grubby otter slides. Though I saw not another human soul, the place had never felt so populated.

In addition to the stone ruins in the coal yard there is a more recent but equally derelict wooden shed with padlocked doors. Its windows are too grimy to permit a view of what's inside, but around the back, I find a broken panel has created an opening just large enough, if I duck and twist sideways, to slip through. Inside is a work bench and shelves filled with bottles and tins, their labels, if they ever had any, long lost or faded or rusted away. Arrayed against the workbench are a garden fork, a filthy car battery and an early model strimmer. There are carrier bags from a supermarket chain that hasn't existed for 15 years. The electrical wiring looks 50 years old, and there's a 1980s radio with a design that is familiar but a lifetime distant.

My first thought is that the whole place is a health and safety nightmare. Old tools and old wiring and who knows what dubious chemicals. But what bothers me more is that the place has no sign of recent childish occupation. No caches of treasures, no sweet wrappers or crisp packets, no footprints or finger marks in the dust. On one wall a grinning skull has been daubed in dayglo orange, but it looks decades old.

Children don't play here anymore, it seems, not even in lockdown. At least not by themselves. But that wasn't always the case. Mischievous pencilled graffiti still adorns the inside walls of the weighing hut, including a little cartoon labelled 'Mr Vause' (the name of the coal merchants). One of these children was Norman West, who grew up here between 1937 and 1955, in one of three small cottages on the river side of the railway. COVID means we can't meet up but we speak on the phone and he tells me the houses are gone but the place is easy to find. 'Just look for my Mam's damson tree, it's still there.' I find the tree and the outline of the buildings next to a tumbledown storehut. They had no electricity or sanitation, says Norman, being on the wrong side of the railway, and their water came from a well. 'We were told after many years that the well water wasn't good – they fitted a mains tap for us but it was half a mile away, so of course we didn't use it.'

The children were always told the river was dangerous, and many of them saw for themselves. 'I remember when a soldier perished trying to get across in a borrowed canoe,' says Norman, 'Then another night in the war some friends and I tried to salvage a tailor's dummy from the water, only for it to roll over and reveal a human skull in a rotted face – it was an evacuee boy who'd gone missing months before. But worst was young Michael MacKillican from next door who also got drowned. I remember his dad. He lost a leg in the war and the other one didn't work well – so he worked his garden sitting down.'

In Norman's day, the Derwent ran swift and unobstructed, even in low flows, because silt dredging had been routine, partly as a source of sludge for use as fertiliser but mainly to keep the channel clear for boat traffic. From the Bronze Age to the mid nineteenth century, the Derwent was the main cargo route in the area. Barges once plied its course at least as far as Malton, carrying 50-tonne loads of grain, potatoes, gravel and coal. But the railway changed all that, and by the 1940s and 1950s most of the boats that remained on this stretch were small, rented pleasure craft which, following severe deterioration in the condition of navigation infrastructure, especially lock gates, were effectively trapped above Kirkham.

The York to Scarborough railway was one of many projects instigated by local boy George Hudson, born three miles downriver in the tiny farming village of Howsham. Orphaned at eight, Hudson was raised by his brothers before leaving home and being apprenticed to a draper in York. The drapery business boomed, Hudson became a partner, and began investing his profits in railways. By the mid 1830s he was not only a pre-eminent businessman, but also alderman then lord mayor of York. He became a friend and partner of George Stephenson, the so-called Father of the Railways, and by the mid 1840s at the height of Britain's railway mania he had a nickname of his own – the Railway King. Between 1844 and 1846 the government granted permission for 6,220 miles of track, equivalent to half of today's existing network. This included the 42-mile line from York to Scarborough, campaigned for and built by Hudson's York and North Midland Railway (YNMR) at astonishing speed. It opened on July 7th 1845, just one year and three days after the Act of Parliament allowing construction to begin.

George Hudson's star ultimately fell almost as far as it had risen, and perhaps his most potent legacy is a cautionary tale of overreaching ambition. In both business and politics his careers were marked by dubious practice and ultimately overshadowed by financial ruin. He initially avoided imprisonment for debt through his status as a sitting Member of Parliament, but lost his seat in 1853 and fled into exile. He attempted a return to politics in 1865, but was arrested days before an election in which he was standing again as a parliamentary candidate. He later absconded from jail and left the country again, only returning in 1870 when the punishment of debt by imprisonment was abolished. He died a year later and was buried in the churchyard at Scrayingham, two miles downriver from where he was born.

The significance of the railway for the future of the Derwent was immense. The new freight services had an immediate effect on river traffic, but the switch was not fast enough for the YNMR, which bought control of navigation on the Middle Derwent in 1855 and immediately increased tolls for water cargo – effectively forcing freight onto the rail. Flood damage in the early 1930s led to many locks being temporarily closed, and in 1935 the statutory right of navigation above the tidal limit of Sutton upon Derwent was formally revoked. Since then, as on around 97 per cent of rivers in England, if you wish to travel this waterway, which has served as an artery for thousands of years, or to slip into its satiny green water for a swim, and you do so without explicit permission, you are trespassing.

Howsham is three miles downstream of my home and has a water mill George Hudson would have known well. It is unusually ornate for such a functional building, having been rebuilt in 1755, in what the then owner of Howsham Hall considered a more aesthetically pleasing gothic style. The wheel now generates electricity, along with two big Archimedean screw turbines more recently installed in the weir. As you approach the mill you hear first the rush of the weir then, as you get closer, a superimposed triple heartbeat that signifies the production of enough electricity to power the village three or four times over. It's a good place to watch kingfishers and grey wagtails, the occasional smirking cormorant and, if you are lucky, otters. The restoration of the mill was the work of a small charity, the Renewable Heritage Trust (RHT), brainchild of hydropower specialist Dave Mann and his wife Mo MacLeod. Dave's company pioneered the use of Archimedean screws for hydropower in the UK and the original screw at Howsham in 2007 was the first to be installed in the country for this purpose.

I served as trustee of the RHT for a few years and, along with other volunteers, helped maintain the mill, guide weekend visitors and develop a programme of educational events. One October afternoon I was working there with Dave and Martin, another of the trustees, when we saw a huge salmon attempting repeatedly to jump the weir – a broad slope over which water runs far too shallow to be swimmable. To see such a creature this far upstream was remarkable – other weirs downriver are generally regarded as impassable to fish. Having already defeated the odds the great fish – a male judging by its pinkish undercarriage – leapt every few minutes, close enough that we could almost feel the damage sustained to its body with each thud and battering backward slide off the stonework. The worst of it was that the RHT had offered to construct a fish ladder while installing the second screw turbine – something the Environment Agency recognised an urgent need for. Our offer would have saved the public purse hundreds of thousands of pounds. But getting the necessary permissions proved impossible in a reasonable timeframe and so the turbine went in without the fish pass and to this day any salmon managing to get as far as Howsham in anything other than extreme flood conditions will still beat themselves to exhaustion on the weir.

It was on this stretch of home water – Crambeck to Howsham, sometimes as far up as Malton – that Roy and I started paddling again. We began using our old open canoe, which had room for both of us and Lochy. Then my kayak, which had been on long term loan, came home. Boats become like old friends. This one is a yellow Pyranha H3, old now, battered but sound. Plastic white-water boats are made in spin moulds, like wheelie bins, only the plastic is thicker and barring major impacts they are extremely tough, and serviceable for decades. I put off getting back in mine for a while, but when I did, and felt again the familiar slither and buoyant plop of a seal launch off the bank, it was like I'd never been away. The weight of the boat is more of a challenge than it used to be, and my older joints complain when I sit in it for too long, but the simple fact of being back on the water was a joy. We bought a small kayak for Lochy, and began getting to know the quiet, green, willow-lined corridor on which we seldom saw another human soul.

Howsham is the place Roy first taught me to paddle straight. Having moved to York to be with him, it was immediately obvious I'd see more of him if I learned to kayak, and besides, it looked like fun. But it's not as easy as it looks. On moving water novices invariably find the boat turning too far left or right as the flow catches one or other side of the hull. The instinctive reaction is to paddle harder to try and correct the yaw, but that makes things worse. Every paddle stroke creates a turning force. The trick is to balance these forces, and use subtle corrections – paddling wider, more steadily, adjusting the angle of the blade within a stroke, or dragging it slightly – or altering the balance of the boat using your hips so that more or less edge is in contact with the water. It's a lot to think about, and it didn't come naturally to me at all. The river spun me left and right, weed snagged the paddles. The boat was uncomfortable, the water was wet and cold. It didn't help that Roy seemed to be able to place his boat anywhere with a couple of effortless strokes. Sometimes without even making a stroke. But gradually I learned. I got my first boat, an aging red Microbat with a rounded hull described as 'forgiving' because it lacked the aggressive carving edges that make some other boats highly controllable, but too twitchy for most novices. In that faithful old tub, I could bounce down most things. Roy helped me fit it with footrests and hip padding, which wedged me into the seat. I learned that you don't sit in a white-water kayak, you wear it, and it becomes part of you. You lean, it leans. You twitch a hip or a knee, it gouges the water on the other side. In the same way, paddles become extensions of your arms – instruments of power, yes, but also of fine control. There's a fast chute down the middle of the weir at Howsham – a glassy slide with a bouncy flush you can whoosh down without any real skill at all. The hard part is moving from that fast-moving water to the slower flow either side, or trickier still, crossing the flow from one eddy of slowly recirculating water to another on the other side. Doing so, there is a moment where the bow is pushed one way, the stern another, and if you're not ready to harness those flows and use the carving edges of the boat, your own bodyweight and momentum, and some appropriately judged paddle-power, you become flotsam, unstable and liable to capsize.

Taking control also requires commitment – leaning and edging both feel horribly counter-intuitive to the beginner. At Howsham, I capsized and swam time and again. Twice in as many months I hit the bottom (which is scattered with the rubble remains of the original seventeenth-century weir) with my face, earning the blackest of black eyes – the kind of damage that startles people in the street. I learned belatedly to adopt a defensive capsize posture with my face tucked in to my knees.

But the biggest shock at Howsham came on a summer evening when I suggested to some canoe club friends that we might paddle down the river to Buttercrambe – make a trip of it.

'We can try. But we'll probably get grief from a bailiff.'

'A bailiff?' I thought of burly men in black confiscating televisions and stereos.

'A water bailiff. They sort of guard the river. From poachers mainly but they often try and stop paddlers.'

'Because they think we're poaching?'

'No, because we're trespassing.'

'We are?'

'Mostly. Technically. Yes.'

The first I knew of trespass as a child was as something to be forgiven, in the Lord's prayer. Then there was the mysterious Trespassers William in A.A. Milne's *Winnie the Pooh*. In the story where the Hundred Acre Wood gang try to catch a Woozle, Piglet explains to Christopher Robin with great assurance that a gradually disintegrating sign reading 'TRESPASSERS W' refers to Trespassers Will, who he thinks is his grandfather. I guess that means they were all trespassers – perhaps Milne included. I saw those 'TRESSPASSERS WILL BE PROSECUTED' signs too, but perhaps because Piglet was unconcerned, they never bothered me. Those signs couldn't mean me. I was a good girl.

I remembered the license number I'd been sent with my membership of the British Canoe Union (now British Canoeing). I was sure the information pack said it gave me some kind of permission. There was even a permit sticker for my boat.

I was about to learn that this official looking piece of paper gave me a right to paddle on less than 3 per cent of English rivers. Large, flat ones mainly, plus tidal waters. Even a few months into the sport I knew there wasn't a great deal of white water in such places. Which begged the question, what was the point in having a licence at all?

For the kinds of rivers we paddled, it transpired, there pretty much wasn't one. The BCU were, I was told, trying to do something to improve river access. A big step forward nearly happened in 2000 with the Countryside and Rights of Way (CRoW) Act, which was originally drafted to include rivers as well as land, but this got stripped out. Private access agreements had been made with public-spirited landowners in some places, such as the half mile between Howsham Bridge and the mill, but the big picture was of massive exclusion. It was a long conversation, that. Full of baffled indignance on my part, and open-palmed shrugging from the others.

'Can't you get prosecuted?'

'Nah. The thing is, trespass is a civil offence but not a criminal one. So they can tell you to leave, and then you're obliged to do so – sticking around would then *become* criminal, but usually the fastest and safest way to go is to carry on down the river. If they threaten the police you just say fine, and suggest you meet them at the get-out. By that time you're actively complying with their request that you leave, so there's no crime. The police know that and so do they.'

I was warned that the angriest people I was likely to encounter were not landowners or farmers, but recreational anglers, especially the ones that pay to fish, and here perhaps is the rub. Paddlers do make economic contributions. For the ten years I paddled intensively, we spent every free weekend driving hundreds of miles, usually with a group, eating in cafes, restaurants, take-outs and pubs, staying away once or twice or more a month in hostels, inns and campsites, buying supplies, buying kit. Roy and I were relatively cautious spenders but some more affluent paddlers routinely invested thousands of pounds a year on equipment, coaching, books and subscriptions, accommodation and travel. But they don't generally pay landowners simply for owning the river. Anglers often do. From the paddler's perspective, fierce defence of the system by anglers can appear to be a kind of Stockholm syndrome.

A much more legitimate concern is that of damage to habitat. It is important to consider the impact of any access on wildlife. There is no danger to fish or other aquatic life from a passing kayak, or even a fleet of them, but scraping over gravels could certainly disturb spawning areas and damage eggs. It's a bad idea to paddle when there's not enough water to float. It's no fun for a start.

In some places long-lasting access agreements are highly workable. However, because most rivers flow through the land owned by many people, negotiating new ones is far from easy. I got to know the local access officer for the Derwent – he is another of the trustees of Howsham Mill RHT. A brusque but vast-hearted Yorkshireman, Paul is a consummate fixer – of broken things and broken situations. In many ways he's the ideal go-between – but I have never sought advance permission to canoe, kayak or swim because doing so seldom makes sense. Any river sport should be contingent on conditions – not just to suit your ability but also to manage risk and protect the environment. On the Derwent heavy rain brings sewage downriver from Malton and sometimes flooding. In higher catchments, many rivers need rain to be runnable at all. You can't plan the weather, which makes the palaver of arranging access in advance, even where the possibility exists, really clumsy. You couldn't design a system better if your sole aim was to discourage and obstruct. So with a few exceptions, the process gets bypassed, and paddlers fall foul of the straw-man argument that they haven't sought permission through a system that is unfit for purpose. Little by little, like so many others, we lost faith in the ability of the BCU, or British Canoeing as it became, to ever get a breakthrough because the landowning and angling lobbies were never serious about giving up control and these are people with friends in high places – indeed many large riparian landowners sit in Parliament.

Across much of the physically paddle-able river network in England, the option left open to kayakers is to wait for the right conditions, and just go, taking every effort to ensure that you treat the river and the adjacent land and communities with respect, but accepting a risk of confrontation. For decades now, this is what most have done. The responsible ones (I like to think that was us) park carefully, collect litter, rescue sheep and children's toys, clear obstructions, report pollution, spend with local businesses and support grassroots campaigns against ill-advised development. Clubs provide training in water safety, offer public taster sessions, raise money for charity – this kind of thing was all in a year's richly enjoyable work for York Canoe Club and its members during my time there.

Inevitably this uneasy and complicated status quo sometimes breaks down. Verbal challenges range from polite objections to shouted abuse. I was never assaulted physically, and our cars never got their paintwork keyed, their windows broken or their tyres slashed. I never got hooked by a line flicked at me (though we'd often snag line discarded in the water or cut tangles of it from bankside vegetation). But stories of all these things and worse were rife in the kayaking community. Rocks and bricks thrown. Threats or claims that rapids had been booby-trapped with barbed or razor wire, forcing paddlers to abort, just in case it was true.

I have good reason to fear barbed wire.

The River Mint in Cumbria is a small, rocky, rollercoaster with jinking bends and feisty rapids. It's one of those rivers that needs a lot of rain to come into condition, so by definition, it runs fast. Paddling it one winter in a small group, I was following PK, a hugely experienced river lead, when I saw him raise a hand and make a swift circling gesture over his head, the signal to get into the safety of an eddy as soon as possible. He was shouting something too, but I couldn't hear what, and I had no time. I saw the wire at the last moment, running taut across the entire river, 10cm above the surface. I back-paddled – not because there was any chance of avoiding it, but to buy myself thinking time. Roy was close behind, shouting. 'Over! You've got to get over it!'

It is possible to make a kayak jump. Normally this kind of move is used when paddling over an abrupt drop – you use momentum and coordinated hip thrust, leg lift and abdominal crunch to 'boof' off the edge and skim the soft pile of aerated water rather than tipping off and pencilling down the fall line, where gravity and flow will carry you down, and you have little control over what happens next. In this instance I needed to raise the front of the boat over the wire with enough momentum that my weight would push it down, after which a hip thrust and a couple of paddle strokes could get me off the other side. But having hesitated, I wasn't going nearly fast enough. As soon as the hull touched the wire, the force of the river swung me sideways. I was going to get broached on the barbs. Normally when broached sideways the best course of action is to lean on to the obstacle and lift the upstream edge of the hull so the river can slide underneath. Otherwise, water piles up on the upstream edge, pushing it down and forcing a capsize up against the obstacle. But to lean on this time would have meant laceration. So, I did the only thing I could think of. I dropped my upstream edge, capsized and scraped under the wire, upside down.

We were lucky. At lower water levels the wire could have been at garrotting height. In higher water we'd maybe not have known it was there, unless one of us had the misfortune to be swimming. To give the benefit of the doubt, possibly it was meant as a stock fence – in summer when the river is very shallow cattle might walk in and use the channel as an escape route. But this was the winter paddling season, and anyone who runs barbed wire close to water level in a swift river either hasn't thought too hard or doesn't care who or what gets caught on it.

The pandemic brought the issue of river access to much wider attention. At Kirkham, as at accessible beauty spots across the country, as the strictest phase of lockdown eased, people came in their hundreds. And who can blame them? It's a perfect picnicking and swimming location. You can park nearby, there is a broad field with a public footpath running through it, and the river is wide and slow. Teenagers tested their mettle by jumping from the bridge. Families sprawled. There was boozing and snogging, squealing and yelling, music and gales of laughter. There were huge amounts of litter, which some locals stepped in to help clear up, while others joined what seemed to be a new epidemic – of vilification, othering and super-local xenophobia.

Litter is offensive. By its very definition, it is the stuff we do not wish to see, which we wish to dispose of in the most expedient way possible. But whether we bin it, flush it, put it in a recycling bin, lob it from a car window or fly tip on a country lane, those discarded items continue to exist, and we are relying on someone else to take care of the problem. That 'someone else' is a system, and as frequent scandals suggest, a failing one. Is shipping tonnes of waste meant for recycling thousands of miles overseas to be dumped or burned any better than leaving a crisp packet on a riverbank? I understand the rage. I've tried stuffing takeaway wrappers back in through car windows and Roy has delivered bags of canine excrement back to the offending address. But those acts of retaliation don't fix the problem. As individuals, and as a society, we just want our waste to disappear. It is not OK to drop litter. But neither is it OK for water companies to release raw sewage into rivers (which they admit to doing for millions of hours a year). It is not OK for farmers to dump or bury waste on their own land to enrich the water with fertiliser or poison it with pesticides, or for industries to leak other pollutants. It's not OK that water-loving pet dogs are treated with doses of inadequately regulated spot-on flea treatments capable of killing tens of thousands of aquatic invertebrates. But blaming the public is easier than sorting out systemic failures.

Into the storm of hostility about post-lockdown access to natural places on my social media timeline came a stylish black and white linocut illustration with the hashtag #RightToRoam. It was the work of Nick Hayes, author of *The Book of Trespass*, who had partnered with environmentalist and activist Guy Shrubsole to launch a new campaign opposing government plans to criminalise trespass and proposing instead a significant expansion of the statutory right of responsible access in England. I felt an instant affinity with the ambitions of the campaign, and especially its focus on responsible access and a shared love and care for the land.

We meet for the first time via video call. Both Nick and Guy are affable, irreverent, focussed and sharp-witted, and they explain that their campaign is framing the argument as a matter of public health as well as social justice. The current right to roam in England covers a measly 8 per cent of land area, and most land accessible under the CRoW Act is in upland areas far away from centres of population, while the need for green space is greatest where people live. Nature, they say, shouldn't be something you have to travel for. I tell them about a contribution I made in 2018 to *The People's Manifesto for Wildlife*, formulated by the naturalist and TV presenter Chris Packham. Chris had appointed me 'minister' for Social Inclusivity and Access to Nature – I had proposed that the latter should be recognised as a human right.

Time spent in nature keeps people out of doctors' surgeries and hospitals. It reduces sick leave. There is therefore a compelling economic argument for promoting activities like walking, wildlife watching, fishing, swimming and kayaking. And, as we plunge headlong into the climate and biodiversity emergencies, the action required to turn things around will only be taken by people who know, love and act on behalf of the ecosystems on which our survival depends, both locally and globally.

Nick and Guy intended to make a particular case for greenbelt land, woodland and rivers. Nick lives on a boat and is also a swimmer and kayaker. In reading his book, I learned that rivers were established in Roman law as the shared property of all citizens – only one step removed from air and sea, which belonged to all humankind. As *res publicae*, rivers could not be privatised. And yet somehow, here, they have been. The owner of land through which a river passes owns the riverbank and its bed, and for the short time it passes by, they may also lay claim to the water. If the river is a boundary between properties, then landowners on opposite banks each own the bed up to a midline. In practical terms however, a river is a poor choice of feature to service something as rigid as jurisdictional boundaries or property law. Levels and courses change, making a mockery of such boundaries. Scrutinise the high-resolution maps of England and you'll see that parish and county boundaries often follow strange kinks – the shape of a river whose course has long since changed, naturally or through artificial straightening.

As soon as I began supporting the Right to Roam campaign on Twitter, I experienced a slew of vitriolic, patronising, gaslighting responses. A popular comeback was 'How would you like it if I came and trampled all over your garden?' This is wilfully absurd. In countries with a right to roam, including Scotland, that right applies only to large areas of land, and there is still a right to privacy that prevents intrusion close to homes. In Scotland and elsewhere, access is codified so there is seldom any doubt about what constitutes responsible behaviour.

The online fishing community were far from impressed, though as is usually the way, those with moderate opinions tended to keep their heads down. In the real world I meet plenty of anglers who have no problem with other river users. A neighbour, Arran (not his real name), works in environmental services and river flood risk management. He's a kayaker and an angler, and he confirms what I suspect. The fishing community is huge, and even a small percentage of such a large group can make a lot of noise. Arran comes up against these antagonists professionally and personally 'They just don't want to hear that the world doesn't revolve around them. They are usually the same ones who complain vocally about otters without bothering to understand that otters only live where there are a lot of fish, and, as top predators, are never going to become abundant enough to threaten fish stocks. They don't want to do the work of understanding ecology. And they are hostile to sharing the river with anything other than fish. Unfortunately, when it comes to things like access it's easy to see how member organisations like the Angling Trust might be tempted to play to that vocal minority. I mean – just look at UK politics! But the thing is, there are a huge number – a majority probably – of thoughtful anglers out there who are perfectly happy to play nice with other river users, but I understand why they often don't speak up. There are fewer kayakers than anglers, but as a rule I don't see the same levels of ignorance or shoutiness from them.'

The hostility I was seeing locally and in the media towards people just trying to get a bit of badly needed air and space reignited old memories – the brittle edge of defensiveness that comes from a challenge to one's right to exist in a place is not conducive to a quiet mind. Then one sleepless night, something clicked. I sat up in bed and swore, and announced to a groggy Roy that every single access challenge I've ever encountered on a river was from a man. A white man, most often on his own. Access to rivers, and in fact to countryside in general is profoundly patriarchal, and it is policed by lone entitled males.

'I've had enough.' I announced, and went soundly to sleep.

The maleness and paleness of gatekeepers is not surprising. Most large landowners are men, as are a majority of farmers, and certainly anglers. After a couple of months of supporting the Right to Roam campaign I'd also noticed that the most hostile and time-consuming interactions were from accounts whose profiles were anonymising – they didn't use their full names and their avatars were mostly dogs, tractors or fish. I don't necessarily doubt their claim to care about rivers – but they seem incapable of understanding that others could legitimately love them too, and that we could do a far better job of looking after them together.

To save my sanity, I resolved not to engage in social media debate with anyone who wasn't prepared to identify themselves, and immediately things improved. I found farmers, land managers and anglers willing to share perspectives in a constructive manner. I also found wild swimmers, kayakers and paddleboarders, ramblers, other writers, poets and artists, naturalists and filmmakers, conservationists, citizen scientists, grassroots activists and high-profile campaigners: passionate, respectful, diverse and determined people.

The shifting balance of public opinion towards river access owes much to the rise in recreational wild swimming and stand-up paddleboarding, with sales of boards skyrocketing during the pandemic. Both activities appeal strongly to women, in fact long distance open water swimming is one of few sports where women out-perform men at an elite level. There is little bravado in either sport and both lend themselves to discretion. On quiet water, there is no stealthier vessel than a kayak or a canoe, except perhaps a coracle. All were originally designed for hunting and fishing from, so in that way, paddlers share heritage with anglers. Inflatable kayaks are also gaining rapid popularity, and like paddleboards are relatively easy to transport. Basic models are less expensive and less conspicuous than rigid plastic boats. While white-water paddlers still have little alternative but to use access points relatively close to roads, and to arrive with roof-racks stacked with brightly coloured plastic, the inflatable user can park discreetly, walk some distance with their boat or board in a backpack, and slip onto the water. Swimming of course, has the potential to be less conspicuous still, trespassing or not.

Organisations like the Outdoor Swimming Society are providing excellent resources on safe, responsible access to water. There is also a code of conduct for paddling. This needs to be updated and promoted more – especially the need for biosecurity, which receives far less attention here than in other countries. In New Zealand, river users are meticulous about cleaning and drying kit to prevent transfer of invasive species, in particular the diatom *Didymosphenia germinata*, known as didymo or rock snot. Reminders are everywhere – boats are slapped with stickers, and clubs, guides and coaches all preach good practice. We have equally heinous invasive species here: American signal crayfish, quagga mussels, water primrose, giant hogweed and Himalayan balsam to name a few, but the threats they pose and the often simple measures needed to restrict their spread are poorly known. This is a failure of public information. Such education is not expensive. But given that from 2010 to 2020 the total UK government spend on publicising the Countryside Code was a mere £2,000 every 18 months for printing leaflets, we have a long way to go.

I ponder this often. This river feels like my river, in that I feel responsible for it, I know it well, and love it dearly. Those feelings connect me to thousands who have lived, worked and played on this short section for thousands of years, and to the wilder lives here – some long, some very short. But the law says I have no right to stick my foot or my paddle in these waters. Words on paper say this is no longer a river for everyone.

Summer on the Nene

In summer 2020 I visited the schoolteacher to whom I owe much of my love of nature. As the coordinator of the school's Duke of Edinburgh Award Scheme group, Liz Doherty also helped introduce me to mountains and adventure. She's retired now, and living with her husband back on her family's farm in the Nene valley, Northamptonshire – a pastoral idyll of big hedges, grand old trees, honeyed stone, thatched roofs, generous gardens, wide floral verges, and the sleepiest of rivers, winding through it. This is where Liz's own love of nature grew, and where I've come to visit. The 800-acre farm is now managed by her brother, John, and his son Michael. Liz's dad, Bob, was a farmer and naturalist, whose grandfather first began farming here in 1900.

It's the first time I've properly met John – he's good looking in a no-nonsense way and he speaks with warm, rounded Northamptonshire vowels. I can tell within minutes we're not going to agree on everything – badgers for a start. But I also sense this is someone I can simultaneously like, respect and disagree with and that he's willing to make space for that too.

He is initially puzzled by my interest in what he calls 'the most boring river in the world', then tells me he once paddled the Nene from Flore to the Wash, camping along the way in a wooden canoe he made at school.

He's not sure exactly how the farm became a wildlife haven: 'Dad just chose not to move with the times. He's always had an intense love of wildlife, but he was also a shooter. He used to skive school sports, to go wildfowling. As a young man he was often out gameshooting with BB.'

'*The* BB?' Otherwise known as Denys Watkins-Pitchford, BB was a countryman and hugely popular author best known for *Brendon Chase* and *Little Grey Men.*

'Oh yes – they were great friends. He wrote a lot about Dad and the farm, and he also wrote about Elizabeth. '"A comely country girl," he called her.'

'Oh John, don't!' Liz protests, but he's grinning, warming to the tease as though they are still kids.

'"With no stockings … "'

'Stop it!'

Alas for Liz, BB really does describe her thus, in *The Quiet Fields.* The farm and its surrounds also feature in *A Summer on the Nene,* in which BB travels the river accompanied by his wife and daughter in a small cabin cruiser. On this stretch he recounts the novelty of two birds relatively recently arrived in his day, which have since become widespread – the collared dove and the little owl. The dove colonised of its own accord in the 1950s, while the owl had been given considerable help by local aristocrat and ornithologist Thomas Powys, Lord Liliford, who made a habit of releasing 'a considerable number' annually until the species was well established. It was even known for a while as the Liliford owl.

Liz takes me on a farm tour. Her little Suzuki four-by-four rolls through fields waist deep in midsummer grasses and wildflowers – knapweed, drifts of bedstraw, buttercup and bird's-foot trefoil. The fields alongside the river are in higher-level stewardship schemes, whereby John and Michael are paid to manage them for environmental gain. For John this is a no brainer. 'The river is our main asset from a conservation point of view, but a challenge from the farming one. We couldn't do anything intensive here even if we wanted to, with flooding possible any time.' The flowers look great, and the fields are full of butterflies. I decide that I'm going to sleep in one of them tonight because COVID restrictions mean I'm not allowed in the house. Liz tells me that come mid July the hay will be cut and sheep and cattle allowed on until the winter floods arrive. 'We've switched to low intensity breeds – native Lincoln red cattle and easy-care sheep, which don't need shearing and only need dipping once a year.' Where the stock are grazing, they've been fenced off from the river bank and provided with water from drinkers they operate themselves with snout or hoof. The banks are now thick with vegetation – mostly aggressive weeds because of high nutrient levels in the river, but much less prone to erosion than before, and busy with small birds. The biggest commitment, they tell me, has been working with the local Wildlife Trust to create several long scrapes in one of the flood meadows, designed to hold water on the land even longer. There are oystercatchers there today. There are frustrations and crossed wires from time to time; 'the wrong sort of seed mix went down one year, but they never could explain what was wrong with it, and it was massively cheaper.' But the willingness to try, and to share their land with nature is impressive and it extends to people too.

'We feel total privilege to be here', says John, 'And I love the idea of sharing it. We do a lot of educational visits – the more townie the better, I reckon. Other farmers would just point out all the things they think we're doing wrong, whereas people with little knowledge of the countryside seem to really get a lot out of it.'

At Wadenhoe there's a picturesque mill and a ford, which the local farmers use from time to time to move cattle. Liz points to signs forbidding fishing and access to the river printed in several languages. 'They're aimed mainly at Polish fishermen who like to come and catch supper, and cook it there and then on the bank. In their culture this is entirely normal, and the English system of permits and trespass is baffling to them.'

'It's so lovely here. We should share it, but it can be hard. In lockdown it became a bit contentious. So many people came and not everyone behaved well. A few locals heard we'd identified hemlock water dropwort and that it was Britain's deadliest wild plant and they were delighted – they wanted to put signs everywhere to frighten visitors off.'

The challenges of allowing public access aren't new. In *A Summer on the Nene*, BB wrote of the problems posed to Liz and John's dad – walkers leaving gates open, out of control dogs and floods resulting from boaters failing to properly close locks. It sounds familiar, and it's hugely to the family's credit that they've not been put off.

'What's the answer?' I ask John later while we drink G&Ts in his garden.

'Communication, for sure,' he says. 'After lockdown there was a load of kids in our fields by the river, drinking, leaving bottles and cans. Michael went to talk to them, asked why they couldn't go to a park or just clean up after themselves. They said they were underage, so it had to be private and they knew it was wrong to leave the trash but there were no bins and they couldn't take the evidence home. And I guess I can at least understand that.' The empathy makes me want to hug him.

'Still bloody annoying for you, though.'

'Bloody is.'

CHAPTER 11

Chalk stream dreaming

In early June, as the strictest phase of lockdown eases, I pay a visit to Skerne Wetland — a relatively new nature reserve owned by the Yorkshire Wildlife Trust and managed by Jon Traill. Jon is a man gifted with an aura of kindliness and wisdom: he is measured, composed, considerate, even when he's raging mad. He has a head for detail and tells a great story. He'd probably make an outstanding teacher, arbitrator, politician. But instead he's a conservationist, and a highly effective one. He seems to know pretty much every landowner, manager and river keeper in East Yorkshire and he is always on the move, finding ways and making connections. Jon thinks like water.

Eight years ago, this site was a commercial fish farm. It comprises 115 acres of ponds and reedbeds connected by sluices and gates, skirted and fed by West Beck, a chalk stream tributary of the River Hull. When the farm was in operation, a huge adjustable impoundment weir was used to ensure flow could be maintained through the ponds, even in low levels. Water cascading over the weir caused scouring that wouldn't have happened otherwise, and the precious river gravels below were buried under a foot of silt. Matters were exacerbated by extensive trampling of one of the riverbanks by cattle. Jon had the weir removed, erected stock fences, and fitted coir logs along the banks to narrow the stream. These measures immediately increased the flow, the silt was mobilised and in no time at all, the gravels were clean again.

Aside from that, his approach is highly pragmatic and avoids much tinkering. It is, he says, much easier to manage a reserve if you let the land show you what it wants to be. An area he originally had in mind for wet grassland was rapidly colonised by willow, so he changed the plan and set up a coppicing regime to mix up the age structure and now it is a dynamic and diverse area of wet carr woodland.

Roy and Lochy have joined me on this visit and we are counting the excursion as our permitted daily exercise. We've barely set foot in the reserve when we hear guttural chuckling calls. I grope mentally for a few seconds – what waterbirds creak, hack and chunter at such volume? I can't place the sound at all. But then one of the callers lets rip an epic, gargling belch and I laugh out loud. They're not birds, but marsh frogs, *Pelophylax ridibundus* – a species introduced to the UK in the 1930s. We peer over and between stands of reed into several pools, but the callers are sensitive to the slightest movement and fall silent as we approach. It takes careful stalking to get a decent view, but in time they begin to adjust to our presence. They are huge, luridly green and each wears the faintest of Kermit smiles on a mouth considerably wider than its face. They are the frogs of fairy stories, each in earnest need of kissing. After a couple of minutes the largest begins his serenade again, and through binoculars I see his cheek balloons swell like grey bubblegum while his throat billows to a different tempo, producing the most ludicrous of improvised jazz, a blend of fruity burps and manic squawks – two sounds, two rhythms, from one slippery, smiling windbag of a creature.

I find a shady spot to change into thick thermals, drysuit and a neoprene balaclava, moving slowly, trying not to overheat. Then I scramble down the steep bank, releasing wafts of scent from water mint, and into the blissful cool.

I step onto a submerged rock and crouch there for a few minutes, with the water flowing around my waist, getting my bearings. It's years since I've worn the drysuit. The old neck seal had perished and needed replacing, and the new one is still too tight, making me feel a little panicky. But the buoyancy will help me avoid disturbing the riverbed and the insulation will mean I can stay in longer without any active swimming. Like all chalk streams, West Beck runs at a constant temperature of around 10°C, so it should feel shockingly cold on such a hot day. But there are no goosebumps, no ghastly trickle down my neck, no burning skin. The sense of separation is strange. Sealed into a little package of my own medium, I feel out of my element. Perhaps astronauts get this too, in their composite layers of Kevlar and neoprene, out there, where they are the aliens.

My perch is in the shade of several large willows, which filter sunlight into fingers of blue and gold. On the opposite bank, one of the largest has a half-dozen trunks sprouting from the bank and its roots are partially exposed, forming an overhang. A long shadow scoots upriver and into the dark space there – a brown trout, about the length of my hand and forearm.

Slowly and carefully I kneel, spit in my mask and rinse it – a little saliva helps prevent it fogging up – then press it to my face, and take the snorkel in my mouth. The gear feels ridiculous – complete overkill for entering water scarcely thigh deep. I lean forward, and press my face below the surface.

There are a few moments of startlement where too many things astonish at once. My hands and face, the only parts of my body exposed to the water, register the shock of cold, water trickles icily into my ears. My legs float up and the water takes my weight, and I flail a little to find a position I can hold, hovering, head upstream, and grappling for larger rocks in the riverbed with my hands.

The first couple of snorkel breaths are fast and shallow. I remember when Lochy was newborn, making the expansive jerky movements known as the Moro reflex when picked up from his basket – arms flung out, then tucked in, eyes wide, mouth a little 'o' of surprise at being suspended in the airy brightness of the world without his watery support. It took him about three months to adjust and for the reflex to subside. It takes me about three breaths, before I'm able to properly look.

Given I've planned this for weeks, driven 40 minutes to get here, lugged a bulky duffel drybag the length of the reserve and spent a further 15 minutes wriggling into layers of kit, it should come as no surprise, but somehow it does. I'm *in* the river. Not by it, or floating on it, but properly in. Aided by the mask to keep my vision clear, the act of breaking the surface has transported me a world away. No matter that if I dropped to my knees and came back to the vertical I'd be back in the warm air, thick with pollen, insect drone, birdsong and frog chorus, with the water flowing no higher than my waist: the river has me now, and it fills my senses to the brim.

I begin 'crocodiling' about, touching the bottom with my hands only, legs trailing – a technique that allows me to move slowly, and hold position against the flow, while causing minimal disturbance. From above the water, looking down from the bank or a bridge, you might get a sense of water depth and bed texture, but it's like the difference between a satellite view of a landscape and one from a hillside. The higher viewpoint flattens everything, but from this low angle the topography of the river bottom is a revelation. With my face only a few inches above the bed, I see a rolling riverscape that fades into a slightly milky haze in what looks like far distance, but is probably no more than 15m. None of it is flat. I'm gazing out over a vista of valleys and plains, forests and screes, canyons and caverns.

And oh, *oh*.

In several of the hollows, *every piece* of gravel larger than a five-pence piece has something on it – a small peanut-sized, ovate conglomeration of much smaller fragments, fitted together with the skill of a master waller. They are the cases of caddisfly nymphs, glued with silk. There are about 200 species of caddisfly in Britain, and they are often a predominant life form on the beds of good rivers – but these numbers are astounding. Uncountable.

The gravels of chalk streams are not, for the most part, made of chalk – it is too soft and soluble for fragments to last long in running water. Often there is a lot of flint, chalk's glassy silicaceous companion, which shares the distinction of a biological origin. The silica (silicon dioxide) from which flint is formed finds its way into the seabed in much the same way and in the same locations as the calcite that makes chalk – both via the sedimented skeletal remains of marine organisms – in flint's case, sponges and diatoms. Flint formation occurs preferentially in the infilled burrows of larger animals like worms, bivalves and urchins, and often the nodules take the form of these ancient sanctuaries. Tools made from flint are the defining artefact of the Stone Age: not only do the sharp edges created when nodules fracture make razor-sharp blades, points and scrapers, but the striking of flint against another distinctive and relatively common mineral, pyrite (iron disulphide) produces long-lived sparks that can be used to make fire. The ready availability of flint, the well-drained land and the quality of water made chalk rivers and the landscapes they ran through exceptionally good places to live – as evidenced by the density of prehistoric archaeology.

From this close perspective it is also clear that the riverbed is not the bottom. The river is down there too, among the gravels. I can see it running into the gaps where it percolates down and through, under and up, in and out of sight. In those sheltered and interconnected spaces, whole lives are being lived in single cells and tiny bodies, while others are just starting out. Eggs laid on the gravel settle into secure incubation spaces supplied with a steady flow of oxygen-rich water, cleaned by the flow and safe from hungry eyes.

Close to the bank where I got in, I find a shoal of little square-nosed fish. They look dark from above the water but from my new subaquatic perspective I can see they are boldly marked – mottled above, pale below, with a dark stripe along each flank, and above that, a row of gleaming pinkish-bronze scales. Common minnows. Unremarkable except that some are almost as long as my hand – whoppers, relatively speaking. I sit on my rock on the riverbed with my face still in the water and wiggle my fingers at them. They don't seem frightened, or for that matter even intrigued. But when I take my hand to the bottom and scuff gently at the gravel, dislodging a puff of silt and detritus, they race to investigate, their bull-noses bumping my fingers. I try the same move a few centimetres away, and again they cluster in, more of them this time, wagging tails and shoving with curious snouts. The third time I disturb the bottom, the crowd is bigger still and then several individuals seem to realise that my fingers are attached to something bigger. They start pecking my knuckles and then the back of my hand. It's a delightful feeling – a flurry of little fish kisses, and having them so close and so fearless means I can get a really good look. Their backs are greenish, with darker blotches and stipples. The pale stripe on the flanks comprises a row of rose-gold scales, which gleam as they catch the sunlight. Their eyes are large, with golden irises – like those of teddy bears, making their gaze more alive and alert than I'd ever have expected. The gill covers flutter rhythmically and I can see they are white on the inside. It seems so intimate – like hearing them breathe. Also white are the bases of their fins. In the males, breeding colours are developing – a pinkish flush to the belly and one or two have red around their fin bases. In amongst the minnows are a few sticklebacks – a male with a scarlet chest and belly stands out like a beacon among the greens, the browns, and the pale gold of the gravel.

After what feels like 15 minutes, but turns out to be 45, I clamber out to check on my father-and-son safety team – they are practising throwline rescues and knots on the bank. I knock back a flask of hot coffee to ward off the chill and slide back in. This time I face downstream, lie on my front in the middle of the river, and let myself go. It's just deep enough that I can float over the crowfoot forests – they skim my chest with delicate grindylow fingers. Some clumps are starting to bloom before the floating leaves that lift flowering stems to the surface have formed, and so there are flowers underwater – where white petals have begun to open I can see the startling egg yolk-yellow middles. This must be an accident – pollen and nectar will be washed away – but the sight of this sunlit underwater garden is delightful.

I skim on. The crowfoot beds alternate with more gravelly plains and valleys. The fact that my face is never more than a metre or two from the bottom exaggerates the sense of speed. This, combined with the rise and fall of the riverbed and the way the current swashes me from side to side, gives the sensation of a rollercoaster or a flight simulator ride. Shoal upon shoal of minnows scatter ahead, and there are more to either side. Hundreds of them.

Quite suddenly, the pace picks up and the river deepens – the gravel of the valleys becomes faintly blue, and the numbers of fish increase – there are shoals all around. I'm going too fast to take them all in, but it's like a drone flight over the Serengeti – life abounding. To my left and right are multitudes of dashing forms. Five hundred, a thousand fish. God, no, way more than that. Too many to count... five thousand... *ten*? Each pool seems to thrum with greater and greater numbers – dashing and flickering as I hurtle by, ahead of me and to both sides as I turn my head. I'm flying low and fast over this sun-dappled riverscape, and while the fish dart out from my way, they only part enough to let me pass – they're not fleeing, just negotiating an unexpected piece of flotsam.

The pools become deeper and the crowfoot gives way to ribbon-leaved weed. Much larger coarse fish begin to loom and race – in ones, twos, then sevens and eights. Grayling with their faint horizontal stripes, and deeper-bodied cyprinids with broad flat scales and pinkish fins: chub and perch. The water is becoming greener and cloudier, making it hard to gauge distance and thus their size, but it's substantial – 30cm maybe. I start to think about pike. My pale, ungloved hands feel vulnerable, and I keep them tucked to my chest.

The rollercoaster eases, and I swim the final few hundred metres using slow breaststroke arms, legs trailing to minimise disturbance. Pressing my muscles into use makes me realise how cold I am. I've swum naked in far colder water, but passive floating is very different to active swimming and 90 minutes' immersion has chilled me to the core. I find a cluster of posts that once supported a fishing platform and use them to haul myself out. The sun is strong, but sealed into the suit I can't feel the heat. It takes concentration to unzip the suit with hands that don't work properly, and haul the neck seal over my head. My thermals are damp – the seal might have been throttlingly tight but the seams are showing their age. By the time the boys find me my lips are blue, my breath juddering, my jaw clattering, but I'm laughing, giddy. I want to go again, but sense prevails, and I change into dry clothes, drink more coffee and jog around on the bank until the shivering stops. We set off back to the car, which has been baking in the sun for the hours we've been away – its oven heat is delicious. My knuckles ache and I can feel my bones for the rest of the day, but my mind is lit with where I've been and what I've seen.

I'm still on a high when Jon calls that afternoon. How can a river like this not be the stuff of multiple designations, awards, film credits, I ask? He laughs. These wonders aren't news to him. He tells me that anecdotally, the collected headwaters of the River Hull only missed out on being designated as a Special Area of Conservation because the surveyors ran out of time. Jon is at peace with that though. 'Designations bring visibility and funding, which is great, but they also bring a lot of hoops to jump through – we may just be better off not having our hands quite so tied.'

Water courses that possess all the properties of source, clarity, temperature and mineral content to qualify as chalk rivers or streams are not only the stuff of dreams but also the result of a very particular set of circumstances, and on a global scale, they are extraordinarily rare. Worldwide estimates for the total number of chalk streams range from around 200 to 260, depending how you count them. And of these, around 90 per cent are in England, the majority in the south-east, in East Anglia and the North, South and Wessex Downs, with a handful in the Lincolnshire and Yorkshire Wolds.

The pattern of ancient settlements and ritual sites around chalk rivers suggests that our ancestors understood that they were beneficiaries and custodians of an astonishing treasure. But somewhere along the line since then, we forgot.

In 2019 two thirds of chalk rivers and streams in the Chilterns ran dry, as did others elsewhere. This shouldn't happen: the vast reserves of water in a chalk aquifer are more than enough to keep rivers running in even the driest summer. The problem is abstraction, from rivers and from the aquifer. It doesn't help that the area with the highest density of chalk rivers in the world is also the most highly populated region of the UK – the south east of England. Among the worst affected were the rivers of the Colne catchment in the Chiltern hills, including the Ver, the Gade and the Chess. The Ver gave its name to the Roman city of Verulamium, now St Albans, where my sister lives. Seeing the channel empty month after month prompted local outrage. People wanted to know where their river had gone. It was the same on the Chess. It doesn't help that the water companies of England and Wales alone admit to letting three billion litres leak from their pipes – not every year, but every day. Not only does the regulator for water services, Ofwat, seem incapable of preventing this, according to a water company executive speaking to the Public Accounts Committee on 22nd July 2020, water companies are disincentivised to address leaks because Ofwat penalises them for every repair recorded – in purely business terms, it's better (for them) to ignore the problem.

The Ver started running again in February 2020, when I was there. Similarly the River Chess in Buckinghamshire, after Affinity Water agreed to cease abstracting six million litres a day in 2021, was brim-full and clear by June of that year when I visited. It might take longer for the trout to return, but the solution is simple. We must leave the river in the river. That does present a challenge – but humans are good at solving such things. We can and must use less water. Nobody in possession of a flannel really needs to shower twice daily, or to wash most clothes after a single wearing. Lawns can cope with drying out a bit. No modern building should use drinking water to flush toilets. These are not hard problems to solve.

These rivers are finding champions, sometimes in surprising places. Take Feargal Sharkey, onetime frontman of the Undertones, then music industry spokesman and influencer, who has been shaking things up one way or another for more than 40 years. We met at an event I organised as part of my role with the creative arts and environment charity New Networks for Nature, when Feargal stepped in at exceptionally short notice after our headline guest, Chris Packham, had to pull out. As the member of the team with most knowledge of rivers, I was promoted to interviewer, and I was nervous. It wasn't just that I used to listen to Feargal on the mixtapes of my teens. I was genuinely unsure we'd hit it off, because Feargal's love of rivers stems from his lifelong passion for fly fishing. He is president of the venerable Amwell Magna Fishery – one of the oldest in the country – based on the River Lea in Hertfordshire. Perhaps he was a kayak hater. Moreover, while New Networks audiences are exceptionally warm and enlightened, there was always the possibility someone would give him a hard time about angling and the conversation would be hijacked. I wasn't sure I had the experience to keep things on track. Most of all, not having seen Feargal speak publicly before, I wasn't sure how much he would have to say.

I needn't have worried. The man is a verbal faucet, you just have to turn the tap. Facts, stats, forensic details, quotes, anecdotes, wisecracks, and oh boy, anger; not wasted on other river users, but directed with laser precision at failing corporate and statutory bodies and those leading them – the water companies, the Environment Agency, Defra. In person and on social media, Feargal has kept up the pressure, along with other stalwarts including the journalist and activist George Monbiot and the journalist Rachel Salvidge, and a plethora of grassroots organisations, helping to ensure increasing visibility for our appallingly abused rivers and to hold those responsible to account.

The point Feargal made that really stuck with me was a comparison between the music industry and the conservation sector. 'The thing with UK Music [the organisation representing interests of the creative and production side of the music industry, which Feargal helped set up in 2008] is that for the first time all the people that should have always been on the same side were in the room together, in mutual support and purpose. The conservation and environmental movements have never genuinely managed that. There are big players there, big NGOs with millions of members, but as long as they continue to defend their own territory, obsess over membership, they will always dilute one another's efforts and pull punches they really ought to be landing. When the stakes are so high that's pretty damn sad to see.' He has a point. Maybe one day we'll go chalk stream fishing. Or kayaking. Or both.

Heron

I'm swimming in a quiet backwater near a little weir with a glassy chute. There's a huge willow leaning over the water, and an oak with clusters of tiny, pea-sized acorns and tentacle-like roots spreading left and right along the bank.

The weir means I need to swim downstream first – something that always makes me a little nervous, mindful that swimming back will be much harder work. I don't go far, turning around after 50m or so, just in time to see a heron alight at the water's edge a short way upstream. He parachutes down, placing, lifting and placing again his feet with such ostentatious precision that I'm reminded of a concert pianist's hands. I think he's a male because his back has a particularly long cape of the fine plumes known as aigrets, and he seems keen to take particular care of these, affecting a sort of fastidious feathery origami, folding and refolding his wings before finally adopting a hunting pose. This presents me with a dilemma, because I know herons can't bear to be watched. They never let me get anywhere near them in a kayak, and if I want to watch one from the bank I find it helps to do so sidelong – don't let them see you looking. This one has gone through his entire settling routine, unaware of my presence in the water just a few metres away, but there is no way I can get back upriver without disturbing him.

No creature on Earth expresses disgruntlement more eloquently than a grey heron. I think of Paul Farley's brilliant sweary poem *The Heron* ' . . . fucking hell, all right, all right, I'll go to the garage for your flaming fags,' and resign myself to the recoil when the bird recognises me: the glare, the grudging launch. I speak quietly.

'Sorry, Sir Heron. I need to go past you.'

The bird plays his part to perfection, flinching, scorching me with yellow-eyed disgust, and then after a two-second pause in which I fail to drop dead or vanish, he hunches into his wings as if hoisting on a coat he had only just shrugged off, and hup-hup-hups himself into the air, steeply, to clear the trees on the opposite bank. A spatter of white shit strikes the leaf canopy and I chuckle.

'You missed me.'

CHAPTER 12

Land covered by water

From the perspective of land rights and river access, the Yorkshire Derwent has been the focus of two pivotal battles, almost a thousand years apart. The first took place on 25th September 1066. It lasted all of a few hours, but cost thousands of lives. The second was bloodless, fought in court, but ran for seven years, from 1984 to 1991.

England in the year 1066 was up for grabs. In January, King Edward the Confessor died without leaving an obvious heir. Hoping to fend off a succession battle, the assembly of royal advisors known as the Witenagemot immediately appointed Harold Godwinson, the most powerful man in the country at the time, as king. But Harold was never going to retain the crown without a fight. The first challenge came from his exiled brother Tostig, who attempted an invasion in the spring. This was repelled, but two much stronger challenges were building, from Harold Hardrada, King of Norway, and William, Duke of Normandy. By September both had raised armies and were preparing invasions.

Hardrada struck first, having formed an alliance with Tostig, whose local knowledge was valuable. They arrived on 18th September with an army of 10,000 in 300 Viking ships, sweeping up the Humber and then the Yorkshire Ouse to Riccall, as far as the tide would assist them. On 20th September they covered the final few miles to York, capital of the North, on foot and were met at Fulford, just outside the city by an army led by earls loyal to the King. The Norweigan force won, but the battle was costly to both sides.

Hardrada and Tostig began the process of negotiating terms of conquest, including a demand for English hostages. To avoid the risk of damage to their intended seat of

power, they decided to hold these meetings not in York
but at Stamford Bridge, an ancient crossing place on the
Derwent where there has been a bridge since Roman
times. In a fatal miscalculation they left a large number of
fighting men, weaponry and heavy suits of mail with their
fleet at Riccall. Meanwhile Harold Godwinson had heard
of the attack and moved astonishingly fast. He marched an
army from London, gathering further recruits on the way,
and by 24th September had covered the 185 miles to
Tadcaster, 10 miles from York and 15 from Stamford
Bridge. The Norwegians had not expected to fight again
so soon, and certainly not here on the Derwent. As some
accounts have it, Hardrada and Tostig were approached
first by a lone rider, who offered Tostig a chance to switch
sides and regain his earldom. Tostig asked what Hardrada
would be given. 'Seven feet of English ground, as he may
be taller than other men!' retorted the rider. On hearing
the rider was none other than Tostig's brother, Harold,
Hardrada is said to have commented 'That was but a little
man, but he sat firmly in his stirrups.'

The Saxon army advanced over the wooden bridge. They
were, the story goes, held off for a time by a lone giant
Norseman wielding an axe, until one of the English soldiers
floated under the bridge in half a barrel and speared the
axeman from below through a gap in the planking. The
shield wall hastily assembled by the Norwegians was broken,
and they were slain by the thousand, Hardrada and Tostig
Godwinson included. Others drowned trying to escape, and
reinforcements arriving from Riccall were unable to stop
the rout. The river ran red with Viking blood and the
crushed bones of the dead were said to have turned the soil
of the battlefield white for 50 years.

It's odd to go there. The bridge that crosses the Derwent
now (a single-lane stone structure with traffic lights to
ensure traffic waits its turn to cross) is 200m downstream of

the original fording place, a naturally shallow section, now the location of another salmon-stopping weir. Historians and archaeologists have been unable to find much physical trace of the battle, though the consensus of military experts is that, having crossed the river, the Saxon army would have engaged the invaders over a fairly wide area on the slightly raised ground now known as Battle Flat.

If you walk the riverside path on the south bank now, you pass through highly degraded pasture, and banks thick with a botanical invader: Himalayan balsam. Then you pass the long gardens of a handful of riverside houses where you can look across to a caravan park on an island created by an eighteenth-century mill cut. This is the old fording place. Close by is a village centre with a couple of pubs, a small supermarket, an Indian takeaway and a pizza place. If you stand there by the river, close your eyes and listen, there might be the wail of an emergency vehicle siren. Ignore that, listen again. The jet of a pressure washer scrubbing the flanks of a pale green caravan. Children on a garden swing. Woodpigeons croodling. Beneath all that, the sound of water falling. And in there, somewhere, there are the screams of men fighting and dying for another man's cause.

The victorious Harold Godwinson had little time to rest. Three days later and more than 200 miles south, the Norman army of William landed on the coast of Sussex. Harold marched again; gathered another army. But his luck was running out. The Battle of Hastings on 14th October was won comprehensively by the Normans. William was crowned king on Christmas Day and then, as conqueror or bastard, depending on your loyalties, spent the ensuing years dealing with one revolt after another, building a lot of castles, dishing out land to the church and to his barons (who under the feudal system were owners as long as they offered service to the king) and establishing vast royal hunting forests. It was the beginning of the end of the system of commons and the beginning of the beginning for what remains to this day one of the most skewed patterns of land ownership anywhere in the world. In late 1086 the results of an in-depth survey of land held by William and his barons were written down. The *Domesday Book*, as it became known, is a historical record *par excellence*, containing not only details of land, its value and what it contained, but also who owned it both before and after the conquest. The biggest landgrab in English history is documented, county by county, line by line. In time, the replacement of feudalism meant that land could be bought, provided you could afford it, but laws prevented the owners of modest areas of land from building on it. At almost every stage the losers were commoners. The enclosures that began in the sixteenth century continued right up to the First World War, and as it stands today roughly half of England is owned by less than 1 per cent of the population. Thanks to a law obsessed with property, which (absurdly) equates even the most transient trespass with actual harm to the landowner, ownership carries with it a right to exclude. For the vast majority of the population who own little or no land, the English countryside is a sort of maze, lined with boundaries visible and invisible, peppered with thousands upon thousands of *Private Keep Out* signs. Our extensive network of footpaths disguises the truth that the great majority of what you might see from those paths, 92 per cent of land (most of it behind the walls of large private estates) and 97 per cent of rivers are forbidden to you. Exactly who by, however, even the Land Registry, set up in 1862 to record the national picture of ownership, doesn't always know, because, as Guy Shrubsole, whose book *Who Owns England?* presents an eye-opening exposé of the subject, writes, 'Land has always conferred wealth and power, and concealing wealth is part and parcel of preserving it.'

Despite my instinctive objection to river exclusion across England, it was several years before I understood the unique case on my home river. Here, a battle over the loss of access

has already been fought and decided at the highest court in
the land. And in coming to their decision, the law lords of
parliament spent weeks considering a question I still don't
really know the answer to.

What, exactly, *is* a river?

The story here is not a simple a case of landowners
wanting to shut out the public, though there is undoubtedly
a strong element of that. In this case, the riparian owners of
the Middle Derwent had staunch allies among local
conservationists, including the Yorkshire Wildlife Trust,
thanks largely to highly successful joint efforts to protect an
area further downriver.

The flood-prone Lower Derwent Valley boasts a never-
ending pageant of avifauna, the participants changing month
by month. It is a breeding ground for curlew, redshank and
lapwing, a wintering area for vast numbers of wildfowl and
waders, and a vital stopping-off point for species such as
whimbrel, on their longer migrations between Africa and
the Arctic. Mostly low-intensity agriculture in the area
means it is also still home to farmland species struggling to
survive elsewhere, including a huge number of finches,
buntings and sparrows. There are water voles and otters, and
the floral diversity of the unimproved flood meadows
(naturally managed and largely free of artificial chemical
inputs) makes them among the most valuable in Europe. All
of which makes it astonishing that, in 1970, this was
essentially an unprotected landscape. By the turn of the
century it had been granted scores of new designations –
among them a number of local nature reserves and Sites of
Special Scientific Interest, and an extensive, if fragmented,
National Nature Reserve, which subsequently became a
Ramsar Wetland of International Importance (a global
badge of wetland excellence), a European Union Special
Protection Area for birds and Special Area of Conservation.

It could easily have been different. Prior to the
commissioning of a barrage at Barmby on the Marsh in

1972, the river had been tidal as far as Sutton upon
Derwent, about 24 miles upstream of its confluence with
the Ouse. The main purpose of the barrage was to prevent
salty water entering the lower river. This pleased the water
company, who were able to abstract fresh water from above
the barrage. It also pleased the river cargo operators who
secured an undertaking from the river authorities to
maintain a minimum depth of four feet (120cm) in the
river at all times, improving navigability as far as Sutton. It
pleased developers who smelled opportunity. And it
achieved the remarkable feat of uniting farmers, landowners,
conservationists and anglers against that latter possibility.
An immediate and lasting consensus between these diverse
interests coalesced into a pressure group whose first action
was to draw up a detailed case for conservation. Decades of
ecological study led to many of the protective designations
the river enjoys now. Furthermore, in the mid 1980s the
group campaigned successfully against the installation of
several drainage pumps, thereby curbing the agricultural
intensification that would have seen many areas of
traditionally farmed floodplain converted from seasonal
pasture to arable land, with serious implications for
pollution, biodiversity loss and soil loss.

The biggest challenge came out of the blue in 1984,
when four of the largest landowners on the middle river
between Sutton upon Derwent and Malton were served
with a summons from the Attorney General. The plaintiffs
were a consortium including Yorkshire Derwent Trust Ltd,
a boating lobby that had spent 14 years striving to maintain
navigational infrastructure and permit schemes, and a
group of developers, supported by Malton Town Council.
All were keen to see the river reopened, though their
reasons varied from heritage and recreation to naked
commercial interest. Their claim challenged the revocation
of the statutory right of navigation (and thus of access) on
the middle river in 1935, asserting that navigation was

implicit in the 1932 Rights of Way Act, which established
a right of way across land if it had been used as such for 20
years. A crucial footnote in the Act stated that 'land'
included 'land covered with water'. In his book *The
Yorkshire River Derwent: Moments in Time*, conservationist
and lead member of the hastily gathered defence team Ian
Carstairs, explained that the Attorney General does not
generally take cases where there is a risk of losing, and
matters settled this way carry much greater significance
than those dealt with at a local level between individuals,
companies or other organisations.

The landowners who received the summons were already
allied with conservationists and anglers and they had data in
abundance about the ecological importance of the river.
Unfortunately this mattered little when it came to the
matter of navigation. 'Regrettably, for all of us,' wrote
Carstairs, 'the issue could only be fought through property
ownership, as fundamentally English law is there to protect
private property rights and not to arbitrate over competing
public interests.' The plaintiffs had done their homework.
'Page after page of evidence submitted to support the
[opposing] claim seemed, to our non-legal eyes, to confirm
extensive use of the river for navigation in past centuries.'

The defence took an equally passionate and meticulous
but slightly more eccentric approach, including on occasions,
coin tosses to tip finely balanced decisions, and attempts to
summon the spirit of seventeenth-century angling guru
Izaak Walton to assist. It seems to have worked, however,
because in December 1989 a High Court judge ruled that
there was no superior pre-existing or subsequent right of
public navigation on the middle Derwent and that therefore
the revocation of 1935 stood. Moreover, he judged that the
footnote in the 1932 Act about 'land covered with water'
did not apply to rivers or lakes. The plaintiffs immediately
launched an appeal. When that came to court in July 1990
the three judges agreed with the verdict of the original trial

in all but one instance. They had been convinced that the 1932 Public Rights of Way did indeed apply – for what is a river if not 'land covered with water'?

The implications were enormous, not just in relation to the Derwent, but for rivers across England and Wales. If the 1932 Act was deemed applicable in this case, access to thousands of miles of river would be instated. Now it was the defendants' turn to appeal, and there was only one place left to go. So in October 1991 the case was presented at the House of Lords, and the matter on which so much hung was the legal definition of a river.

On 5th December 1991 the Lords released their verdict. Finding against the appeal court decision, they unanimously judged that a river is *not* 'land covered with water'. The most senior legal brains in the land had considered and judged that, for legal purposes, a river is … a river. The result sent ripples of relief through the conservation and angling sectors, and pleased a great many riparian landowners. All had feared different aspects of what opening up rivers to full navigation and associated development might mean.

It was a victory for many who held the Derwent dear, but also for those who do not wish to share it. Undoubtedly the successful defence by conservationists, landowners and anglers against boaters and developers has limited disturbance on the river and prevented a certain kind of development. There are no pleasure cruisers, house boats or barges, and no marina in Malton. My beloved river remains a lazy green and gold haven. On the other hand, if I wasn't willing to repeatedly trespass on it – in a small boat and by swimming – I would not know or love it in anything like the same way. My personal relationship with nature and place has shaped and informed almost everything I do. And, let's face it, our closed-off rivers suffer anyway, in countless other ways: from industrial, agricultural and domestic sewage pollution, abstraction, engineered flood 'management' and development of other kinds. And they have done so while an excluded public, ever more divorced and disconnected from nature, has been looking the other way. We won't fight for that which we do not love and we cannot love what we do not know. There are twin tragedies unfurling here. In an age of nature disconnection and sedentary lifestyles with uncountable impacts on the physical and mental health of the nation, the catastrophe of mass extinction is passing millions by because they feel no personal connection with what is being lost.

I don't resent the actions of the conservationists working on the defence. They did the best they could within the constraints of laws so lacking in nuance that they fail to register a distinction between speedboat and kayak, cargo vessel and coracle, houseboat and canoe, party cruiser and paddleboard. As Ian Carstairs wrote, 'A right for one boat is a right for all and as many as want to come, from canoe to the largest vessel that can navigate the water'. But current staff of the Yorkshire Wildlife Trust freely admit that the exclusion of low impact river craft was an unintended consequence of their victory.

The case for navigation from the perspective of the pleasure boating and heritage lobby is detailed in *Navigation on the Yorkshire Derwent,* a slim but dense book by Pat Jones. It's a fascinating read, heavy on nostalgia for the puttering, halcyon days of pleasure boating, but marred by a simmering contempt for the defence coalition, described as 'organisations obsessed with nature conservation and environmental issues (to the exclusion of all else)', and 'the fanatical so-called conservation lobby'. The growth of riparian vegetation, in particular of trees, is seen as neglect, and natural flooding as a scandal. It's depressing to see so much antipathy between groups with so much in common. Meanwhile, the establishment gets its way.

The truth is that the environmental protection bestowed on the Derwent and other rivers by the Lords' verdict could still take place if the exclusion applied only to powered and multi-occupant craft. Such a distinction would prevent chemical and noise pollution, bank wash and there would be no need for marinas and other developments associated with powered boats. Small, self-powered river craft such as kayaks, canoes, small row boats, coracles and stand up paddleboards, need no specialist infrastructure, no marinas or jetties or bankside development. Steps and pontoons may be useful in protecting the banks, but these are no more or less intrusive than fishing platforms.

The question of whether it is possible to dovetail river access with ecological restoration needs careful consideration. The answer lies in one word – responsibility. In every access debate, you come across the entrenched idea that people who don't own land cannot be trusted to treat it well. This willfully overlooks both the countless individual and community actions that actively benefit the environment, and the fact that plenty of people who do own land mistreat it appallingly. Property law gives a landowner the legal right to abuse that which they own, and even to destroy it completely, if they so wish. Meanwhile in 2022, the people monitoring pollution and invasive species, those doing their best to raise awareness of catastrophic declines in river quality, are seldom the owners. They are certainly not the regulators or the government. The financially emaciated Environment Agency admits that by its own metric, not a single English river is in good chemical and ecological condition, while failing entirely to do anything meaningful about it. The people stepping up to do monitoring work that the Environment Agency staff cannot are volunteers: grassroots campaigners and citizen scientists. They include swimmers, paddlers, surfers, nature lovers, ramblers and anglers, and many of them are people whose love of rivers involves trespassing on or in them. It is through the efforts of such people that appalling declines in water quality and biodiversity on the River Wye (due mostly to pollution from intensive poultry farming) have come to wider public attention, and that the River Wharfe at Ilkley has become the first river in the UK to be granted bathing water status, requiring the Environment Agency and Yorkshire Water to up their game.

Immersion changes people – symbolically and literally. At the root of the irresponsible behaviour cited as a reason to exclude the public is a dissociation from nature. If you want a society that respects rivers, you must give its people an opportunity to know them. I'll leave the last word to Ian Carstairs, describing his first encounter with the Derwent. 'I have no doubt I was trespassing; I didn't mean to, I was simply carried along with the mood of a fabulous moment in a wonderful place on a beautiful English afternoon.'

High water

Spate *A sudden rise in river levels, often leading to flooding.*

Silt *Fine particles of rock, intermediate in size between sand and clay (4 to 62 microns), small enough to be easily carried in suspension by swift water, but coarse enough to settle out of a slow-moving flow. Silt forms a significant proportion of the fertile agricultural soils typical of natural river floodplains.*

At the end of 2015, it seemed the rain would never stop. Storm Desmond made landfall on 9th December, bringing record deluges to northern England, and the pattern continued: a textbook atmospheric river delivering heavy rain throughout the rest of December, keeping the land saturated and rivers brimming, bridge pillars and flood defences under almost constant strain. On Christmas Eve, another named storm, Eva, struck, and the resulting surge in river levels forced the Environment Agency in York into a grim calculation. By Boxing Day, the Foss Barrier in York, designed to prevent the Ouse backing up into a smaller tributary, was under unprecedented pressure. Rather than risk a catastrophic failure in which the barrier might become un-raisable, the Agency took the decision to open it and allow up to 600 residential and business properties alongside the Foss to flood – hoping to spare many more downstream. Meanwhile Hebden Bridge in West Yorkshire was underwater for the second time in three and a half years, as the Calder burst its banks. Rage here was directed not at the Environment Agency but at the surrounding moorland estates. Many people pointed out that the dearth of tree cover, the drainage of peatlands, and the burning of heather to support unsustainably high numbers of grouse for shooting, had created a landscape unable to hold water as it should. Closer to home, the Derwent burst its banks multiple times, and repeatedly flooded parts of Malton and the old mill at Howsham.

It's hard to imagine the mess left by floodwater unless you've had to deal with it. When Howsham Mill floods, as dated high water marks on the granary door frame attest it often does, the deposit of silt can be more than an inch thick, and clearing it is a Sisyphean task even in this most resilient of stone buildings, which has no plaster, no floorboards or carpets, and no low-level electrics. You can shovel and scrape the worst, then hose it out and wait for what is left to dry – this can take weeks even with the heating on – and then try to vacuum or sweep dust so fine that it just takes to the air and settles behind you.

By 27th December the three-hundred-year-old bridge over the River Wharfe in Tadcaster had been closed amid fears for its structural integrity. A stone's throw from this bridge live our friends Badger and Jenny and their two daughters. In many ways, it's an ideal location, within easy walking distance of the town centre on the other side of the river, where the girls and Jen go to school and work.

On 29th December my phone rang. It was Jen, close to tears. 'The bridge ... I think it's going!' And sure enough, shortly afterwards, footage shared on social media showed the three-hundred-year-old stonework crumbling like piecrust into water illuminated incongruously by the reflected glow of Christmas lights.

What had been a two-minute walk into town for hundreds of Tadcaster households was now a fifteen-minute drive via a complicated diversion to cross the next nearest bridge, on the dual carriageway of the A64. Jen was distraught. It wasn't just the shock of damage to a familiar landmark but a recognition of the time, cost and mental energy involved in having to change a way of life overnight.

The local authorities were quick to assure residents that a temporary crossing would be installed and that fixing the old one would be a priority. Unfortunately, there was an obstacle. It's not unusual for historic English market towns to be owned by single estates and managed conservatively, and Tadcaster is in the grip of one individual, a man named Humphrey Smith. With a fortune based on the Samuel Smith pub chain and brewery, Smith is a man of what might charitably be called traditional values. In his pubs there are no televisions or jukeboxes, and customers are not permitted to use a mobile phone for talking, messaging, accessing the internet or taking photographs. Customers' language is monitored, and you will be asked to leave if staff hear you swear. And if the landlords don't enforce Smith's rules with sufficient vigour, they may find themselves out of a job and a home. He has stringent rules for businesses wishing to operate in his other properties, and if you want to live as a couple in one of the scores of houses he owns – most of them otherwise appealing quaint terraces – you'd better be married. In Tadcaster, there are couples who've wed purely in order to rent a home. A shortage of tenants willing to abide by these rules means the town has more than its share of boarded-up buildings.

Humphrey was less than forthcoming in Tadcaster's hour of need. With engineers standing by to erect a temporary pedestrian bridge, weeks of wrangling ensued. The logical place for the crossing was on vacant land immediately adjacent to the old one. But this was owned by the brewery and Smith refused permission, suggesting instead that a new footpath be created to take residents upstream to an old viaduct he had closed to the public several years previously – a ten-minute detour even for a sprightly walker. In this extraordinary case, the issue of riparian ownership had become a problem not only for river users, but for an entire community.

In the end the temporary bridge went in downstream when another, more obliging, landowner stepped in. The repaired and re-engineered main bridge reopened after 16 months, just in time for Tadcaster to host the start of the Tour de Yorkshire cycle race in April 2017. It should stand firm against further flood events for the foreseeable future. The trouble is, the future is increasingly hard to foresee and there are hundreds of other ancient bridges across the country, whose original builders could never have imagined climate change or a landscape so incapable of holding water. How we deal with these connected crises is a matter for everyone.

CHAPTER 13

Ouroboros

It's one of those sobering September nights where darkness falls sooner than expected, made all the more startling by the speed at which the brand new moon, whose work I've come to see, follows the sun below the horizon.

I'm close to the Gloucestershire village of Minsterworth, on the outside of a bend in the River Severn. There's a riverside path on a high bank, but it's chilly and exposed. I cast about for a few minutes, looking for a place to wait, where I'll be sheltered by the bank and closer to the water. The vegetation illuminated by my headtorch beam looks battered. Reeds, grasses, thistles, tansy and willowherb are bent and coated in dried-out silt, with fragments and strands of flotsam snagged among the stems. I choose a spot high enough to be relatively dry, and sit.

It's strange to be away again. After months in the almost exclusive and constant company of my closest family, I am alone with my own thoughts in the world beyond the home horizon. Time to actually think. It's weirdly intense, and my mind has been on a daylong rampage.

I'm not sure exactly what to expect. I've seen footage of the Severn Bore — a foaming wave sweeping inexorably upstream past crowds of onlookers — but not all bores are equal. Some are big enough to carry flotillas of kayaks and surfers many miles upstream. Others are the merest of swells, easily flattened to nothing by wind or atmospheric pressure. To aid bore-watchers, bore events are graded in advance, 1–5 stars, according to their likely strength and size. There are no five-star bores this year or next, and the next best option has been graded as a four-star, but it's happening at night. How much there will be to see in the dark I don't know. There's another due in the morning, rated three stars, and I almost give in to the urge for an early night.

I check my watch. I'm half an hour early, so I turn off the torch, zip my coat, pull the hood over my hat, stuff my hands into pockets and huddle small to preserve body heat. I appear to be alone, though the sound of traffic on the A48 is close enough that I don't feel exactly isolated. Closer than the traffic, but scarcely louder, I can hear grasshoppers ratcheting in the straggly vegetation at my back, and the hushing of wind in the willows. I recognise the sweet-spicy scent of tansy I must have crushed as I sat down – it smells like apple pie.

Above the trees lining the opposite bank, between swatches of high cloud, Jupiter is glowing bright gold, with Saturn close by. The river is the same iron blue as the sky but appears somehow brighter – as though it has a faint light of its own. That can't really be, but its reflections fool my eye, perhaps because they are closer, and set against the blackness of the bank.

A few miles upstream is an elegant single-span stone arch built by Thomas Telford in the 1820s, which until the opening of the Severn Bridge in 1960 was the lowest road crossing of the Severn. It replaced a series of older crossings at the aptly named settlement of Over just outside Gloucester, recorded as far back as the *Domesday Book*. Telford's Over Bridge is now pedestrianised and traffic on the A40 uses a newer structure alongside. I drove over it earlier this afternoon, when the river was sunlit, and it was strange to imagine that even then, the phenomenon I'm hoping to witness was gathering many hundreds of miles out to sea.

The Severn Bore is a manifestation of extra-terrestrial influence. Every day since the Moon formed, it has been held in orbit by the gravitational pull of the Earth. But gravity works both ways. The Moon also pulls on the Earth, and especially on its water, and as long as the oceans have existed, it has tugged at them like a dog at heavy bedclothes, constantly shifting them this way and that. While tides are dictated mainly by lunar gravity, the Sun also has an influence, which we notice most when it pulls directly with, or against, the Moon, resulting in greater or smaller tides on a monthly cycle (known as spring and neap tides).

The Severn estuary records among the largest tides in the world, at around 13 vertical metres. Only Canada's Bay of Fundy reliably registers comparable range. The bore is a tidal wave, a bulge of water approaching land at such an angle that it funnels up the Bristol Channel and then into the Severn estuary. As the funnel narrows, the water is forced higher, creating a river-wide wave moving upstream at 13 to 20 kilometres per hour. There are around 260 bores a year on the Severn, occurring on the morning and evening tides of 130 days, but most are too small to be visible. They are clustered around the full and the new moon, when the Earth, Moon and Sun are most closely aligned, but also subject to a variety of other influences, including atmospheric pressure, wind speed and direction, flow rates and channel topography, which can change over time. The largest bores of the year are typically those around the spring and autumn equinoxes.

The breeze picks up and the sky clears, revealing a sprinkling of stars. Three are distinctly brighter than the others and I sacrifice some night vision using the star app on my phone to confirm them as the summer triangle of Vega, Deneb and Altair. All of them are bigger and brighter than the Sun but many times further away. From them, the Earth is a mote, and all its life as close to nothing as makes no difference. And yet here we are, infinitesimal fragments of that nothing, making meaning of them. I tuck myself further back into the tansy, and the sleepy stridulations of grasshoppers pause for a few seconds at the disturbance, then resume when I settle.

The river is a dull, scuffed mirror, producing a blurry reflection of the dark trees on the other bank. There's a complete absence of colour now, only dark and less dark. At one minute to the predicted time I pull down my hood, strain my ears to every vibration in the air. I can hear wind in the trees and a now solitary grasshopper, and irregular rushes of noise from the road. The allotted minute passes. Bore timings are not an exact science, so I wait on, taut with listening.

Minutes stream by. Am I foolish to expect to hear it coming? Surely I will see something – at least a ripple in the reflections of the water? Again and again a whooshing sound reaches my ears and I tense, but it's motorbikes, other traffic.

Is a four-star bore ever a complete no-show, I wonder?

What's that? Something – a band of darker water across the river? Surely it won't be silent. My eyes are playing tricks on me. For no reason at all I start giggling. 'Come on, Moon,' I mutter. 'Pull! Or push – whatever it is you're supposed to be doing.'

The grasshopper has a duet partner again – call and response, they saw back and forth.

Six minutes, seven, eight. I fidget.

Nine minutes.

And then there's something new – at least I think it's new – a backing heaviness to the white noise ensemble of wind and road. It sounds slightly ominous, and it's building. I stand up, and the rush increases. Something downstream breaks with a crack like a gunshot – a branch – a whole tree? The noise is becoming a roar, and I take a few hasty steps up the bank. It's suddenly a bit terrifying. I can see almost nothing at all, the world is reduced to pure sound. And then, the roar breaks abruptly into a crash so close I yelp – a primal urge to flee makes my legs skitter under me. There's something pale piling past, against the flow, with a maw wider than I can see and a voice like thunder, a monstrous avatar of the Moon, engulfing the entire river.

Belatedly, I remember my headtorch and flick on the beam.

The transformation is so complete I can only gasp and stare. The body of the bore is following the head, the river is devouring itself, an unstoppable khaki ouroboros. In a matter of seconds the water level has risen well over a metre and the surface is heaving and writhing. The reflections are gone. The water is thick, like hot chocolate, and it is tearing and sucking at the banks and wrestling with itself mid-channel, where the torch beam picks out white-capped waves. Among them, debris starts to flow past: branches, then tree trunks, a flat board that might be a road sign, a large deflated paddling pool and close under the bank an object whose curves are animal, mammal, slicked in wet hair. I dismiss my first thought that it is a beaver, forgetting that there are now some in the Forest of Dean, and scroll briefly through the other options. Too broad for an otter. A badger? A dog? Maybe a small, dark sheep. It passes too fast to see properly – it might be just a mossy log or a roll of carpet, but there's no chance to dwell on it, my mind is too full of the spectacle. It looks like a river in spate but it's all going the wrong way, upstream. The energy required to overcome one of the largest flows of any British river is almost unimaginable. The surge continues and I watch for 15 minutes, still jittery, giggly, and dumbfounded until I realise my trousers are soaked with dew and I'm no longer shivering with anticipation or the rush of adrenaline, but with cold.

In my sleeping bag later I find myself wondering how an encounter with such elemental ferocity would have been interpreted long ago by someone experiencing it for the first time without warning. People would presumably have been used to the rise and fall of the tide and attuned to the phases of the moon – but seeing a river turn on itself and rise so fast – how would they sleep? When did they learn to recognise a pattern? It's not an obvious one because not every tide and not even every full or new moon brings a bore and not every bore is alike. In some years there are scarcely any to speak of, in others there are several. In 2019 there were three five-star spectaculars.

I struggle to sleep myself. Perhaps the longed-for solitude is making me a little crazy. It is certainly giving my imagination space to roam, and I can't shake the thought that I'm mostly water, and that the Moon must therefore be tugging on me as well. It's not just water that responds to lunar gravity. There are Earth tides too. These are deformations of the entire body of the planet, which like ocean tides, occur on a twice daily basis in any given location, thanks to the tug of the Moon, and to a lesser extent, the Sun. There's no such thing as a closed system, I think. Not really, unless you're talking about the entire universe. I'm unsettled and unnerved, in uncharted territory somehow. Aren't we all, though? The Gypsey Race was right. These are not normal times.

Ghosts in the willows

I lived in some part of the Thames Valley for almost 20 years until 2002, but it feels these days like a foreign place; well remembered, but distant. On these blue, high pressure days approaching the autumn equinox in Oxfordshire there's something almost exotic about the billowing willows and rippling poplars of the alluvial plain.

The beginnings of autumn colour are lifting the heavy greens of late summer foliage, and enhancing the movement of branches in a brisk warm breeze. Red kites flash foxily as they tilt over a ploughed field the colour of milk chocolate mousse, and a late cut of green hay in rows waiting to be baled.

The studied quaintness of Buscot village seems to suit neither of the tousle-headed ghosts I'm chasing today. Roger Deakin came for a post-party swim in the 1990s, and wrote in *Waterlog* of a circular pool surrounded by willows: 'the very trees that inspired [William] Morris ... to design his *Willow Boughs* wallpaper'. I know the pattern well. My mum pasted it, somewhat overwhelmingly, over all four walls of the downstairs loo when I was a teenager. I've started seeking out Deakin's swimming haunts, and the double endorsement of Morris makes this an irresistible pit stop in an early-autumn heatwave. The celebrated designer, writer and activist lived most of the last third of his life just downstream at Kelmscott, and called this stretch of the river from the Cotswolds to Oxford the 'Baby Thames'. Others call it the Isis – a name whose recent taint seems already to be washing away as new global bogeymen take centre stage. A river can remove anything. I wonder if it's left any trace of Roger and William.

I cross over what is reputedly the shortest lock on the Thames, into Gloucestershire, and watch a small motor launch passing through on its way upriver. There are three men down on the boat – a fourth, wearing shorts, boat shoes, a hoodie and a captain's cap with scrambled gold on the shiny peak, is operating the lock. He turns a wheel to close the lower gate, then saunters to the upstream one, where two teenage girls are watching idly, and begins to spin the mechanism there with studied ease. The launch rises a short distance, then stops. There's a sound of rushing water and another man, a passerby wearing a t-shirt that says *SAIL FAST*, makes a show of peering down on the lower gate.

'I think it's still open, mate.'

Captain returns, sheepishly, to turn the wheel again. The rushing stops and the little launch rises like a duck in a bath.

Below the lock is an empty staithe where I sit and dangle my feet in the water. It is khaki-gold, clear enough that I can see a steady stream of fallen willow leaves as they well up from below, entrained in a flow leaking from the lock. As they break the surface they become deft strokes of paint, some green, some gold speckled with brown like perfectly ripe bananas, others much paler where they float underside uppermost. The river toys with them, making its own compositions, and I wait, half expecting a proto-*Willow Bough* to tesselate before my eyes. But the river has other ideas. It has decided that what the canvas most needs is a rash of Pop Art pink from some Himalayan balsam petals, then, in an emphatically modernist flourish, the scarlet spot of a guelder rose berry.

The island alongside the lock is so manicured its lawns might have been trimmed with silver scissors, and Lock Cottage, now a National Trust holiday let, is diddy Cotswold perfection. Even the pink roses in its garden are a miniature variety, and they make giants of the red admiral butterflies flickering there. The style is more chocolate-box than Arts and Crafts, and a bit saccharine for my taste. Even the weir looks like a wedding cake. But there's nothing twee about the trees surrounding the oval millpond: elder, guelder rose, hawthorn, and arcs of dog rose, all heavy with fruit, and willows. I scan the branches for a hint of *Willow Bough*, but the trees refuse it. They don't do decorum or pattern repeat. They thrash in the warm breeze like headbangers at a tea dance. I have no trouble sensing Roger's unruly spirit there, next to one of the muddy chutes into the water, which he wryly described as 'the sort of thing known to opponents of wild swimming as bank erosion.' I plunge down one, then pick my way along the water's edge where people tend not to go, clambering and limbo-ing among willow stems and trampling mint underfoot – the scent clings cool to my bare soles. The water surface around the pool edges is cluttered with willow leaves and several large, exquisitely soft feathers, downy and palest grey. Between them I can see reflections of the trees they have fallen from against a bright sky, disrupted here and there by the movements of pond skaters – the dimples caused by the four long legs they stand on are more widely spaced at the front than the back.

Crack willows are well named. The heart of the largest here has long gone, leaving sinewy remains, split and rent apart, but alive all the same, explosions of new growth shooting from its once-pollarded top. Its roots are hawser-like, but they divide into a mat of cords and fibres in pub-carpet colours – deep burgundy, faded in places to magenta. There's scarcely any soil; there's no room. It's almost all willow root. Their sheer density is amazing.

I change quickly. I've chosen to interpret a *No Swimming* sign as referring to the lock and not the millpond, but don't want to give anyone a chance to challenge me. I'm picking a spot to get in when a golden retriever galumphs past. His accompanying human tells me his name is Sparkles. The water is somewhat less sparkly in his wake, but he has shown me what turns out to be the easiest way in and out.

I make a few slow laps of the pond, pushing aside leaves and sky reflections. The sun is strong enough that I can feel it through the water as my arms extend. There's something pleasing about swimming in a circular space – you can make circuits or transits or just float in the middle, like an embryo, or the gleam in a great watery eye. Hawker dragonflies skim low, making lightsabre sound effects. When I tip upright again I see I've been joined in the pool by a swan and four well-grown cygnets – the casters of feathers. The adult steps out onto the first step of the multi-tiered weir, white plumage against white water, and sips from the next level. It's the most ostentatiously beautiful thing in this absurdly beautiful place.

CHAPTER 14

The silver fish

A phan daw dydd fy nghladdu, torrwch fy meddrod i,
Ger dwy lan afon Clettwr, yn swn ei dyfroedd hi.
And when comes the day of my burial, break my grave,
Along the banks of the Clettwr, in the sounding of her waters.

Trad., *Song of Praise for the Clettwr*, translated by Owen Shiers

On the long drive down to see the Bore I'd spoken to my friend, the folk singer, song collector and naturalist Sam Lee. At some point in a wide-ranging conversation, Sam had mentioned another singer he thought I should meet and soon after we rang off my phone bleeped, with contact details for Owen Shiers. And so it was that two days later I found myself driving to Machynlleth, listening to Owen's new album on a loop. The songs were all in Welsh – a language I know only a few words of based on place names, map features and basic courtesies. Owen's performing name, *Cynefin*, is a word with no English equivalent, which he translates as a sort of path worn through repeated use, usually by animals. In that sense it is similar to the English terms *smeuse* (a small passage, often through dense vegetation, made by animals) and *desire path* (a track worn by passing feet, usually human, marking a preferred route and often cutting corners created by less-convenient official paths). But for Owen, *cynefin* also represents a literal home, and forms a counterbalance to the more widely known Welsh concept of *hiraeth* – a sort of bittersweet longing for a place, which came into common use in the nineteenth century when people were forced from their lands, often overseas or into towns and cities. In Owen's interpretation, the paths, or *cynefinoedd*, form a kind of web that bears not only people, but also culture and song.

It was another blazing day and the heat and the glare of a long drive brought a maddening desire for cold water. The beach at Aberystwyth was packed with students returning for the first academic year in the era of COVID, spaced out in small household groups like nests in a bird colony. There was nowhere to park and eventually I gave it up, drove on to Machynlleth, and found a quiet campsite in the valley of the Dyfi (Dovey) overlooking hills and forests. I still needed to swim, so as soon as my tent was pitched I followed a signposted footpath, only to find after 15 minutes another notice saying the onward path was closed. It had the look of a temporary sign that had been there a long time, and with no alternative offered other than retracing my steps in the wrong direction I stepped around it, clambered over a broken bridge across a small stream and into a riverside pasture. I found a place where flat pebbles had accumulated on the inside of a bend, and, concluding that the footpath closure meant other walkers were less likely to happen along, skinny dipped off it, swimming against the flow while going almost nowhere, like running on a treadmill only infinitely more restorative.

Nightfall brought a low crescent moon the colour of pink grapefruit, and as it set, a dense swathe of stars that might have been sprayed across the sky with an aerosol can. It was a spectacular night, but now the dream state I'd drifted in through the last few days had lifted I found myself wondering what I was doing here, so far out of my way. All I knew of Owen was that he cared about a particular river enough to spend three years of his life gathering, arranging and recording some of its ancient songs. His text messages had been entirely friendly, but he was clearly busy and was setting time aside for me between meetings. What was it Sam meant us to talk about? I tried to replay the conversation in which Owen's name had come up. We'd talked about chalk rivers, and Scottish salmon, the Severn Bore and our shared love of the Moon. But my mind had been half on driving and all I could remember beyond those was the unseasonal heat and the motorway glare.

I dreamed of trying to catch a fish in my hands. Its scales gleamed so bright they made my eyes ache. More lustrous than silver, and whiter, like the light from an old magnesium flash bulb, it swam in water the colour of night, leaving after-images of itself in faintly glowing magenta and green. It slipped through my fingers, over and over, until I realised that it wasn't really a fish at all, but a reflection of the Moon on the water.

In the morning Owen messaged again to suggest we walk up the Afon Cletwr to *Bedd Taliesin*, or Taliesin's grave.

And suddenly I understood why I was there.

The story of Taliesin is one of the oldest in the British Isles. It's the tale of a boy, Gwion Bach (Little Gwion) who undergoes a series of magical changes, travels down a river, then out to sea and eventually returns as Taliesin, possessed of a magical way with words and destined to become pre-eminent among bards, advisor to kings and – some say – tutor of Merlin. I encountered his story first the old way: told rather than read, by master storyteller Malcolm Green, and liked it so much that I went in search of more and found a translation of the *Mabinogion*, a collection containing some of the oldest and weirdest surviving prose stories in Britain. Written versions in Middle Welsh date to the second half of the fourteenth century, but oral versions are much, much older. They share some characters and tropes with the tales of King Arthur and other Celtic myths, but have their own completely unique character.

Part of the role of myth and folklore is to show us ourselves, and often there is an element of repetition that echoes the cycles of seasons, generations and history. In the mythology of our own island this is perhaps nowhere more apparent than in the *Mabinogion,* in which tales of golden sons, of blessings, curses and transformations layer and braid and circle back imperfectly – it is more accurate to say they spiral than cycle, the story never quite returning or repeating but making close passes of where it has been before and will come again.

In the version I have read, a poetic English translation by Matthew Francis, the reader or listener joins the story at the death, on a river crossing, of a hero called Pryderi, son of Pwyll, Prince of Dyfed, and Rhiannon, a witch with power over time. It's clear immediately that this is not really a beginning – just a point on the circumference of a circle bigger than we can easily grasp. The subsequent narrative cycles and eddies – it sometimes flows out of sight, other times vaporises and condenses elsewhere, and yet eventually returns, with a sort of grandiose inevitability, to a place very similar to where it began, a ford on a river, where the sun gleams and water trips and slides and riots its way around smooth rocks, and there we are left with a vision of another son, his lifeblood ebbing as 'he lay in the swirling place where stories begin.' It's not really an ending, just another point on the circumference of a circle bigger than we can easily grasp.

It's hard to follow. Even Francis's magnificently visual version is like watching an epic movie with bad broadband or satellite signal – what you see is marvellous, but there are bits missing. In this it is reminiscent of the water cycle. Most of the world's water is dark, held in the deep oceans or the deep underground. Some flows take shortcuts back to where they have recently been. And some go into deep storage for longer than the span of civilisations, or even species. But from time to time, they linger long enough in the light that we notice them. Such are the gleams of revelation to be gained from mythology, and many of those gleams are gleams of water. As well as reprising our aquatic origins world myths tell us, repeatedly, of great floods, and of lands and civilizations under the water. Parallels between the deluge myths and scientific evidence for prehistoric sea level rises or inundations caused by tsunamis are striking, and it's hard not to conclude they represent a folk memory of actual events, thousands of years ago.

It is the day of the autumn equinox, Mabon. Owen is waiting for me in a drizzly car park in Machynlleth, and because of COVID we drive separately, a few miles south, to the foot of the Afon Cletwr, which makes a short, turbulent descent into a coastal plain, and then into the Dyfi estuary. The name Cletwr is virtually the same as that of Owen's home river, the Clettwr, though the latter flows into the Teifi, about 50km south of here.

Owen moved to the tiny village of Capel Dewi in Ceredigion at the age of six, because his father, one of only two concert harp makers in Britain, needed a bigger workshop. If there appears to be a kind of romantic inevitability to a harp maker's son growing up on a steep Welsh river going on to forge a career combining music and place, Owen insists otherwise. 'I was an outsider,' he says. 'We'd come from Cardiff, we spoke English at home, and I was this weird art kid who listened to Nirvana. As a teen I couldn't wait to get the hell out of there.'

Getting out meant studying music and then a dream job working for the singer-songwriter, record producer and human rights activist, Peter Gabriel. At that point, Owen says, he had no thought of coming back to Wales, let alone to rescue old songs. He credits a change of heart to experiences and insights gained during a year and a half at Embercombe – a free-spirited retreat and education centre in Devon. 'My mentors there asked me bigger questions than my culture or upbringing ever had. And the answers to those questions led me back home. It was a massive decision though. Thousands of people would have given an arm for the job I had.'

In English you 'play' a musical instrument, in Welsh you 'make it sing'. Owen realised that what was making him sing was a longing for the place and culture of Wales.

Hiraeth. 'Perhaps I had to go away for that to happen,' he says. By the time he did return, he had a mission in mind.

'Folk songs were meant to be performed', Owen says, 'and by definition it seldom occurred to anyone to write them down. The danger for these often very ancient songs is that if they stop being sung, they die with the singers.' He began seeking songs from as close to the Clettwr Valley as possible, and found scores of them. Some came from recordings and manuscripts archived at institutions like the National Library of Wales, and St Fagan's museum of Welsh history and folklore. More came directly from residents of the valley old enough to have learned them when social singing was still common. 'The academic collections are important, but too many songs collected that way exist now only on paper. Some of them probably haven't been sung for centuries. I wanted to restore them to life.' The result of three years collecting is *Dilyn Afon*, 'Following the River', the album I'd been listening to.

After half an hour of climbing steadily we pause where a gap in the trees gives a glimpse of the estuary. Out beyond that, says Owen, is the mythic sunken kingdom of Cantre'r Gwaelod, location of one of the better known inundation myths that endure from prehistoric cultures worldwide. Sea levels rose well over 100m between the peak of the last Ice Age and the time around 8,000 years ago when Britain was islanded. Cantre'r Gwaelod was low-lying, fertile land, protected from the tides by a system of dykes and sluices, but eventually overwhelmed. Was it real? Well, we know for a fact that there are preserved forests and graves and causeway-like structures out there in Cardigan Bay – parts of them exposed from time to time by low tides and storms.

It's still drizzling but too warm for coats, so we continue uphill, getting wetter, and talking about folk memory. 'You'd think we'd treasure that stuff,' Owen says, 'But we're experiencing an epidemic of cultural amnesia. Many holders of disappearing knowledge don't realise what they have. For example, there's this old farmer who's the only one I know still growing Welsh black oats and possibly the only one still practising the old method of tying an oat stook. But when I ask people like him about old practices or stories or pieces of agricultural equipment, they're surprised. "What that old thing?" and I'm like, "Yeah, *that* old thing!" They don't realise it's cultural gold. They'd rather tell me about their brand-new truck.

'I don't blame them. That oat farmer only got electricity in 1968 and his forebears grew up in absolute poverty. But there's a dichotomy now, where indigenous folk in the valley build these horrible pebble-dashed houses and want jacuzzis in them, while the incomers have romantic ideas of Wales and are doing restoration work. There is a groping for culture in that, but like my family, these people generally speak English. Our village is typical. When we came there, about half the inhabitants spoke Welsh. Now, it's probably 30 per cent. They say there are critical thresholds for language, and as soon as usage drops below 40 per cent it becomes non-functional. At the other end, 70 per cent is a key threshold for viability.'

Owen pauses to check a map on his phone. I remember dire predictions that both Welsh and Scots Gaelic were dying out in the 1980s, but I also know that my younger Welsh friends were all taught their native tongue in school. So how, I ask, is it still being lost?

'The language isn't in freefall the way it was, and from 2022 it will be reinstated in schools across Wales as a dual first language alongside English. It's easy to translate twenty-first-century life into Welsh and we think that in doing so we're sustaining Welshness, but that's an illusion. A language needs culture to sustain it. Immigration and second-home ownership are part of that. The Welsh are generous – they tend to switch to English when they hear it, so it's still easy to move here and not hear Welsh spoken and not understand that it *needs* to be spoken. I use it every day, but you have to make a conscious effort. It's the same with the songs, many of which still have very real relevance.'

'How so?'

'They are familiar stories – of people, place but also of birds and animals. Blackbird, cuckoo, swallow feature strongly, as they do in English folk songs. It's love poetry,' he says simply. 'Writing about a swallow returning is about missing someone; the yearning and the relief of being reunited. But because nature is so prominent in these songs, they are also becoming an important way of documenting declines in wildlife. Take the cuckoo, the turtle dove, the nightingale, and the skylark – people were singing very local songs featuring these species, and yet in many of those places the birds are no longer heard. I feel like language loss and species loss are related. They are part of the same problem, you know…'

'Globalisation.' We say the word at the same time.

'Exactly. We're seduced into this progress narrative, and it's relentless. The songs and the stories remind us about things that have always mattered. For example, the estuaries of West Wales once teemed with salmon at this time of year. New methods of netting were introduced by Norman monks in the twelfth century. Those practices continued for more than eight hundred years – for much of that time it was both sustaining and sustainable and there were so many fish that poaching was a way of life. But now there's hardly any left. In recent years traditional netting became more about the spectacle – a tourist attraction – and the last few netsmen on the Teifi are now supposed to return their catches so those fish can go upriver to spawn.'

It seems a strange piece of theatre, this, to catch fish and then let them go. 'It is,' says Owen. 'But by sustaining the culture we are recognising that this scarcity is not normal. It's a check on that shifting baseline syndrome that can otherwise deceive us into thinking that the ecology of our own lifetimes is somehow normal.'

I remember that it's a story about a fish that brought me here. The tale of Gwion Bach and Taliesin is one of the best known of all Welsh myths. Having origins in oral tradition means there are many versions of the tale. Stories set in ink are like butterflies pinned to specimen cards – they can still be beautiful, intricate, colourful, and are much less likely to slip out of your reach when you try and get close. But they lose something too. Taliesin's story was laid out in an illuminated manuscript, whose surviving pages are now known as the *Book of Taliesin*, written by an unknown hand some eight centuries after the events are said to have taken place. Then, a full millennium after the bard lived, Elis Gruffydd wrote another account, *Hanes Taliesin*. But by then the story already had many forms, like those of Arthur and Bran the Blessed, with which it interweaves, and a narrative that tends to shapeshift almost as much as its ineffable characters. If we're looking to history for illumination, the light provided by these stories is a candle flame – dim, flickering, hard to read by, but irresistible in its own right. Like archaeologists and palaeontologists, scholars of myth are permitted some leaps of imagination. But in doing so they can't help but change the form of the thing again.

Before telling the story, Owen says it's important to understand who Taliesin was. 'He's often called *Taliesin Ben Beirdd* – Taliesin, Chief of Bards, and the bards of old were much more than poets and performers. They were immensely important people: advisors, influencers, heroes. The story of Gwion Bach explains how Taliesin came into his wisdom.' The version Owen recounts, and which I have retold in my own words here, follows the interpretation of his friend Gwilym Morus-Baird, scholar of Celtic mythology, who sets the story firmly in the landscape between Llyn Tegid, near Bala in Gwynedd, and the valley in which we are walking. The rain has eased and we are climbing a steep slope among small, lichen-covered oaks and hollies heavy with fruit. Droplets of water suspended from the berries are gleaming and when I look closely I can see the whole valley upside down in each one.

The enchantress Ceridwen, wife of Tegid Foel (after whom Lake Tegid is named), has two children. An exquisite daughter, Creirwy, and a son, Morfran, whose looks are a blight. But Ceridwen knows that appearance isn't everything, and sets out to ensure that Morfran will have other advantages. She prepares a potion in her magic cauldron, that will give the recipient the gift of inspiration, knowledge and foresight. The potion must be boiled and stirred for a year and a day, after which the first three drops will make her son all-knowing. She devotes herself to gathering the necessary herbs, and allocates the task of tending the cauldron to another boy, Gwion Bach. Gwion is a good boy. He does his job diligently, keeps the potion on a rolling boil and after a year and a day he is still watching and stirring as he waits for his mistress to come. But boiling liquids are volatile, and as Gwion stirs, a splash of potion catches his hand with three scalding drops. Without thinking, he tries to soothe the burn by licking away the hot liquid. The deed is done. Just as Ceridwen approaches, Gwion is filled with the wisdom and inspiration meant for Morfran. He knows it, and in a moment he sees what was, is and will be: the past, the present and future. A moment later Ceridwen understands. Gwion flees, and in a white-hot rage, Ceridwen pursues him. But Gwion is no longer an ordinary boy. He uses his new power to transform himself into a hare, the faster to run. Ceridwen becomes a greyhound. Gwion zigs and zags, dashes and darts, but Ceridwen keeps up. She is so close he can feel her hot breath. He leaps for the river, transfiguring himself a second time, mid-leap, into a fish.

We pause. We're close to the brow of the hill, and soft views of Snowdonia are opening up to the north. I glance at the OS app on my own phone, which suggests we're some little way off the path. But I guess that's what Owen intends, so I don't mention it.

Gwion is in the river, a fish swift and silvery as thought. Ceridwen shapeshifts too, into the lithe form of an otter, still relentless in pursuit. They hurtle on, and down, faster even than the rushing water. If you had been there to see, you might glimpse a silvery flash from Gwion's flanks or the fizz of tiny bubbles in Ceridwen's wake, but you would not know them in the surge and gleam of the river. She is close again. So close he can feel the pressure wave pushed in front of her ferocious head.

We've located a track and use it to approach a farm. A dog rouses to meet us. Her barks come in a torrent, her tail not wagging, but lashing, and she is making herself as big as she can. We continue; steadily, talking quietly, occasionally throwing her a word or two (Welsh seems to register slightly, English not at all) and she follows, unnervingly close behind, wolfish, furious, and barking relentlessly. I have no doubt if we run, or try to head in any other direction, at least one of us will be bitten. I daren't look back at her – eye contact seems like a bad idea. 'We're going, we're going,' I repeat as calmly as I can, keeping moving. The barking only stops when we pass the gate.

There's no respite for Gwion Bach. In panic he leaps from the water, now a bird. Again, like a nightmare he cannot wake from, Ceridwen follows, in the form of a hawk. He has no hope of outflying her, so he drops to the ground and makes himself as small as he can. He is a grain of corn, a mere kernel of life. But Ceridwen can see through the disguise and now he is helpless to escape. She becomes a hen, and swallows him whole. It is the end for Gwion Bach.

And yet, and yet ... the power of Ceridwen's own potion is now working inside her. She becomes pregnant and knows the child is Gwion. She resolves to destroy him as soon as he is born. But another transformation is happening. The baby, which possesses both Gwion's spirit and his

magical wisdom, is being nourished by Ceridwen, in spite
of her fury. When he is born, he has become Taliesin, and
Ceridwen sees a child so beautiful she cannot do the thing
she intended. So instead she casts him again into the water,
this time in a little coracle. He travels out to sea and when
the tide turns he is washed up, alive and well, in a fish trap in
the mouth of the Afon Dyfi.

'That's just north of here,' says Owen. Below us the Cletwr
now runs straight as a ruler from the base of the hill to the
Dyfi estuary. But Owen tells me that the flat coastal plain
was once a convoluted wetland, no doubt full of fish, and
only drained about 150 years ago.

> Taliesin is found by a prince, Elffin ap Gwyddno, son of King
> Gwyddno Garanhir, of Cantre'r Gwaelod. The infant
> immediately begins talking and singing to Elffin. His
> eloquence and poetry are irresistible – verse after verse fills
> the prince with hope and promise, and so he adopts the
> magical child. Taliesin grows up to become both a teller of
> stories and a protagonist in them, and in doing so he lives still.

We reach the high point of our walk and its principal
destination, a large grey stone on the slightest of humps
on a grassy slope. The stone is flattish, and propped at a
slight angle above a cist grave lined with smaller stones.
On the OS map this spot is named in the gothic font
used for ancient monuments as *Bedd Taliesin* – Taliesin's
grave.

For all the wild weirdness of the story, Taliesin appears to
have been a genuine historical figure of the mid to late sixth
century. He is mentioned by another poet, Aneirin, and is
listed among the great poets in a ninth-century history of
Britain, the *Historium Brittonum*. His journey, I discover later,
continues well beyond present-day Wales into the region
known as *Hen Ogledd* – the Old North, covering much of

what became northern England and the Scottish Borders. Taliesin had a particular affiliation with the court of King Urien of Rheged, whose kingdom straddled parts of what are now Cumbria and North Yorkshire, but historical details of both men are overlain and interwoven with mythology and the poems, which Taliesin himself appears to have composed and performed. While Celtic identity has been all but erased from northern England by waves of conquest, Wales remains high ground culturally as well as topographically. A refuge for stories that are not only Welsh, but British.

The intermingled stories of Taliesin himself and the characters in his poems are futher intertwined with those of King Arthur and Bran the Blessed, in which, for example, Urien is married to Arthur's sister, Morgan la Fey. Taliesin also serves their son Owain mab Urien, otherwise known as Ywain, Knight of the Round Table. Some further accounts give Owain a son, Kentigern, also known as Mungo, founder and patron saint of Glasgow. All these stories shapeshift and braid to form a mythology whose origins are as difficult to identify as the beginnings of a river. Like water, each story carries far more than itself.

So I don't ask Owen how much of the tale of Taliesin he thinks is true. Or whether the mortal remains of the real-life Taliesin ever lay here. This grave is evidently much older than sixth century (I'll later find out it's Bronze Age), and I'm sure Owen knows that. So instead I ask if there are other claims to the bard's final resting place – other sites called *Bedd Taliesin*.

'No, just this one. And other places and names in this landscape fit the story.' He outlines some of Gwilym Morus-Baird's work, explaining that the route we have just taken is part of an ancient trackway called the *Sarn Ddu*, the Black Road. It seems likely that this was a funerary route linking several graves and barrows to the places people lived and farmed down on the plain, possibly even before the rise in sea levels that took place around 8,000 years ago. Low-lying

wetlands and floodplains would have made for good hunting
and productive farmland, meeting many of the needs of
daily life. Burying their dead up here would have taken a
huge effort, so it must have been considered important.
From here the Black Road continues, connecting to other
places whose names recall elements of the journey of
Gwion/Taliesin from Llyn Tegid via the Afon Dyfi, out to
sea and back. The story sits in the landscape as though made
from it, and it seems perfectly plausible that people
recounting it a thousand years ago would have looked at this
impressive grave and made a connection.

I ask Owen what he thinks the story is really about. 'I
guess the chase and the shapeshifting are an initiation — a
pilgrimage whereby Gwion Bach learns what he needs to in
order to become Taliesin. But it also emphasizes the
importance of the river as the lifeblood of the living,
animistic world of which the historical Taliesin was part.
Life would have revolved around it.'

'It's pretty far out, though, isn't it?' I say.

Owen laughs. 'It's a complete acid trip!'

Salmon are a recurring motif in the ancient stories of these
islands. In Irish mythology Fintan mac Bóchra, or Fintan the
Wise, survived the biblical great flood by transforming into
a salmon and living a year under the water. He went on to
live a further five and a half millennia, into the time of
Fionn Mac Cumhaill (Finn McCool), with whom he shares
the ancient wisdom of fish. Like Taliesin, Fionn gains his
inspiration accidentally, in his case by ingesting a drop of oil
from a magical salmon as it cooks. The fish had previously
eaten nine hazelnuts that had fallen into the well of wisdom.
Thus the young Fionn gains magical insight and leadership
of the Fianna, the disparate bands of landless young warriors
who roved medieval Ireland. Meanwhile a mythical hermit,
Tuan, also survived the flood, and underwent many animal
incarnations over many centuries, the last of which was a

salmon eaten by a mortal woman from whom he was eventually reborn as a man, Tuan mac Cairill.

It's not hard to see why salmon feature so prominently in myth. Their life story conforms closely to the oldest and most pervasive story format of all – the monomyth, or 'hero's journey'. They travel, they overcome adversity, they grow and change and return. They never forget where they are from. They are an embodiment of hiraeth.

We take a selfie – I want to frame the shot with the Dyfi valley behind us in the misty distance, but it proves impossible to capture that without also including an unedifying and unmagical stack of silage bales in black plastic. We can't help being when we are.

We get lost again on the way back down, finding ourselves on a farm track heading uphill and I reopen the OS app and try to make sense of Owen's suggestion that we can pick up the river from here. We drop into a meadow and a wood with a tiny spring running through it. We could follow the spring to the river, I think, but Owen's phone says otherwise, and for the first time I realise he is following not the Ordnance Survey or a satellite map but a sketch with a set of loose instructions. Combining his sketch and my app, we find a route across a series of steep pastures and arrive back at a farm we passed a half-hour earlier. Only this time, to get back to the road, we have to cross a concrete yard, and to get into the yard we have to climb a wire fence and jump down from a 2m-high cinderblock wall. Owen goes first and holds up a hand to help me down. Without thinking, I take it and leap. His grip is warm and dry despite the drizzle, and the sensation lingers as though he's transferred hot wax to my skin. I'm suddenly aware of all the handholds and handshakes, the hugs and shoulder nudges and cheek kisses I've missed and will miss in the age of COVID, and feel a pang for the here-ness and now-ness of physical contact that no quantity of warm words and smiles, elbow bumps or *namaste*s can replace.

We talk about pandemic-induced xenophobia, and Welsh valleys flooded to supply water to England, and about *Cofiwch Dryweryn*, which I saw painted on the wall of a school in Machynlleth. Owen is confident nothing like the loss of Capel Celyn will ever be countenanced again. 'The threat now is different – it's gone from that kind of geographic, resource-robbing colonialism to something more insidious. It's a sort of steady erosion rather than a great destroying wave, and harder to spot. The thing is, I have no problem with open borders. Decent people come here for perfectly understandable reasons and with no ill intent. Wales has a declining birth rate, so without incomers, the population would be shrinking and aging, and we'd have fewer people paying tax, supporting more and more elderly – that's going to be a problem. But if the cultural tide is all one way, then those people become, however unwittingly, part of this insidious force eroding something that is precious – not just to Wales but to Britain, and I think the world.'

I'm touched by this brand of nationalism, if that's what it is. It's not raging or defensive. It is open hearted, outward facing and vulnerable. It knits landscape and human lives with biodiversity and culture, and it connects rather than isolates.

Before we say goodbye, we sit for a while on the mossy bank of the Cletwr and share a flask of tea. The water seems in a terrible hurry just here, intent on raising the ocean higher still than that which covers Cantre'r Gwaelod. We find ourselves again at a point on the circumference of a circle bigger than we can easily grasp.

CHAPTER 15

Light and water

Etymologists have traced the origins of colour words in a variety of languages and concluded that their appearance in evolving tongues follows a consistent order – black and white first, then red, presumably because an association with both food and danger incentivises its distinction. Then come yellow and green. Blue, it seems, is consistently last among the primary hues to be named. Many old languages and some modern languages fail to separate it emphatically from green: in Old Irish *glas* covers hues we'd now call green, grey and blue and in Japanese, *ao* and *aoi* serve as noun and adjective for both blue and green. The politician and four-times British prime minster William Ewart Gladstone, also a classical scholar, suggested that terms for blue were absent from the works of Homer, illustrating his point with the poet's description of the sea as 'wine-dark' and concluding that the Ancient Greeks simply didn't perceive colour the way we do. In fact the Greeks had more than one word for specific shades of blue – much as in Russian, where light blue and dark blue are considered different colours. Interestingly, native Russian speakers are able to colour match swatches to one or other category of blue much faster than anglophones. The Himba people of northern Namibia and southern Angola, on the other hand, genuinely have no word for blue, and 'see' night and water as black or dark, and the sky as white. According to research by cognitive neuropsychologist Jules Davidoff of Goldsmiths, University of London, the Himba easily pick out shades of green that to a European eye blend almost imperceptibly with others, but cannot separate sky blue from a sea of greens. All this suggests that despite our shared optical physiology, humans can see colour in different ways, and these seem to relate to language. It is as though, without a name, the concept of blue may as well not exist. This is true in other areas of life, for sure. We remember people better when we know them by a name, and as a naturalist, a name is a huge aid to fixing a species in our awareness. Naming is not simply a matter of convenience or classification, though it serves both. It is an act of conjuring, of meaning-making, startlingly close to the magic described in Ursula Le Guin's *Earthsea* books, in which mage-power over a person or a creature comes from knowing its true name. Names give us the power of recognition.

Even with a convincing explanation for the absence of blue in Himba consciousness I can't imagine not knowing it instinctively. It is the only colour that is there, day and night. It is the colour of air and distance, my art teacher once told me – make each hill in a landscape a little more blue and they will look further away. In water, blue is the colour of volume, density and age. Fresh snow is white but it sinters into blue – as Robert Macfarlane wrote in *Underland* of glaciers and ice cores: 'Ice has a memory and the colour of this memory is blue.'

In evolutionary terms we've been sensitive to the blue-green-yellow part of the spectrum far longer than other colours. The ability first evolved in ancient single-celled algae that needed to harvest sunlight but avoid the harmful UV component of midday rays. Modern phytoplankton still make vertical migrations up and down the water column in order to catch morning and evening light (red and blue wavelengths are especially important in photosynthesis) but avoid darkness and the high levels of UV in noonday glare. Red wavelengths do not penetrate through more than about 5m of water. This explains why so many deep-water animals are red. At depth, redness confers invisibility. In animal evolution, it seems sensitivity to red came long after our emergence onto land, and the discerning red vision of humans – actually rather rare among mammals – developed sometime in our fruit-eating primate ancestry. But we can't see ultraviolet as birds and bees do, or perceive infrared as snakes and mosquitoes can. Salmon see both, but at different stages in their life history.

The nature of blue was a particular obsession of Swiss polymath Horace-Bénédict de Saussure. Saussure was a measurer and an adventurer – one passion fed the other. A year after Chamonix mountain guides Jacques Balmat and Michel-Gabriel Paccard became the first to summit Mont Blanc in 1786, Sausurre hired them to guide him to the top. Among the simplest but most ingenious of the recording devices carried by his team was a 'cyanometer' – a flimsy, hand-made circle of 53 paper swatches, each dyed a different shade of Prussian blue, grading from white to black. With it, Sausurre intended to test his theory that the blueness of the sky bore an inverse relationship to the density of particles in the atmosphere (mainly dust and water droplets). At low elevations, skies with a lot of moisture appear pale, while deeper blues are indicative of dry atmospheric conditions. But Saussure was also well aware of the effect of altitude on sky colour – whereby blueness increases with elevation. At the summit of Mont Blanc, Saussure recorded the most intensely blue sky he had ever seen, equivalent to 39 degrees on his cyanometer. This observation, and Saussure's more-or-less correct assumption of why it occurred, predated the formal explanation and quantification of atmospheric scattering effects by John Tyndall and Lord Rayleigh, whose papers are usually cited in answer to the question of why the sky is blue. His was the first attempt to measure a familiar phenomenon, which had led to a local superstition that at the greatest of heights, the sky would eventually turn black, and that anyone climbing so far would risk falling up, into the void. The idea is not so silly. Walking on a clear winter night in Dalby Forest, not far from where we live, I looked down into a void at the side of the path, and felt a jolt of vertigo so intense that I almost fell over on level ground. A pool of water there was reflecting the sky so perfectly that it appeared bottomless – an inky never-never, similar in colour to Saussure's 39-degree summit-blue.

Blue may be the colour of atmosphere, and it is a colour most of us associate with water almost unthinkingly. But it is not the true colour of water. That is perhaps closer to *glas* and *aoi* – it is aquamarine: not-quite blue and not-quite green. Is it coincidence that these in-between shades have always been my favourite? That I am always wearing them, painting them on furniture and walls? Aquamarine is relatively seldom seen in rivers, because in addition to itself, H_2O gives us both reflected and transmitted light, in which we see not only the water, but also its content and its context. We see solutes and suspensions, sky and riverbed, weed and rock. We see sunrise and sunset, moon and stars, fish and trees, and all the colours there are.

The rivers and the sea on the fourteenth-century Gough Map are shown in murky green. It's a marked contrast to modern maps where they are invariably depicted as bright blue, and much closer to the reality of British rivers, which are mostly green and gold and olive and bronze, sometimes amber or purple, and a thousand shades of beverage brown. Just occasionally, sometimes in chalk lands, but usually in mountains, there are streams clear enough for water to be itself and then it is at its most extraordinary. Then it is the colour of clarity. Then it seems you could immerse yourself and not understand why you were suddenly seeing so clearly until you were drowned.

David Miller understands the effects of light on water better than most. We first met at Birdfair, the annual festival of birdwatching and nature on the shores of Rutland Water, sometimes known as the 'Wildlife Glastonbury'. The art marquee always lured me in, and I'd make a systematic tour from stand to stand, wistfully admiring one amazing display after another. But on this occasion I'd barely made it halfway along the first row, when over the heads of other visitors I caught a gleam of light on water. It was so luminous and compelling that I abandoned my tour and made a beeline for it. The stallholder, a slim bespectacled man with neat greying hair and a light tan, was also the artist. The pictures were of seabirds and fish, all rendered with startling realism, but it was the water I couldn't resist. David explained that as well as a painter, he was an angler and a diver. Most of the paintings on display were of the sea, but he told me of the Welsh rivers he dives in to photograph sea trout and salmon, and offered to show me one day.

Snorkelling in West Beck has given me an inkling of what David might be seeing down there, and my walk with Owen has left me with a yen to swim with salmon, so I drop him a line and ask if I can come. By pure good fortune, he says the conditions are perfect.

We meet in a pub car park near Carmarthen, a short drive from one of his favourite rivers, the Afon Cothi. David is boyishly excited. It was access to the sea and rivers like this that brought him to South Wales 20 years ago from Oldham, but he still has a light Lancastrian accent. As we scramble down a steep bank using the exposed roots of oak and beech for hand and footholds he tells me he hasn't dived here since last year, and that timing is critical.

'I have an understanding with the fishery – they don't mind me coming as long as it's before the gamefish season – so I have a narrow window to see the big fellas before the season starts. Then there's the light – the gorge is so steep that the water only catches the sun for a couple of hours – I have to be in at around midday. And of course absolutely everything is weather dependent – water levels affect the migration and I need the sun, if I'm going to get anything worth painting.'

We emerge on a rocky bank. The river is sublime – under a canopy of green and gold, there's a rapid above us and another below, and the pool between is close to the elusive aquamarine.

'I'm almost frightened to bring people here,' he says, 'in case they just look and go "yeah, whatever".'

I look. Take in the green-gold shot-silk surface of the river, the dancing cascades, the shimmer of reflected light on overhanging trees. 'Yeah. I can't imagine why you'd bring me here, David. It's horrible.'

He grins. 'I always think it's a Land that Time Forgot,' he says. 'Sometimes, after I've been down there a while I feel like if I come up and met a Stone Age hunter crouching on the bank – like Stig of the Dump – I wouldn't be surprised. This river, and these fish, would have been so important to them as a source of food. It's like they are still here somehow. Like all times exist.'

Most of David's pictures sell to anglers, and the fish are undoubtedly the commercial stars, but I tell him it was the water that drew me across the marquee at Birdfair. 'I'd love to try some big canvases without the fish, he says. 'Just capture the drama of this place. The rocks, the water, and the light.'

It takes a while to get kitted up. David is using full scuba kit and has to lug heavy tanks and a lot of camera equipment down to the river. He's wearing 6mm-thick neoprene. I have a skinny 2mm-thick swimming wetsuit, a mask and snorkel, and the fins I meant to bring are still lying forgotten in the garage at home. I borrow a belt and some weights to counteract the buoyancy of the suit. I can tell David is a little concerned, but I promise him I normally swim without extra insulation, and that I have no intention of staying in until I'm hypothermic. He gives me a rough description of the layout below the water and assures me I'll be able to climb out all the way along. We agree a plan, in which he'll submerge and I'll swim above him while he takes me on a tour of a 25m-long pool between rapids. It looks deep – but not so fast I won't be able to swim against it.

'You'll see my bubbles, and the flash when I take pictures.'

He enters the water and disappears beneath the surface reflections. I lower myself in carefully, checking I've got the weight right – I don't want to sink like a stone. But it's perfect. I adjust my mask and snorkel and look down.

There is a gloomy green nave below me, where David hovers – easily holding position with slight movements of his big fins. The water is clear and faintly gold-green. The walls of the channel are worn sculpturally smooth. We begin exploring. The rocks are variable in colour – slatey grey-green and rusty, occasionally maroon. There are scoops and circular bowls worn over millennia by the action of gravel and pebbles tumbling round and round, and the banding of rock in some of these concavities calls to mind the growth marks on mussel shells.

In the larger bowls and crevices and along the bottom of the canyon there are rounded pebbles, distributed as through they've been carefully sorted and counted by river fingers. There is virtually no fine sediment, but everywhere, to my complete surprise, there are acorns. Thousands upon thousands of them, green and gold and brown, some nestling among larger stones, more rolling merrily from saucer to trough, queuing in orderly fashion for their turn down the slides, collected in dishes and hollows, like olives at a party or bowls of food placed before a shrine. Votive offerings from forest to river.

The water glimmers briefly – it's David's camera flash. I find him on the riverbed a little way downstream with his head under an overhang, and duck dive down to see what he's found. It's a female trout, tucked in against the wall. She's already losing the silveriness that she would have acquired while at sea, and now she wears the grubby gold of a tarnished pound coin. The pattern of her scales gives the impression of perfectly fitting, exquisitely tooled chainmail – the mithril armour worn by Tolkien's dwarves. She has a few dark spots on her flanks. By the time she is ready to spawn she'll be browner still and spottier. Her face is blunt, her mouth slightly down-turned and her large eyes gold-rimmed and froglike. Her pectoral fins splay and rest lightly on the smooth rock of the riverbed and under her tail in a depression, as though she were brooding them, is a handful of acorns. I want to cry into my mask – there is something so sweetly and essentially melancholic about all this. Death and fecundity, river and forest, rock and water, light and dark. Old partners, holding space together.

I leave David to his photography and swim past looming, fantastical shapes. Castellations and gullies, portholes and arches. On a pillar in the middle of the river, is a throne for an aquatic god. And then as I round a buttress of smooth rock it's like a switch has been flipped or a skylight opened. Shafts of light illuminate the grand space I'm swimming through. If Henry Moore had taken after Gaudi and designed a cathedral it might look like this. Grand, compelling, not a vertical or horizontal to be seen. The slight surface ripples are lensing the sunlight into a reticulated pattern on the floor – a swaying net of bright gold.

After about forty minutes we surface to talk. David says he's going to drive downriver a short way – he can't negotiate the rapid in his scuba gear and his tanks and weights are too heavy to carry far. But from the bank I can almost see the pool below, and ask if he minds me making my own way downriver to meet him there. He's relaxed a bit about my safety and agrees. And so, for a short while I have the place to myself.

I want to dance in that underwater space, if only my breath would hold out. There are leaves already doing so. Oak, beech and hazel; gold, crimson and green; swirling as they might on a windy day in an autumn wood – but in slow motion. I can reach out and catch them, or swim around them as they tumble, like Keanu Reeves and Carrie-Anne Fisher ducking bullets in *The Matrix*. I have fly-reactions. I can see the eternity in an hour.

At the end of the pool there's a chock of boulders and then a rapid formed from a series of bedrock slides. The water is shallower here, and thus by simple mathematics, flows much faster. I could stand in it, knee deep, but that would be an old view and actually, with the risk of being swept off my feet, no safer. I take to crocodiling again, facing downstream, and bracing with my arms to slow my descent. The river is busy here, and from this position I can see what it has been working on these past few thousand years. The rock bears the mark of the river's stride, reciprocates its bellies and arches. I'm moving along the impression fossil of a river, created where water and land have lain with each other for a very long time. The shapes are familiar. The riverbed might be a mould from which the first otter or eel was cast, where spirits leapt into curved shadows to animate watery flesh.

The rapid steepens, becomes swooshy and it's harder to control my speed. I'm very conscious of being bareheaded: in all those years of kayaking, sliding down a river without a helmet would have been unthinkable. Then it spits me out into a pool bright with bubbles. In my peripheral vision I glimpse something large. It's so fleeting I'm not sure how much of the grey-blue zeppelin-like after-image is real, and how much is my imagination reaching for something. It slips from my sight, and I cannot find it again. Later, David says 'Did you see it? Big salmon!'

I don't know. Maybe. I can't honestly say.

A little later, we walk up the river and find a place to set up a stove and make coffee to go with our sandwiches. David tells me about sea trout. They are the same species as brown trout, but behave more like salmon: spawning in rivers, but spending much of their lives out at sea, where, like salmon, they become silvery. The colour change is all about camouflage – drab hues with countershading (dark along the top of the body, paler below, cancelling out the effect of being lit from above) are the best bet in rivers, and spots and speckles are a good facsimile of gravelly riverbeds. But in the sea, as most fish inhabiting the sunlit upper waters know, the most effective trick is to bounce light around: to blend in by reflecting the blueness of the surroundings. The shimmer of fish scales is achieved with

layers of guanine – better known as one of the four bases
that spell out the genetic code written in the nucleic acids
DNA and RNA. But in fish it is pressed into another
purpose, laid down in crystal form in flat, multi-layered
sheets that reflect all wavelengths of visible light. The
guanine can be broken down and re-laid as the fish comes
and goes between fresh and salt water.

Unlike most salmon, sea trout are survivors, with good
numbers of them making the same spawning migration year
after year. Like salmon, they stop feeding when they come
upriver. That seems just as well to me – this river is
extraordinarily beautiful but doesn't seem biologically
productive – there's no sediment, and thus no weed; the rocks
are scoured and the clarity of the water suggests there are
barely even any algae. Not much to build a food chain on, and
certainly not enough to sustain something as large and
carnivorous as a salmon or trout.

'Exactly,' says David. 'That's why they go to sea to grow.
But the scarcity of other big fish here also means it's relatively
safe for their young. That's pretty wise, don't you think?
They are amazing. When you meet them and imagine where
they've been, what they've seen, what they've survived, how
many times they've escaped being eaten – you realise each
one is a miracle. How anyone can look at them and just see
something for the barbeque is beyond me.'

We talk about the privilege of being here on a week day
and at this time of year, like kids playing truant, when the
weather and the river levels have been so kind.

'I'm always after the perfect shot but there's something
aggressive in trying to catch the moment. Creativity is
hungry like that,' says David. 'It's good sometimes to just be
there without trying to make anything of it. That's when the
water is most redemptive. I get anxious, I worry a lot, but I
never come away from a river like this not feeling better –
energised, more at peace, more connected. It's strange to say,
but water *earths* me.'

He sips coffee, watches the water slipping by. 'I sometimes think we're living as shadows of what our bodies can do and feel. It makes us forget that we belong out here, and with that sense of belonging we've lost a sense of the sacredness of places. But it's everywhere, isn't it? The sanctity, magic, whatever you want to call it. You just have to be awake to it. That's what it is, when I've been down there. I'm awake.'

Yes. We've been in a sacred place. Divinely lit and furnished with offerings. But unless I count that fleeting blue shadow, which I'm not willing to do, I haven't seen a salmon. October is coming, and I need to go north.

Damnation

Our last day paddling in Ladakh was without raft support or local knowledge. Our guide was Daz Clarkson, a hugely experienced expedition paddler, but he was usually based in Nepal, so we were running this big water section of the Indus on hearsay. The Indus is one of the world's great geographical and cultural arteries, and it didn't disappoint. More than twice the volume of the Zanskar, it provided a day of huge wave trains, pocked with crashing, mashing holes. Towards the end, we rounded a long bend and ahead of us, entirely unexpected, was a gigantic dam – or rather two-thirds of one under construction, with the entire volume of the river funnelling through a tight squeeze to its left.

Daz went for a look, then signalled us over to climb out onto vast hewn boulders that formed the base of the dam. I was incredulous. How come no one had mentioned a colossal infrastructure project on a river section we'd made no secret of our intention to paddle? We had no option but to climb up the angle between the riverbank and dam, which had been chocked with more boulders to protect the structure. It wasn't easy, scrambling and balancing while lifting, shoving, hoisting and dragging the boats. Three-quarters of the way up, dizzy with exertion, we began to come across turds. Human ones, in varying states of desiccation and decay. They lurked in every crevice; some had been deposited jauntily on boulder tops in the manner of otter spraints. Of all the routes to take, we'd picked one directly through the construction workers' toilet area. After ten minutes' climbing, lugging our boats through shit, we crested the dam and emerged into the building site. Smiling sheepishly at bemused dam builders in short-sleeved shirts and hard hats, we picked our way around a few sections of gappy security fence, past diggers and storage containers to a place downstream of the dam where the bank was less steep. I was aiming for a rounded brown rock at the water's edge but veered abruptly downstream when the rock resolved itself into the prodigiously inflated carcass of a horse – its head stretched out, teeth exposed.

'Well,' commented Daz with typical understatement. 'That was interesting.'

Hydropower seems to offer a lot of solutions. It's one of the oldest forms of power-generation, it's cleaner and more sustainable than methods that involve burning and, once the infrastructure is in place, has a lower carbon footprint. But at scale, it is problematic. Large dams change landscapes, flood homes and habitats and wreck rivers. Upstream of a large dam, a river disappears into a reservoir which may actually become a major source of greenhouse gases, especially methane, as a product of biological decay. Downstream, hydrological regimes are drastically altered and the river and its floodplain are starved of silt – the fine particles of sediment that provide natural substrate for ecological processes. And of course the dam itself is a barrier to movement – of water, of energy, of sediment, of life.

At the same time as massive structures like this one on the Indus and more colossal still are being constructed on some of the world's largest rivers, others are already being demolished elsewhere in order to restore the rivers they have stifled and starved. I think of the dams children seem to build compulsively on small streams or beaches where trickles of water drain towards the sea. It makes me wonder if any of these new dams will stand long enough to offset the true cost of their construction. Whatever we build, it will only ever be temporary. Long-lasting enough to power the development of a city perhaps, or to drive an industrial or technological revolution. Enduring enough to drive local species to extinction, for sure. But in the life of a river, no time at all.

CHAPTER 16

Anadrome

A month passes after my trip to Wales and I'm still dreaming about salmon. Voyagers, shapeshifters, crossers of boundaries. Even as embryos, I've read, they orient like compass needles.

Dusk is falling when I arrive in Braemar, and the place is aglow with the late October colours of aspen, beech and birch. I check into my hotel and use the last of the light to stretch my legs and lean on the railings of the bridge to watch the Clunie Water powering beneath on its way to meet the Dee. It's running high, which is just what the fish need, but discouraging for me – I can't swim in water like this.

The Atlantic salmon is one of a global group of closely related species with an anadromous life history: they begin their lives in fresh water and almost all spend a period at sea. That individuals return to the rivers of their origin has been known empirically for more than 300 years. Izaak Walton, author of seventeenth-century angling blockbuster *The Compleat Angler*, wrote of early marking experiments in which 'a riband, or some known tape or thread' was used to mark fish heading downriver in spring, allowing them to be recognised when they returned. A seminal experiment performed on the Tay in 1905 made clear that this applied to all returning fish, and that any that find themselves in the wrong river or tributary try to correct the situation, even if it means making a long detour.

When they first return from the open ocean, both male and female salmon are silvery and fat – this is when they make the most succulent and nutritious eating. But before entering the rivers they must run a gauntlet of dolphins, orcas and seals, then otters, and – where they still exist – bears. This is also when they have been traditionally netted in coastal waters, estuaries and lowland rivers. But at this time the salmon themselves have stopped feeding – the same flood of hormones that turns their attention to home from far out at sea also seems to put them off their food.

The return to fresh water triggers further changes. As their colouring darkens from silver to slate, and they begin to move up from the lowland rivers, they become increasingly sensitive to the cues that lead them home. Males develop mottled pink and orange breeding colours and a hooked extension of their lower jaw, called a kype. Their capture becomes a matter of sport rather than feasting – the fish survive by metabolising their own flesh, which becomes less good to eat. Fly fishing is fishing made difficult: old-school equipment and etiquette dictate a deliberate inefficiency that requires, on the part of the angler, an attention to detail bordering on obsession. Because the fish are not interested in feeding, they are difficult to tempt. They spend long periods lying in pools, inert, conserving energy and who knows, perhaps coming to terms with what is ahead. Pursuing prey is the last thing on their minds.

Sometimes they linger at confluences, waiting for certainty, but as the year wanes they enter the final stage of their journey, which for most will also be the end of their life. The higher tributaries are often obstructed by large drops, and the fish require spate or flood conditions to help them climb. Autumn rain provides this, usually bringing the levels in higher catchments up within a matter of hours. The fish respond accordingly.

The females decide where to spawn, and usually arrive before the males. When she is ready, a female creates an elongated depression in the gravel known as a redd, by lying on her side and beating her tail hard enough to shift even quite large pebbles. Males vie for the right to pair up and the successful suitor will align himself just behind and alongside the female, releasing a stream of milt to cover the eggs as she expels them – anything from a few hundred to several thousand. The eggs settle into the redd where they are covered by more gravel dislodged from immediately upstream. The work is usually done by mid November, and most spawners will die in the ensuing days or weeks, certainly long before their offspring hatch in spring.

The spent fish are known as kelts. A very few, most of them females, will survive and return to the sea to come again, but for most, the circle ends where it begins, in pools with pebbly, gravelly bottoms, flushed by swift, clean oxygen-rich water. As dead and dying adults, as eggs, as larvae (alevins), and juveniles (parr) the generations become part of the signature scent of the water that will bring future spawners home. Parr between 10 and 20cm long (usually two or three years old) develop into smolts, their barred markings disappearing as silvery guanine is laid down under their scales in preparation for going to sea.

I drive along Deeside the next morning. The road is swishing with spray, and what looks like old snow heaped at the roadside is actually foam, catching the light, such is the torrent of water in the gutters.

I meet Edwin Third, river operations manager for the Dee Fisheries Board, in a car park on the Glen Tanar estate. He's softly spoken, with Peter Pan eyes and a slightly lopsided smile that reaches his eyes every time – I'm glad about that, as we spend a good part of the day in facemasks, riding socially distanced in his four-by-four with me in the back seat diagonally opposite the driver's seat, windows open. We live this strange way now.

Our first stop is a place where the Tanar passes through a remnant of ancient Caledonian pine forest. There are, says Edwin, still capercaillie on the estate.

'I got chased by one once. It was seriously intimidating,' he laughs. He knows some pools the salmon use for resting, and when we planned this excursion two weeks ago he thought it might be a good place for me to try and swim with them. I already know that's not going to happen, but there's something else Edwin wants to show me. We meet the river in the forest as we approach – out of its channel, flooding between pines and over bilberry. We wade through a backwater to the edge of the main channel and Edwin points upstream to where the carcasses of a few dozen pines lie higgledy-piggledy on a slight bend in the river where an even higher flood has dumped them. It looks like a giant game of pick-up sticks.

'I spent years of my early career tidying up that kind of chaos. Now though ... ' he smiles the way Lochy sometimes does when revealing a new LEGO® creation ' ... we're leaving it be.'

I laugh. 'Crikey. What does the estate owner think?

'He thinks it looks a mess, which it does. But he's going along with it, as long as nothing threatens the bridges.'

Woody debris, Edwin tells me, is a big deal. But to understand why, we need to take another drive.

We head back over the Dee, upstream along a few miles of spectacular tree-lined road, past huge beeches and aspens exploding with colour, then take a turn up alongside another tributary, the Gairn. We stop briefly near the bottom to look at a wide, shallow river with water stained the colour of cola. On the opposite bank a fenced area of a few acres has been planted with trees in plastic guards – pines and birches, willow and rowan, right to the water's edge. Edwin opens a folder to show me a photograph blown up to A4 of what it looked like before – just heather and short sheep-cropped grass. I try to sound enthusiastic. It's a little underwhelming, if I'm honest, but I don't like to say so.

But then we drive upstream, into the bleakest, hugest expanse of land I've seen in a very long time.

'They call it Mamba,' declares Edwin, gesturing expansively to the horizon. 'Miles And Miles of Bugger All.'

It's shocking. I mean, I know what grouse moors look like. I live close to the North York Moors. But the emptiness here is on an entirely different scale. Edwin runs through some deforestation statistics. The average forest cover in Europe is 35 per cent. In Britain as a whole it is 12 per cent. In the Dee catchment it is 8 per cent, and in Glen Gairn it is 2 per cent.

'Those trees at the very bottom? That's pretty much it for the whole glen'.

I start to see why that small area of planting he showed me is significant. Up here there is only heather and rough grass, grouse and sheep – the latter Edwin explains are not farmed for meat or wool. 'They're here as tick mops. Treated so as any ticks they pick up die, reducing the threat to the grouse.' After several miles we pull over at a point where we can look down on the Gairn. The bottom of the valley is flat – at some point in its history the river must have sprawled all over it. Now its channel is very uniform, shallow, almost featureless and very exposed. But in it, spaced at intervals of a few hundred metres, are dozens of dead trees. Big ones. Edwin starts to tell me how his team got them there, felling, transportation, excavation – but I have to stop him, ask him to go back a bit, thinking I've misunderstood. He seems to be saying that, at great expense, they have imported trees from elsewhere, dug trenches in the riverbed and wedged the trunks into them.

'Yep. That's right. They have to be dug in, rootplate upstream, trunk angled down and deeply buried so there's no chance of them washing away and doing damage downstream.' He produces another photograph, of an orange digger on caterpillar tracks, swinging a tree into place.

'But ... that sounds ... mad.'

'Aye. It is. But let's go and have a close look, you'll see.'

We drop down to river level and stop again, near where the river splits around a small, flat island, on either side of which a dead tree has been installed. And I do see. I see that downstream of the rootplate, extending for perhaps five or six metres in the middle of the flow, is an area of smooth water. An eddy. And in the eddy, already, because the sudden slowing of the flow permits it, are deposits of fine shingle. 'There's shade there', says Edwin, 'and a refuge – a place to rest.'

I understand. With a bit more water this river could be paddled, but I wouldn't really want to. It's not technical, but there is nowhere to stop. No bends tight enough to create differential flow, no eddies. It's like an airport travellator. The power of the extraordinary interventions being made by Edwin's fishery team is in demonstrating, with immediate effect, why a river needs trees. It's not much, but in the otherwise relentless conveyor of this naked and skeletal river, the imported timber has created the beginnings of structure. And as a kayaker I can think a little like a fish. These eddies make so much difference.

We drive on to a place where two oddly unfinished-looking buildings gaze blankly at the river and the moor. They are a shooting lodge and a bothy and from a distance I can't work out why they look so awkward in the landscape. They're stone, and not new. Then I realise, it's the exposure and the complete lack of vegetational setting. Not a tree, not a shrub. No ivy or other climbers. Not even a bed of nettles. As a result the buildings look as though they've just been dropped there. To my eye, it's astonishingly bleak.

Edwin seems to be reading my thoughts.

'There's a deeply ingrained idea that this kind of emptiness is somehow natural,' he says. 'And until recently the idea of planting trees was anathema. Or rather–', he corrects himself, 'it was more a disbelief that trees could actually grow here, despite there being obvious pine roots right up the glen. Sure, some of them are thousands of years old. But this Mamba-scape is how it's been in living memory, and that lived experience is incredibly powerful.'

He produces another A4 printout, this one showing a map of the Dee catchment, with rivers marked in shades of blue, green and yellow.

'This map is based on climate models including projected water temperatures and ecological data,' he says. 'It rates all the rivers in Scotland according to the priority of action needed to improve their resilience to climate change.'

Then he shows me another version of the same map, zoomed out to show the entire north of Scotland. There's a huge rash of yellow, amber and red across the northern highlands. 'Blue and green are relatively low priority, yellow is more urgent – orange and red – well – you get the idea. All these yellow tributaries on the Dee are our spawning and nursery grounds.'

Water temperature matters hugely to fish. Experiments suggest that the eggs of salmon and trout survive best when incubated at around 8°C, and that survival declines rapidly over 10°C to near total mortality at above 12°C. Moreover, larvae hatching in the upper end of the survival range are significantly smaller than those at optimum temperatures (trout hatched at 12°C are barely half the weight of those hatched at 8–10°C). As parr, they can tolerate a wider range of temperatures, but their growth is affected. Young salmon will feed between 4°C and 21°C, but growth at the cooler and warmer temperatures in this range is non-existent. Exposure to temperatures above 25°C for more than a few days can be lethal. At over 30°C, the water carries so little oxygen that death can occur in minutes. Edwin's team monitor river temperatures of spawning and nursery areas and have already recorded summer highs of 27.5°C on the Gairn. If that starts to happen regularly, it will make most of these spawning and nursery grounds unliveable.

'The thing is, the Gairn is "only" a priority-four stream – if we're hitting those temperatures already, imagine what we're facing in the near future,' says Edwin. 'This map is changing everything. It's terrifying for the salmon estates, a picture of catastrophe, *if* we don't act. But when you say that tree shading can reduce the temperature of water by several degrees, suddenly, they are listening. Look down there.'

I follow his gaze. Down near the river there are a series of small, fenced enclosures. There are more upstream, dozens of them as far as I can see. Each one is about 3m by 3m, and inside, penned, are small trees.

'The deal here is that we've been allowed to try. Planting, that is, but in a super-controlled fashion. Birch, willow and rowan, only in enclosures, each of which costs more than three hundred pounds in labour and materials. This isn't a forest – it's not rewilding. It's the least useful and most expensive step we could take really, but we're at the limits of what the traditional estates can stomach – even with years and years of relationship building. It's the lowest rung of the ladder of change, but it is doing something instead of nothing – creating a seed bank, so that soon, we hope, there will be something to spread from.'

On the way down we pause again, overlooking part of the glen where the valley bottom is particularly flat and wide. 'Look at that. Can you imagine that filled with trees, with water braiding through them?'

I can.

'Can you imagine ... ' he almost whispers ' ... beavers?'

I very much can. I like this man a lot. He's one of those individuals willing not only to build bridges, but to be a bridge. He's receptive, proactive, and collaborative, keen to point out he's only part of a small team. But it's easy to see why he's trusted. The restoration journey he's coaxing these estates on is about giving tradition a viable future. Wildness, if you want to call it that (he doesn't) is a by-product.

Our last stop is Balmoral, the Queen's own Highland retreat. Edwin has security codes, and we drive through gates, past stripy lawns and the castle with its many gables and turrets (smaller than you might expect, but with a sort of CGI perfection) and beyond the formal grounds into Ballochbuie Forest. When Queen Victoria came here, Edwin tells me, this wasn't part of the estate. But Victoria realised its value as one of few remaining fragments of pristine Caledonian Forest – rare even in those days – and bought it.

And what a forest it is. Huge pines, dripping with lichen, cowberry clumps that are taller than I am. And cascading through it is the river we've come to see, the Garbh Allt. It's a scene of Landseer grandeur, but when we walk downstream towards the confluence with the Dee, we come across a digger at work, tearing into the banks. On Edwin's instructions, the operator, Hans (who also buried the trees on the Gairn) is creating channels that the river can spill into when it runs high. It's working already – water in a new channel is cutting down through the stony soil, elsewhere spilling over the grass and rush, and pooling in other places. Once again, Edwin seems childishly excited – like a boy building canals and dams on a beach, breaching them to see where the tide runs.

He explains that the last stretch of the Garbh Allt has historically been engineered – flood banks added to prevent it spilling into the forest. But this canalisation was scouring away gravels and in flood conditions unwanted silt was washing into the Dee. The carefully devised new plan, approved by the estate factor and the royal family, is to give the river more space, slow it down, so the gravel beds can establish in the channels and excess silt washed down from above in high water will be dropped in the forest.

'It looks a bit of a mess now,' he says, 'But sometimes you've gotta just take a brave pill, and cause some upheaval to achieve a long-term improvement. When we've made this physical restoration we'll let nature get in here and finish the job – that'll mean excluding deer for a while, but this will all regenerate and create a woodland with fingers of water braiding through it. What a place it will be! And to get salmon spawning right here, that would really be something.' In a few weeks' time, he will email me to say that salmon did indeed spawn on this section of the Garbh Allt, and on another restoration site on the Beltie Burn. In the case of the latter, the 15 salmon and sea trout redds counted after meanders were restored may have been the first since canalisation in 1860.

We walk down to where the Garbh Allt meets the Dee and out onto a gracious white footbridge. Edwin talks about trust.

'The kind of work Hans is busy with takes a few days; making a good plan takes months; but the groundwork – the building of trust and momentum – that's the work of years or even decades. But it has to be done. The river and the forests, the fish and the trees, are interdependent. The estates have no trouble recognising salmon as lynchpins but the fish need the forests to provide structure and dynamism to the river – to provide refuge and shade, and of course to play their part in nutrient cycling, which gives back to new generations of fish. It's a very beautiful cycle, which has been badly broken. But we can put back that core interaction. We can put back the trees.'

It's been an illuminating day – Edwin is a wonderful guide as well as a getter of results, and for all his insistence that none of the progress could have been made without the rest of the small Dee Fisheries Board team, he has renewed my faith in the power of individuals to make change. But I haven't seen a single fish. That evening I look up another phone number I have, for Duncan Ferguson, Operations Manager for the Spey Fishery Board, the other side of the Cairngorm plateau from Braemar. Something tells me Duncan is more conservative than Edwin. But I call anyway. He has a big voice, as fierce to my ear as Edwin's was gentle. The voice of a bear. I tell him I haven't seen any salmon. It sounds like I'm complaining.

'That's no surprise.'

'I don't think I have much chance of swimming with them this weekend either.' I imagine bear eyes rolling.

'You can keep your wetsuit in the bag. Ye'd be better just drinking some whisky.'

'Yeah. Except the bar is closed because of COVID.'

'Ach well, best get along to the Co-op then.'

That, I decide, is a very good idea, but for now I say, 'I've been looking at maps, wondering where I might have a chance of seeing salmon running from the bank.' I repeat what Edwin has told me about fish leaping mostly on the rising and falling arms of the flood, and ask if Duncan can suggest anywhere on Speyside.

He describes two places where I might be lucky, *if* the levels are right. He asks me not to name them, then hesitates a moment before adding, 'Look. Ah'll check the levels for you in the morning. Call me first thing, save you comin' around the hill if there's no point.'

In fact I don't even need to call. A text from Duncan arrives next morning while I am cleaning my teeth. *Upper Spey has dropped a lot. I'd say you have a 50% chance.* This feels as close to a certainty as I'm going to get.

I drive 'around the hill'. It's an 80-mile trip for what is a mere 30 or so miles as the crow or the eagle flies, so I appreciate Duncan's concern about wasting my time. The rain turns sleety as I pass the Glenshee ski centre and the car pings an ice warning as if on cue. A half-dozen disconsolate-looking grouse are hunched in the gravel of the car park between grey puddles and there is something pale on the road, ruffling in the wind. It turns out to be the smashed body of a mountain hare, hind legs splayed at an atrocious, girdle-cracking angle and one eye bulging from its skull.

The trees are less colourful than yesterday – partly because of the heavy cloud but also because the rain has brought leaves down and compacted them into a mulch at the edges of the road. Just before Pitlochry a sodden red squirrel leaps across the road like a flicked length of frayed rope, or the tail of some much larger beast.

I stop for coffee in Pitlochry, where it's *pissing* rain on the few waterproof-clad shoppers, and I'm despondent. There's no way any of the rivers I've seen are dropping today and it's hard to imagine anything going my way. But as I merge onto the A9, a swatch of baby-blue sky appears, cloud draws up like a lid being lifted, leaving a few drifty wisps snagged on forested slopes. In a matter of 60 seconds, visibility increases from metres to miles and I feel the pressure change in my head, as though a window has been opened.

Duncan's directions were careful, and precise. Where to park, which gates to take, paths to follow and ending with 'then if you're not feared of heights, you creep out on the rock spit, and peek over' – a hesitation, and the bear growl softens a bit – 'do watch out for tree roots, you don't wannae trip just there.'

The car park is one big puddle. But after less than two minutes walk I pass through a gate and another of those magical transitions take place. I'm in a woodland as it might be painted by Klimt, the floor golden with the leaves of birch and aspen, lacquered with light and water. The leaves that remain on the trees – maybe half – tremble in the air and the effect is of a shimmering golden mist. The path weaving between the trees is trimmed with heather and mosses and it reminds me of the contrived fairytale perfection of a garden woodland I saw in the grounds of the Imperial Palace in Kyoto. Only here it seems to be entirely natural. Or supernatural. The birches speak:

We have gilded this path for you, with leaves made from sunlight and water and air. Follow where it winds between silvery trunks, and then steeply down.

The mosses speak:

We have cushioned the rocks with our green, but not too much – it is good for you to pay attention to where you put your feet.

The river is snaking through a narrow, twisting defile under a bridge whose height is a clue to the volume of water that sometimes surges below. Under the bridge is a pool, its dark surface pulsing gently with upwelling currents, and a seam of spume snaking down the middle. A huge larch with drooping brassy tresses, like Rod Stewart in his glory days, trails in the water. The surface flow is insignificant, pedestrian, but it runs deep, and the undercurrent is probably significant. At the end of the pool the river slicks into an even narrower channel like a slurp of black treacle. Leaves carried in the flow accelerate through a rick-racking slot no more than a metre across, though I'd have to be under pursuit by wolves to consider jumping across, as it leads directly to the falls.

I find the rocky spit Duncan described, where spindly Scots pines cling by their bare knuckles, and roots run over the ground in all directions. Larger trees have sinewy roots that extend snakelike, far from the parent trees. I follow one up 15m of cliff and am surprised how small a tree it serves – I think of the many plantation pines I've seen toppled with a saucer of root plate no more than 2m across. Growth is prioritised differently here, and perhaps some of these immense roots were grown by trees that no longer stand. The soil is almost non-existent – just a sprinkling of pine needles settling into crevices. Seams of pink glittery granite run through darker grey and brown rock.

I reckon I can get closer to the main drop from the other side and cross back to where wooden steps lead down, so I pick my way through bilberry and ferns. Tits ping around the pines and birches, their high-pitched, wheezy calls audible above the water. The rocks more than a metre above the waterline are daubed with grey lichen, lower down it's white crustose lichen, feather moss and clubmoss and a decoupage of golden aspen leaves. And close to the edge they are slick with rain and spray.

The river speaks:

You have remembered, have you not, that is it not for you to decide why you are here, or what will be? If you wait now, I will show you something. You can decide afterwards, if you must, whether it is the thing you came for, but in the deciding, understand that you may miss much that it would serve you to see.

I settle on a wet rock by the bottom of the falls, as close to the water as I dare. The fish speak:

You don't know it yet, but we are here, where she writhes and surges, spits at your dangling feet. She hides us in white foam, white noise, white thunder. We nose her billows and folds, scenting the tangs and flavours of home. We press our bodies to her rise and fall, her twist and curl, feeling her seams, acknowledging her denials and testing the allowances she offers. We search for possibility, no more than that. It is hard. There is the clench of emptiness. But that is a distraction. Our wealth is flesh, and we spend to ascend. It is home calling. It is love. The higher we go, the clearer it becomes. We know where we are bound. Do you, in your ancient brain, know it too?

The first body rises like a missile, close to the face of the fall. It's exactly what I was hoping to see and yet the surprise of it takes my breath. The snout is pointed like an arrowhead, the body deep, tail broad. I have the fleeting impression of a projectile, something thrown rather than something leaping. It is not silver at all, but heavy grey. Twenty seconds pass, then another, browner with a flush of rouge around its undercarriage, a male. It rises a metre and a half then drops back, and comes again, closer to me – at least I think it's the same fish. He is jumping from further out and I wonder what his water-adapted eyes see on each leap – enough to assess the challenge? To understand he's going to need a bigger leap? Are these trial runs to scope out the challenge, or does he just read pressure, water speed and angle? Salmon run mostly in the dark, they do not need to see.

More come. They range in size, I estimate, from 50cm to twice that. I've no idea what that might be in weight. The biggest yet, a dark grey female, makes a series of leaps – the first more of a bob – a spyhop, just the head and first half of the body snouting at the fall, then again, from further out. As she drops back a second time I see her back with the larger dorsal fin at the front slightly raised skirl away, and am amazed that such a solidly built fish can bend so easily – she has a turning circle half her body length.

I begin to develop a picture of the hidden structure of the drop – the fish are teaching me. What looks like a curtain of falling water is just that – a curtain I cannot see behind – but as fish after fish drops through I realise that behind that veil, there must be a whole snakes-and-ladders architecture of sills, clefts and slipways, steps, refuges and tongues. From the river's right, water slides in and angles across the fall, forming a crease, which several of the fish seem to be aiming for. From the left water drops into a frothing cauldron in which there is as much air as water – nothing on which to gain purchase. In the centre there's a sweeping tongue of dark water in which there would be something to beat against – but moving so fast it's hard to imagine overcoming it. But I'm thinking like a paddler, not a salmon. A salmon can swim faster than I can run and a salmon can use its whole body to push water.

There's a quote sometimes attributed to Albert Einstein, and normally used to deride, that 'insanity is trying the same thing again and expecting a different result.' But in the case of these fish, there's no expectation, only motivation. They have no concept of failure, only a will to press on. And sometimes circumstances do change. The river rises and falls in ways beyond their control, but seemingly not beyond their ability to comprehend. Rain makes unassailable drops achievable. Today is one of those days.

After half an hour I've seen maybe 20 fish, and then suddenly, for no reason I can discern, there are many more. Some rise almost vertically up the face, others seem to take a running jump from a metre or more out and I wonder if individuals are consistent in their style of jumping and which techniques work best.

One that leaps at the far side of the river falls back sideways. The meaty thwack of muscle on rock is audible even above the roar of the water, and I can't help but flinch. Bruises and scrapes are almost inevitable. These wounds are how fungal infections get in. Salmon often begin to rot while still alive, shedding skin and flesh in pulpy discoloured ribbons.

Every striving, beating leap pulls on my diaphragm – I can't not cheer each effort. Mostly they are in view for less than a second, but occasionally one manages to hang, beating, impossibly, agonisingly long, as though dangling from a line. It's like no one has told them they can't, so they do. These fish don't know impossible.

A sign near the bridge explains that 98 per cent of salmon reported caught on the Spey are now released. NatureScot have used some of their last EU funding to buy netting rights in order that they are not actually used. As in Wales, culture has been forced into conflict with nature – both are threatened with extinction. This year these running salmon will make it. But the water into which they are ascending is getting warmer. The fungal infections and other pathologies will get worse, hatching rates and the growth and survival of alevins and parr will decline – there's even a risk that intense heatwaves will kill adult fish. Saving them means changing the entire landscape, and it is a race against time. But the solution is one that nature has been working on for millions of years. Trees.

CHAPTER 17

Riverwoods

I pull up on the driveway of a tidy white croft house and am met by a Labrador with a head like a furry half breeze block. His name is Fin, and Fin's human is wildlife photographer Peter Cairns, with whom I've worked from time to time without ever actually meeting. They both tell me in their own way that it's time for Fin's walk, and so we head straight out into a light, bright drizzle, the kind of saturating sunshine that is a speciality of Scottish uplands.

Pete has lived here on the edge of the Feshie floodplain for the last 27 years. It's transformed in that time, he says, as we walk past stands of birch and meadows where a vestige of summer lingers in the fine flowering grasses, bowed by the rain but not yet beaten down by it. With fellow photographer Mark Hamblin, Pete is the driving force behind rewilding charity, SCOTLAND: the Big Picture. 'It was never meant to be a charity,' he says. 'It started as a feature-length film about rewilding generally but we soon realised two things: first that it was impossible to do justice to all facets of the topic in one film, second that it risked preaching to folk already in the church, while turning off those we really want to reach.'

Rewilding – the restoration of land to an uncultivated, self-willed state with a full complement of ecological components – has a degree of toxicity, especially in Scotland, because of echoes of the Highland clearances – the mass evictions of tenants in the eighteenth and nineteenth centuries. People, and especially those in government, fear anything with a whiff of de-population, and rewilding is often represented as an authoritarian 'wolves in, people out' narrative, says Pete.

'It's deeply problematic. But wild salmon are very different. We needed a storyline that would engage farmers, gillies, land managers, keepers, and communicate the philosophies and principles of rewilding…without even using the word, and these fish provide it. They are politically non-sensitive, culturally valuable, with an astonishing narrative of their own, but more importantly, they carry a story about the processes and cycles that govern the state of whole catchments.'

The idea that salmon live in trees has become an ecological meme. The story that goes with it is usually told in a North American context, where a key element is the role of large predators, especially bears, which gorge on running salmon, scatter partially eaten remains and go off to do what we all know bears must in the woods, thus contributing significantly to the nutrient cycle. The nutrient wealth of the oceans is brought to the forest by fish, and the forest then helps to nurture more fish. The film Pete and Mark have made plays heavily to this ecological communion and when Pete tells me its name, *Riverwoods,* I feel a little electric buzz.

A tree is a river and a river is a tree.

It's stating the obvious, but we don't have bears in Britain, and any suggestion that they should be reintroduced is hardly likely to calm the rewilding debate. 'Surely', I say, 'you're not going to be able to sell that idea to anyone already opposed to wolves or lynx?'

Pete smiles. 'The film will briefly show bears eating salmon in an Alaskan forest, but we don't actually *say* bears are what Scotland needs.' Behind the half-joke, he's serious. 'We're navigating a thin line. Weaving all the messages without preaching or dictating, and keeping a sympathetic ear to different perspectives. We've focussed on the interaction with trees and once we began teaming up with people like Edwin we realised that perhaps the most powerful thing with the approach you saw on the Gairn – those tiny cages of trees, and the dead wood planted in the river – isn't the progress towards restoration, but the willingness of fisheries and estates to engage. Their involvement is an exemplar for others to be reassured, informed and inspired by. And already there is a realisation that those small steps weren't so bad, and maybe those little tree enclosures *are* a bit silly.'

On the face of it, this cautious approach seems to be working. In addition to big, well publicised projects on the Dee and Tweed, several smaller ones are taking place. A changing of the guard is underway in terms of estate ownership and of intent, says Pete, with a younger generation keen to make an impact.

'Owning large areas of land, and in some cases whole river catchments, means there's much less politics to negotiate – for some of them it's possible to effect change at will. They may not use the word rewilding or like what they think it means, but they are into nature recovery and have a keen eye on the economic horizon. They can see that the ways of their parents and grandparents aren't going to stay viable.'

We've taken a loop around the floodplain, through birches and alder. A turn brings us in full view of the Feshie, braiding over its rocky channel, just as the sun reappears and water on tussocky grasses and rushes sparkles like a million trembling diamonds. Even after 27 years Pete is still moved by it. He gazes out with water beading on his hair and eyelashes. I can sense weariness in him – the kind that comes from a passion that means work always comes first – but he's in the right place. This valley, with its rainbows and jewel light, its dancing birches and its restless river. The energy of the place is palpable.

I ask where I can go to see the change happening. He laughs 'Right here! Take a look up Glen Feshie.'

The 42,000-acre Glenfeshie estate has been owned since 2006 by Danish billionaires Anders and Anne Holch Povlsen, whose holdings now also include a further 180,000 acres elsewhere in the Highlands, making them Scotland's largest private landowners. The estate is run by WildLand, a company established for the explicit purpose of managing ecological restoration on a grand scale. As the longest-owned estate in the WildLand portfolio, Glenfeshie has been a testing ground for a bold approach, in particular to reafforestation.

It's almost four o'clock when I park at the trail head – I only have two hours of useable light, so I pack quickly, call home while I still have phone signal, and walk.

By four-forty the sun is dipping below the forested whaleback hill to my right, while the bald high flanks of Càrn Bàn Mòr and Meall Dubhag, western outriders of the Cairngorm massif, are still bathed in golden light. A sign at a gate welcomes me to the Glenfeshie estate, asks me to keep the gate shut to prevent sheep from getting not out, but in. It also warns that the bridge from Carnachuin, marked on older maps, was washed away in a spate some years ago.

Almost immediately I have a ford to cross. Coming straight after the warning about the missing bridge it sets the tone. This is not somewhere you can expect help in crossing water whose flow is a dominant force here and it's up to you to negotiate it as best you can. The water overtops my boots and I think ruefully that my feet might not be dry again until tomorrow night.

Close to the path up ahead I can see what looks like a short cane with a scrap of bright red surveyors' tape at the top, fluttering in the breeze. I'm almost on top of it when I realise it's not a cane but a tiny tree. A stripling rowan, beside a pool of black peaty water, its scarlet leaves so bright they seem to shout. And it strikes me suddenly that there is something to shout about. *Here I am!* it says. *I've not been nibbled off!* And now I've noticed this little tree, I start to see others, mostly pine and birch, some seven feet tall, some just a few inches. But the more I look, the more I see and after another few minutes' walking, they are *everywhere*.

The few people I've seen are all heading the other way: a couple of mountain bikers and three cheerful young nuns, the white of their wimples gleaming in low sun. That was half an hour ago, and as I walk on, I'm aware of a swelling sense of solitude, but not of loneliness. In fact the opposite. I have a profound sense of being at home. I feel welcome.

I linger on a bridge, which is now the last (or the first) on the Feshie, not because I want to cross, but because the view upstream is a stonker. The river, it seems, is a restless inhabitant of a huge, generous space, with a penchant for moving the furniture, knocking down walls. Everywhere are signs of recent watery renovations: gravel banks and islands, boulder gardens and land slips. It's dynamic, untidy, wild in the original sense, of a willed thing.

The path winds among young trees for a stretch and I'm surprised to see a temporary-looking laminated cardboard sign: *Steep Drop Ahead*. It seems a strange kind of warning, given the general nature of the place, where surely steep drops are to be expected, but as I round the bend and descend a few rocky steps, the path disappears. The 'steep drop' is in fact a ten-metre cliff of recently exposed glacial deposits with the river clawing at the plum-pudding mix of ancient silts, gravels and boulders at its base. Steep drop? *Bloody hell!* I chuckle at the understatement and find the way others have obviously climbed down. Immediately there is another obstacle: a gushing burn, which my map identifies as the Allt Garbhlach, ripping down a cleft in the side of the glen, with an apron of variably striated, washed-out boulders in humbug and bonbon shades of black, white, pink and grey. There's no bridge, at least no man-made one, but a huge multi-stemmed pine has toppled across the torrent, as generous in death as in life, offering a way across. I climb slowly and carefully along the branches. There are thousands, no, hundreds of thousands of holes in the bark where insects have emerged, and woodpeckers have probed and excavated. It feels like an unearned intimacy, a trespass into the private anatomy of the tree. I find myself begging pardon of this uprooted matriarch and, once safely across, I pat the trunk.

'Thank you, Granny Pine.'

I scramble up another heavily eroded bank into an area of much younger pines, a plantation, judging by their uniformity, where the path glows rufous with dead needles through a vivid green carpet of knee-deep bilberry and moss. It's very quiet in amongst the trees after the pummelling, boulder-rattling rush of the Allt Garbhlach, but water is running here too – a soft trickling, tickling sound from several sinuous, crystal-clear watercourses winding though the moss, each just a few inches across, a baby step. There's heather too, flowers still with a faint blush of ashy pink. The trees have craggy lichenous bark around their ankles and a natural ombre from grey to mauve above head height, then higher up still they flush a gorgeous flaky red. And here too there are tiny new trees, mostly rowans, presumably sprouted from seeds defecated by birds. They flicker gold and lemon and red, like candles in the green.

I take a turn in the path towards the river and hack my way down an overgrown four-by-four track through a thicket of broom, thick with pods, and emerge on an expanse of grassy meadow starred with powder-blue scabious and buttercups. Ahead, on a slight knoll by the river is a huge old pine. It's a lovely spot, and I decide immediately to stop.

I make a perfunctory job of trampling the long tussocky grass before pitching my tent. The pegs sink easily into the fibrous grassy matt. Too easily really, I should know better.

I eat rehydrated risotto under the pine, along with a half-bag of fiery wasabi peas, washed down with slugs of river water so cold it burns my throat. The tree has a trunk 3m around, and descendants clustering close by. There's a another of similar size but dead on the opposite bank, dumped there by the river, several metres above the current level – a souvenir of what must have been epic water.

By the time I finish eating, the river is black and silver and a half moon has risen, with Saturn and Jupiter close by. Clouds begin to pile up on the southern horizon like servings of mashed potato. The moon is hidden for a while, but then pops up again, dazzlingly bright and illuminating a whole luminous country in the clouds. In the future hurly burly of life, I think, I must remember that this enchanted place exists, with its gleaming river, its resurgent, generous trees and its indigo star-spattered sky.

The wind rises soon after I go to bed and it brings rain in gusty buckets. It wants to rip the tent from the ground, it paws at the flysheet and occasionally swipes underneath it, blind but fierce, like a cat trying to hook a mouse from a burrow. Twice it unzips the flysheet, and I'm roused by the whipcrack slap of wet nylon. My sloppy pitching on tussocky ground means the pegs work loose and I have to get up three times to resecure the guy lines. Some nights it's hard to know if you've really slept at all.

Dawn is grey and grudging. The wind drops, but the rain doesn't let up. I clip the door open and sit in my sleeping bag and down jacket, watching the rain and the river. I make and drink four very small cups of instant coffee, one after another. My jet stove can boil 150ml of water in seconds and since there's no rush, this is better than making a big mug that goes cold before you finish it. I relish every piping-hot sip. The opportunity to just sit is rare, but I've been in the tiny tent for 12 hours and begin to deeply regret not bringing a book. I study the map instead, imagining walks I won't have time for on this trip.

Eventually I give up waiting for the rain to ease. It takes two minutes to collapse and pack the saturated tent. I set off in a steady downpour and after pushing through a cluster of small pines emerge, unexpectedly, in a place of sheer grandeur. The trees, all Scots pine, are nothing like the spindly forms anyone living in England might imagine the species to be, but immense, sprawling beasts, somehow filling the aesthetic of both willow and oak. Most have a marked directional growth – leaning southward, but also riverward. To find decent numbers of such trees is joyous – they add

gravitas to balance the explosive vigour of the new growth
here. It's sobering to realise that many of these monumental
specimens only avoided felling a century or more ago
because their growth was too crooked to be valuable for
timber. Here, as with tiny remnants of once dominant
Caledonian pine forest across Scotland, a unique habitat is
being saved at the very last possible moment.

There's short turf beneath the trees, neat and mossy,
sprinkled with red needles, and eruptions of hard fern – an
ancient woodland indicator with a preference for damp acid
ground, recognisable by its narrow evergreen foliage, a
sprawling rosette of dark green sterile fronds and an upright
central crown of paler, spindlier fertile ones. It's one of many
plants eaten by red deer, so I wonder if its abundance here is
new. There's plenty of dead wood, in varying stages of decay,
most of it thick with moss and lichen, and the fallen trunks
and boughs in more advanced stages of decay are sprouting
with rows of bilberry like oversized growbags.

A little further on there are signs of past habitation or
industry. A pair of rectangular pits near the river and some
ancient five gallon cans that might have held fuel oil or
pitch, but now so rusted and fragile I can break off flakes
of metal with a finger. They could be 100 years old, but
what's striking about this human detritus is the way it is
disintegrating and returning to the Earth – the way plastic
never will. I feel a strange sort of nostalgia for old-fashioned
trash. Close to the pits, along the faintest of paths is a
rectangular plinth – the foundation of a small house or hut
draped in a thick blanket of moss. Most of the trees in the
immediate area are young – a few decades old, but there is
one granny, which must have stood alongside the building.
The sink is still here – a huge square double butler-style, in
cast concrete, with a tiny pine and a goat willow growing
in it, and on its rim, *Cladonia* lichens with fantastical
hooter-shaped fruiting cups, like something drawn by
Dr Seuss.

Nearby I find what looks like an art installation. It's a two-dimensional red deer, cut out of inch-thick sheet metal. The head is level with mine, the eye brassy. It is covered in many layers of peeling, clot-red paint, and pockmarked all over where it has been shot hundreds of times. On the other side it has been braced and riveted together. Built up to be shot down.

It looks alert, as well it might, because the spectacular regeneration of this valley is dependent on the relentless culling of its kind. In 2004 it was estimated there were as many as 95 red deer per km^2 on the Glenfeshie estate. Not only was the intensity of browsing and grazing preventing any regeneration of trees and threatening the survival of the precious scraps of ancient forest, but when it rained, water was racing down the denuded slopes into the river so fast that the flow was washing away spawning gravels. The Forestry Commission demanded a cull, part of which was carried out from helicopters because of snowy conditions – a move that outraged the highly traditional deer stalking community.

With the estate in the Povlsens' hands and managed by WildLand, the intensity of culling increased. Every deer was now a target. While elsewhere forests are protected by fencing out deer, enclosing an estate of this size and topography would be astronomically expensive and require a constant programme of maintenance and inspection. And it would create a barrier to movement in the landscape, including by people, who have a codified freedom to roam responsibly in Scotland that the English wanderer can only dream of. Moreover, the cull is not intended to eliminate deer completely, just to severely limit their numbers. A few nibbling teeth actually help a regenerating forest develop a varied structure. Meanwhile, the shooting policy meant that the estate retained its stalkers – it is a mark of the Povlsens' approach that environmental restoration should not be at the expense of a traditional way of life. Deer are still free to enter the estate from neighbouring land, and once the forest is established, numbers may be allowed to increase again. Even so, this pockmarked dummy is the only deer I'm likely to see in Glen Feshie.

I'm back on the riverside, where a dirt road ends abruptly at a drop into the water – the onward route obliterated at the whim of the river. But there is another track, which brings me in time to a clearing where a pickup truck is parked next to a well-stocked woodstore and a neat stone building with smoke trailing from its chimney. It is the Ruigh Aiteachain bothy.

Through a window I glimpse a balding head with white hair, and by the time I get to the door, it is flung open. A man neatly dressed in a green jumper over a checked shirt beams at me though wire-framed spectacles. 'Welcome!'

I express surprise that the bothy is open, and he looks incredulous. 'But we're always open.'

'But, um ... the pandemic?' I'd checked the website of the Mountain Bothies Association before I left home, and it implied all bothies were closed until further notice.

The man smiles again. 'Well, we like to say that in Glen Feshie we do things differently. So let me pose you a question: are y'in need of shelter?'

I look down at myself. I'm so wet I may as well have swum there. He holds the door wider.

'I'm OK,' I say, 'But it might have been nice last night.'

'Oof! Were y'out in that?' he exclaims. 'You'll perhaps be in need of a coffee then. Mebbe some cake?'

And I find that I cannot refuse.

Two minutes later I'm ensconced on a bench in the cosiest of kitchen-living spaces. The place is so warm I have to peel off three sodden layers in a hurry to avoid passing out. I spread my waterproofs on another bench, where they dry in minutes, and put my boots by a glowing wood stove on which a huge kettle is rapidly coming to the boil. There are four other people there, two couples sitting spaced apart but otherwise they seem relaxed in a way I haven't seen in a public place for months. No one is wearing a facemask.

The man who invited me in is called Lindsay, and he has been here since February. 'When lockdown happened, we were told to go home and stay there,' he says. 'So I did.'

'You live here?'

'Oh, I have an address in Glasgow where the taxman sends his letters.' I get the feeling these are well-worn responses, but that he enjoys giving them.

'You're a warden?'

'No. I just like it here. I've been coming for sixty years. I've been retired thirty of those and these days I'm here about eleven months of the year.'

'What's it been like this year?'

'The first three weeks of lockdown I was entirely alone. We've had 350 overnight guests since March. Normally it would be 150 a week. But apart from those first few weeks, people have kept coming. A place like this meets certain needs, you know.'

'I bet you've seen some changes here in sixty years.'

His eyes light up. 'The last fifteen years have been absolutely wonderful.'

'Does everyone feel that way?' I ask. 'I mean, some of the changes can't have been easy for everyone.'

'Well, no. There was some resistance. The gamekeepers kept their jobs but they were told to stop doing all the things they'd been doing to benefit the deer and to start shooting them. These are smart, skilled people, but the complete change in mindset is a big ask. But I think everyone working here now can see the effect – the natural regeneration is amazing and the two million trees they've planted are doing well.'

I'm startled by that – I haven't seen anything that looked like recent planting. Lindsay explains that a lot of it is behind the existing blocks of plantation, so that when the time comes to fell or more likely to thin them, the visual impact won't be so great. 'But you've seen them alright,' he adds. 'You'll maybe not have realised because no deer means none of those plastic tree guards, you see. The planting is much less conspicuous.'

'What about voles?' asks one of the other guests – I get an impression he's an ecologist.

'Voles? Lovely!' grins Lindsay.

'Yes, but I mean, don't they strip the bark and kill the saplings?'

'Well they maybe do. But two million trees is a lot. Enough to live with some loss.'

The ecologist and I sip coffee and digest this.

'There were plenty of naysays,' Lindsay goes on. 'It's a very different way of doing things and lots of people said it was pointless and that some of the trees would never grow, especially higher up. But you can see the result.'

The bothy has been recently renovated and Lindsay is keen to show me round. There are two pine-boarded and resin-scented rooms upstairs, with room for several sleeping mats on the floor, and two rooms downstairs – the one we are using and another, similarly sized, both with deep benches along the wall. There's a storehouse outside and two continental-style squat toilets with buckets for flushing. It is the cleanest, tidiest, most homely bothy I've ever seen. Most are basic and some are outright hovels. This feels like the kind of place you could bring a family. I say so. 'Of course,' Lindsay beams, 'And people do. We still get groups of lads turning up expecting a squalid drinking den – some bothies are like that, you know, but when they arrive to find baby clothes and nappies on the washing line outside, they look at each other, there's a bit of muttering and they move on.'

I resolve to come back one day and stay. But the day is already half done and I want to see more of the glen before walking back out. I enquire where I should wash up my coffee cup, but Lindsay says 'Oh, leave it – Mary will be in later to clean up, she's a wonder.'

I'm trying to process the idea that this place has a housekeeper, but the conversation has moved on, and it's time I did as well. Fortified, and with a promise of tea and more cake on my way back if I need it, I continue up the glen, fording regular spills of water and little chugging burns. There are thickets of juniper and birch and dense patches of alder and willow scrub, alive with the *peee zee-zee, peee zee-zee-zee-zee* calls of long-tailed tits. A little further on I encounter a pair of bullfinches who keep up a back-and-forth *piuuu-piuu* either side of the path while I stand between them. But the grandees of this place are the pines. Broccoli-headed titans, spreading their arms wide to maximise the efficiency of their solar arrays. Passing through one stand of these giants I hear another, less familiar call – *p-chink, p-chink*, like pennies dropping into a piggy bank. Crested tits! I dig out my binoculars and use Nan Shepherd's technique of sitting against a trunk and waiting for them to forget I am there. It takes only a minute or two before the branches flicker with small feathery bombs of life with punky coifs and needle bills, moving incessantly in a sequence of dart, peer, probe, repeat.

I'm not sure if it's the confiding nature of the birds, the lifting of the clouds, or the warmth of hospitality at the bothy, but I'm feeling a kind of exultant belongingness. I've found my feet since yesterday, especially on the water crossings, where I suddenly seem able to hop from rock to rock without breaking stride.

The sun breaks through early in the afternoon and the hills arch their backs to it like cats stretching. When I drop my gaze from them back along the valley I've walked through, the whole place is popping with colour: the blue-green and russet-mauve of pine foliage and bark, *spumante* fountains of lemony birch, the fresher green of broom with its glossy black pods, the scarlet-pink of rowan leaves and the furnace red of rose hips. The birches growing higher up in more exposed locations are starting to show their naked beauty – a fuzz of purple that blurs with distance. There are fat fungi in chestnut brown, yellow and scarlet. The boulders are black, white and candy pink. And the river has all these colours and more, mingled with sky blue and peaty brown. The next shower of rain falls like wet glitter out of a mostly clear sky, there are rainbows in the mares' tails of water pouring off the side of the glen. I hold my arms out. It's an absolute wonderland.

Eventually, I run out of trees. The river is steeper, and narrower and I come to a place where it surges through a constriction and over a sill – a whooping thunderous flow, the kind that robs you of thought. I lie on the slab of rock with my head hanging over, wondering if I might see more salmon and mentally picking the line I'd paddle if I had to. Not that I ever will, but old habits die hard.

This is as far as I have time to go, but as I begin to retrace my steps a delicious thought occurs. I don't *have* to leave until tomorrow. I have a room booked in Aviemore, but I could cancel it if I can find a bit of phone signal. I retrace my steps to the bothy, where the kettle is still on, and ask if I might stay after all, and I am welcomed like an old friend.

The German couple I met in the morning are still here – it turns out Selina and Rob are regulars, with an easy, almost familial relationship with Lindsay. They've lived and worked as tour guides in Scotland for eight years – this year they have cancelled everything and are spending as much time in Glen Feshie as they can. Today they've been out collecting mushrooms, which are spread out to dry on the benches, filling the room with a cool, savoury aroma.

As dusk falls, Lindsay starts rummaging for provisions in several large tin boxes, and by five we are all eating. I'm given fish soup to go with my emergency noodles and a glass of wine, then Selina makes pancakes. I have little to offer but the remaining half-bag of slightly damp wasabi peas – they take a few, I suspect just to make me feel better.

The bothy is candle-lit, absurdly cosy. Lindsay fusses gently over everyone. Topping up glasses of wine, and then port, whisking away empty plates, washing and drying while we chat, refusing help. *Mary will be in later to clean up.* Of course, I twig, belatedly, there is no Mary.

I remember what he said this morning about being retired for 30 years and ask what he retired from so early. 'I was an engineer. I spent my career drilling oil wells, back when going down six hundred feet was a challenge. Now they drill in twelve thousand feet of water and thirty thousand into the rock. Even I can see it's a dangerous end game.'

'So, all this … giving and care-taking you do now. Is it–' I check myself. The question seems impertinent after all his kindness. But he's read me.

'– making amends? Maybe it is.'

There is talk of pine martens and golden eagles, of otters and water voles, and of a badger who spent three solid hours feeding on a deer carcass left nearby after they had taken the best cuts. 'It was so full it could hardly walk,' laughs Selina. They tell me black grouse are spreading out into new areas of habitat. That there are now 13 leks – smaller than before, but much more spread out.

Lindsay loves talking about salmon. He tells me about a researcher called Jane Grant who spent three years monitoring 140-plus redds in the valley and used to swim in the pool and feel fish bumping her.

'I taught her to girdle salmon – tickle them, you know – just for fun, of course. You'd lose your job, car and house for poaching around here.'

I ask what he thinks about fishing. 'Of course we netted too many. I know folk who supported their families on twelve weeks' netting a year. That kind of taking can't be right. But the fly fishing, that's different. It's about appreciating the fish, and they get put back.'

Selina plays with a candle, incinerates a dead fly.

There is always work to do, they tell me. Repairing footpaths and other mischief done by the burns and the river, maintaining the bothy. They have plans to plant apple, cherry and plum trees around the bothy. 'We already have currants and gooseberries.'

I wonder how all this is funded, and again the response is puzzlement. 'We don't need funding. We just do it.'

'It's Glen Feshie ... ' says Selina. 'We do things differently.'

By eight o'clock it feels like we've talked late into the night. Perhaps sensing the previous sleepless night catching up with me, the others all say they are ready for bed. After they turn in I hang the rest of my damp kit out to air and settle on a bench. In the candlelight it looks like the house in a fairytale. The remains of Selina's fly are wicking wax, flaming like the moth in Annie Dillard's towering essay, 'The Death of a Moth'. I fall into a solid, exhausted sleep.

I'm woken by a thunderous sound. Having experienced a couple of night-time earthquakes before, I'm on my feet even before I'm awake, before I've remembered where I am, heart racing, convinced something seismic has happened. I find my torch and cast it over the room – over the huge painting of a stag on the wall, the gingham tablecloth, the candle lanterns, the clean pans hanging motionless in an alcove beside the chimney breast. All is still, and silent. I can't hear the wind or the river, and yet the sound I'm sure I just heard replays in my head, crash by rumbling crash. I think it came from higher up the glen. If not an earthquake, then a rock fall, I reason. A big one, down one of those steep gullies. The clock on my phone says 3.50 am. Ten to four. Again. There's no sound of movement from upstairs and after a few minutes I sit down, then get back under my sleeping bag and drift into an uneasy doze, hearing that smashing rumble over and over and wondering what new shape the world has taken, out there in the dark.

The others appear at seven, and to my astonishment not one of them heard a thing. I can't have dreamt it. I try a few ways to describe the noise: like simultaneous thunder and lightning; like an earthquake; like an explosion in a quarry. They look blank until I say, 'Like someone tipped a hundred tonnes of rock down a mountain,' and Lindsay laughs.

'Ah, I bet that's exactly it. That'll have been Dave, the estate manager. Contractors are coming to make a new access track up there. I expect he thought he'd get an early start and deliver the stone up for them.'

'At ten to four in the morning?' What kind of madman moves bits of mountains around by himself in the dark, I wonder.

'Well, he often starts at five and he'll maybe not have realised the clocks have gone back. He'll be wanting to get as much as he can done before winter comes,' says Lindsay.

'It's Glen Feshie ... ' says Selina, smiling.

Yes. They do things differently.

When I walk out a little later, there is a rainbow, because of course there is. It spans the whole valley, like a grand gateway. This place is the antithesis of preservation, of ecological conservatism. It is change, but at nature's mixed pace, some fast, some slow. There is balance here, but a dynamic kind, achieved through something like faith. A bit like kayaking; you have to let go a little in order to feel the flow. Lean into the turns. Embrace the mess. Don't fight it, ride it. Use the eddies to rest or read what is coming. Push at the right time. And never, ever give up.

Flowover

Drain *An artificial channel created and maintained to remove water from a wetland. Also dike; dyke; rhyne; main; ditch; grip.*

Like beavers, we've been tinkering with flow for thousands of years. Not just in Britain but the world over. Since ancient Sumerians, inspired by the benevolent, nutrient-rich flood waters of the Tigris, began creating irrigation channels in southern Mesopotamia, now northern Iraq, around 7000 BC, we have sought to modify, control, contain and divert rivers to our own ends, for farming and for power – energetic, political and economic. In Britain, most of our tinkering has achieved the opposite of beaver workings, resulting in the drainage of vast areas of floody land and a paring-back of biological richness.

The drainage of Holderness in East Yorkshire started at Meaux Abbey, where monks first entertained the idea that the surrounding carr, bog, fen and marsh might be engineered into something else. Something more productive and biddable; less hostile and wild. The technique spread, and huge areas of wetland across the region were developed into viable farms. I visit one with Jon Traill.

In almost every way the farm is a model of environmental custodianship – full of birds, organic, focusing on sustainability and biodiversity; there is even a little education centre. But Jon tells me the drains are still cleared of vegetation every year, and this management won't change for fear of relinquishing a tight grip on drainage, not even to help water voles. Flooding is anathema, and drainage trumps all. It's the same in almost any agricultural area. In a blog for SCOTLAND: The Big Picture, hill farmer and conservationist Patrick Laurie recalled a conversation with another farmer who claimed that 'drainage and clearance were some of the fundamental basics of agriculture, and he even implied that I was less of a farmer for failing to do similar work on my own ground.' I know Laurie is far from the only future-facing farmer to experience criticism from his fellows, and Jon nods when I say so. 'But that's going to change. Already in their heart of hearts I think even the most stubborn souls know that they are on borrowed time. We all are. Water will rise, and water will win.'

We reach the corner of a field and he points to the place where two ditches cross. A mundane thing – at first – and it takes a while for me to understand what Jon wants me to see. When I look properly I realise this is not an intersection or a confluence, but a sort of watery flyover. A *flowover*. Somehow these two ditches have converged at different levels so that one crosses the other in a sort of miniature aqueduct. It's a hint at the complexity of a system of becks and drains covering much of Holderness, like a gigantic Escher puzzle. Similar systems exist across other vast areas of reclaimed land in the Fens and the Levels.

Jon explains that the result of intensive drainage is often a perched watercourse – a flow running above the level of land that has shrunk, partly through drying out, but also as a result of centuries of ploughing, harvesting, runoff and wind erosion. The result, in some places like this, is a system of channels on subtly different levels.

'Now try and imagine this system, which runs on gravity, extending over hundreds of square kilometres.' He tells me about a book in which I'll find schematics of some of the drainage systems of the Hull Valley. 'They'll mess with your head,' he promises. I find the book, *Becks, Banks, Drains and Brains*, produced by a local heritage group, and in it the diagrams Jon described. They look like tube maps – with unlikely angles and crossovers. For flows to cross, they must be engineered over a huge area, flowing on tiny gradients and requiring constant and meticulous effort to maintain. Perhaps it's not surprising almost everyone involved is a little paranoid. If land can be said to have a will, these places yearn to be wet.

CHAPTER 18

Confluence and influence

He flew vigorously to one corner of his compartment, and, after waiting there a second, flew across to the other. What remained for him but to fly to a third corner and then to a fourth? That was all he could do, in spite of the size of the downs, the width of the sky, the far-off smoke of houses, and the romantic voice, now and then, of a steamer out at sea.

Virginia Woolf, 'The Death of the Moth'

Rodmell in East Sussex is a mostly flint-and-brick village, but the last house on the right at the bottom is weatherboarded and a little larger than most. Monk's House was for more than 20 years the home of Virginia and Leonard Woolf. On an early spring day in 1941, Virginia left it for the last time. She walked out across the Brooks – a flat expanse reclaimed from the River Ouse – and when she reached the river she loaded her coat pockets with rocks and did what she described in a letter to Leonard as 'what seems the best thing to do'.

That was 28th March. Now it's late April 80 years later, and having parked in the small National Trust car park, facing a verge thick with alkanet and deadnettle in full bloom, and cow parsley coming, I can't help but wonder, naively, what might have been if Woolf had held on a few more weeks. Whether spring might have saved her, even though the war dragged on. Because right now, with the birds singing and the sun warming me through the windscreen, this sheltered spot seems so very sweet. She went while the blossom was still packed tight. Perhaps she saw the violets coming and acted before they summoned an army of other spring flowers to coax her back from the brink. Perhaps it would have made no difference. Her body wasn't found for three weeks, but was still close by – maybe the tide had taken her back and forth through the landscape she had loved as it greened and bloomed and swelled with birdsong and insect murmur.

The house is closed for the pandemic, so all I can do is peek over the fence. The house is pretty but not saccharine, with a grey shingled gable and wavy fascia boards. There's a substantial conservatory to the rear and above it, in the steeply pitched roof, a pair of dormer windows and a small balcony with a sun-bleached wooden rail. It looks an easy-living kind of place.

Those windows though. They remind me of Woolf's essay, 'The Death of the Moth' – published a year after her own passing. Which window was it, I wonder, that she watched a dying hay-coloured day-flying moth cross and cross again, spellbound in its last minutes of life by the great indifferent power of the world beyond the glass?

A temporary sign apologises for the closure of the house and begs respect for the privacy of the tenants. It hadn't occurred to me that people would still live here, and I guiltily pocket the phone I've been using as a periscope to pry.

There's an unmetalled track leading out to the river. I've barely left the village when the wind picks up – a fierce cold blast barrelling down from Beddingham Hill. It's as if I've crossed a boundary into an altogether more harsh reality. I pass some shabby stables and chicken sheds and fields edged with reedy ditches. Rusting skeletons and carapaces of farm machinery lie spaced out like exhibits on a dismal sculpture trail with a gang of crows processing solemnly between them as if following a tour. Behind lines of electric fence horses have their heads bent to grass so short and thin it looks like hard work to make a mouthful. Reeds and silt dredged from the ditches lie in bone-dry heaps. Empty plastic feed tubs and salt buckets roll around in the wind and some of them look like they've been doing so for years.

'I fear I'm going mad again,' Woolf wrote. I picture her walking – coat wrapped around her, or maybe open and flapping in this gnawing wind – and I feel a little mad myself. But it's a grumpy mad rather than a despairing one. A this-isn't-what-I-had-in-mind mad. I round a bend in the track, and the wind comes full in my face.

On reaching a flood bank, I scramble up for a first sight of the river. I've imagined this place so wrong. If you've watched Nicole Kidman sink artfully in to rippling green water in *The Hours*, forget that. There is no Ophelia-esque melodious lay to be had here. It's not green and reedy. There are no trees and no flowers. There is no structure, no riffle or lap. The channel is wide and wholly engineered; the river an incarcerated beast racing low and swift between banks of quarried grey stones the size of small loaves of bread. The lower ones are heaped in wrack and below the waterline I can see tresses of green gutweed. From a swimming or kayaking perspective it's flowing terrifyingly fast – the tide must be ebbing. There are no eddies, nowhere to stop and rest. I instinctively look for safe egress routes. One of the cleft rail fences that seem to be a vernacular feature of the Sussex countryside drops down to the water. Once in the river, grabbing one of those would be the only realistic chance of getting out, but with the tide running like this it would be desperate stuff.

There are rivers like this all around the country, straightened, simplified, walled in, banked up, all to ensure water is moved on as efficiently as possible. You can usually tell if a river crossing a floodplain has been modified, because natural flows have a tendency to curve. Like that moth in thrall to light at a window, the behaviour of a canalised river is simplified, stereotyped. It cannot see out, it cannot speak to the land. It just presses on, head down, responsive only to gravity, and in this case, the tidal tug of the Moon.

The water is a shade greener than khaki. Wrinkles and reflected ripples crosshatch it like anaconda scales. There is a gleam to it, but no joy. There is nothing in this channel for the river to play with, no jink or jostle. Now and then the wind presses flat footprints in the surface and they elongate and curl into question marks.

The path along the flood bank is easy and wide, the kind that invites conversation because it requires so little thought to walk. There is nothing to step over or around. No gradient you'd notice. A couple walk past briskly, collars turned up. 'Well, that's the seven-year itch, isn't it,' says the man. 'That's how long it takes for people to grow in different ways.'

A pair of little egrets overtake me and at Southease Bridge I meet a group of younger people dressed with casual, offbeat panache – one in a white Panama, one a folded beanie, girls in skinny jeans and deep turnups. 'Yeah, he did the whole Nazi thing, greased-back hair, moustache, leather coat...'

'No!'

'Yes, he really did.'

The bridge is a pale green iron structure, but with wooden piers to deflect the flotsam that must routinely smash into it. It once swung, I gather, to allow boat traffic to pass, but was locked in place in the eighties. A dense hawthorn offers some respite from the wind, and I use a bench beneath it to eat my packed lunch. A couple of bikes rumble over the bridge and I hear young, strong voices ringing with all the relief of spring sunshine and another lockdown over.

'Today is a good day!'

'A day of days!'

They shake me out of my mood. It *is* a good day, I think. There's really nothing of Woolf here, why would there be? Then my eye is caught by a movement over my shoulder. A day-flying moth flickers by, grey and primrose-yellow, with nothing but the width of the sky between it and the downs.

Cambridge is an awkward city to drive around and after a wrong turn I find myself lost among the glittering steel, plate glass and curved concrete of the Biomedical Campus that continues to grow around Addenbrooke's and Papworth Hospitals. I pull over to consult the map on my phone and spot a familiar name: Nine Wells Wood, the setting of the final chapter of Robert Macfarlane's *Underland*. I have some spare time, and remembering the springs Rob described, I can't resist going for a look. I find my way around a tract of chalky farmland to a layby and set off on foot. I skirt a field so vast and empty it makes my stomach clench. The recently tilled soil is bonemeal dry. Enthusiasm for this little exploration starts to ebb and I try to focus on the skylark song that is raining down – imagining their hearts as tiny steampunky engines attempting to produce enough of the stuff that souls are made of to bring life to the desert below. At the bottom of the field is a more substantial hedge – a really good one, with tall ash, hawthorn, hazel, beech and dogwood, all in fresh spring leaf. A waft of warm Mediterranean scent leads me to a mass of ground ivy, thronging with eager bees and bee-flies. When I raise my head from them I find myself staring into the crusty sockets of an almost fleshless skull. The carcass of a bird is suspended in the branches just about head height. The tree is a dogwood, named *Cornus sanguinea* for the bloody colour of its branches, whose straight growth was ideal for making arrows. The colour of the stems and the posture of the carcass create a sense of ceremony – this is a sky burial. The trachea is exposed, and with its annular ridges it looks like a component from some early electrical device. How did it come to be here? The skeleton appears to be complete from beak tip to small claws. The body feathers have fallen away with the flesh, but the wings and tail are intact enough to identify it as woodpigeon. There's no firm perch above from which a bird of prey might have dropped it. Was it shot? Or was it struck down and lost by one of the peregrines that nest around the city? The empty skull isn't telling.

On the other side of the hedge is a chalky path lined with more ivied ash and also blackthorn, dogwood, field maple, guelder rose and wayfaring trees in full flower. The soundscape becomes closer and more intimate, including the excitable helter-skelter of dunnocks, the free-form flutey-toot of a blackcap. It's a surprise to come to a new wood, not marked on the map. It is densely planted and incredibly species-rich. I walk on, conflicted by this place that seems to be both desert and oasis, with life and death in overt competition for my attention.

The feeling intensifies at the entrance to Nine Wells Wood itself. There's an interpretation board explaining that it was once a Site of Special Scientific Interest but was stripped of its status after losing the unlikely stars of its invertebrate fauna, a rare caddis fly and two species of flatworm, as a result of the drought of 1976. The site is even smaller than I expected, at three acres, scarcely bigger than a rugby pitch. And yet, crossing the threshold you find a place that feels not only bigger on the inside, but older, and deeper.

The springs have steep banks, whose topography suggests that the water is lower than it should be – no surprise in this incredibly dry April. For the most part the banks are clad in moss, ivy and hart's-tongue fern, but there are a few slithery access points where the geology is exposed: chalky clay with embedded pebbles and boulders – some so closely set they might be a human-made wall. The water is crystal clear and so still that at first glance you'd think there was no flow at all. So still that a smooth blue rubber dog ball on the bottom has collected a cap of fine sediment to match that lying thickly over the bed of leaf litter.

According to the information board these leaves, mostly from beeches planted many decades ago, are problematic, causing acidification of the water. The channel leading away from the springhead narrows and the flow becomes more obvious where it finds its way around weeds or trailing branches, resulting in fingerprint whorls, and slight wrinkles in the surface. Stems of dog rose loop out over a pair of mallards rummaging among long, lobed leaves of water weed. There's intense bird activity in the trees: I can hear the *wheeep* and *creeeeek* of greenfinches, see-sawing chiffchaffs, and the furtive rustles of a blackbird fossicking in the crispy beech leaves: toss and pause, toss and pause – quick movements that appear bad-tempered but probably reflect a need to listen for danger between bouts of noisy rummaging.

These springs were, for 250 years from the early seventeenth century, the main source of clean water for the city of Cambridge. There's a monument in a corner of the wood commemorating the construction of the conduit that channelled their flow via a series of sluices, gutters and runnels into the market place and the basements and yards of colleges and the old hospital. But over-abstraction from the aquifer has dwindled the flow and most of these are now sealed off.

I find a larger springhead at the southern edge of the wood. It is a grey and solemn sort of rising – no rush or gurgle – the issuing of water so slight that the flow is scarcely perceptible. But I sit and watch for a while and begin to notice trembling and darting movements in the grey silt. There is life there, though I'm seeing water disturbance rather than the animals that make it. After a few minutes I notice flashes and sparks, and having trained my eye, I realise these are happening several times a second across the pool-bed. It takes a while to understand they are the result of very small objects striking the water – particles of dust perhaps. The impacts cause minute concavities in the surface tension that momentarily focus sunlight into intense flares, but they happen so fast that by the time I fix on them properly there is nothing to see but tiny spreading ripples.

It's not creepy in this little enclave, exactly, but mysterious. It seems scarcely possible that just a few hundred metres away are the gleaming architecture, frontier science and helipad of the Biomedical Campus, a new flyover, rumbling trains and the barren expanse of that prairie-like field. Part of the magic is the size of the trees – some big old hollies, alder, cherry, ash and towering beeches – but mainly it's the way that water, emerging after so long in the dark, plays with light and vice versa: a strange, silent merging of the essence of a planet and the luminous song of a star. It feels like a natural waypoint, a transition, but also a place of communion – a mingling of flows from limitless beyonds. A point on the circumference of a circle bigger than anything I can hold in my mind, but whose completeness I can sometimes, almost, sense.

Several of the beeches bear arboroglyphs. I feel a pull to make my own mark, but this is my first visit, and a short one, and I haven't earned any right to impose myself. So instead I stand at the edge of the water with the sun behind me and my shadow waves in it. The flow carries the salute off and away, to wherever it goes next.

In Grantchester, I park near the pub named for the unreasonably beautiful Rupert Brooke who never grew old, and push through a clattering metal gate onto the meadows. A herd of dark red bullocks, some standing, some lying down, blink long lashes at me, making slow sounds of bovine content: huffs and soft belches. Starlings whirr up from amongst the herd, where they have been raiding cowpats for insects.

Virginia Woolf was part of the Grantchester set as well as the Bloomsbury. After the bleakness of the Ouse, I want to imagine her happy, that's all, really. She swam here in the Granta (which becomes the Cam in Cambridge) with Brooke, who wrote longingly of the setting while homesick in Berlin in *The Old Vicarage, Grantchester*.

The water is the green of a lapwing's back, with a faint hint of oily blue. It's not entirely attractive – there are peelings of brown scuzz similar to those I'm familiar with on the Derwent, whose origin might be storm drains or sewers, but the water is otherwise clear enough that I can see the bottom a couple of metres down.

In the willows on the opposite bank a sedge warbler is shouting its tiny head off. It has bold head markings like those intricate hairstyles with close-clipped tramlines favoured by urban cool kids. The song is extraordinarily loud and abrasive, and between whistles and flutes there are chacking, churring, buzzing raps. The singer moves irritably from branch tip to base and descends often among the tangle of bare, grey branches that hang in the water – submerged too often to bear leaves. They look like mangroves. The bird dips its narrow beak into the water and I wonder if that's because singing so loud makes its throat raw. Cooling sip, and go again. Or perhaps it's not drinking but feeding – the aquatic larvae of various insects could be clinging to those branches. A moorhen approaches, gets harangued by the tiny gangster-warbler and retreats with a reproachful-sounding *puuuuurrrrrp*. There is the richer flutier song of a blackcap too – now *that's* a warble. This would be a drowse-inducing spot were it not for the sedgie's ravings.

The banks are grazed to neat turf and the places where cattle drink look like bitemarks in the bank, made by some fluvial leviathan. These embayments are shallow and warm and teeming with tiny fish, which gather in the hoofmarks on the muddy bottom to feed on algae. After watching for a few minutes I move too abruptly and they explode like an underwater firework then coalesce again into a cyclonic school. These gently sloping dips could provide access for swimming but I fear I might sink beyond my knees in the mud and have to beg one of Grantchesters' exceptionally well-dressed dogwalkers for rescue. So I walk on.

A minute or two later I hear whistling. Not absent-minded or tuneless noisemaking, and not the kind of whistle you'd use to call a dog, but a real melody.

A man with a ponytail is lying on the bank on his belly, head and shoulders out over the water, and whistling a tune

with a twirling *Blue Danube*-y vibe. I pause, hoping he hasn't
noticed me because I want to listen longer. A pair of mallards
with a flotilla of new ducklings have approached to circle
beneath him – there's an exchange of some kind going on,
unspoken. When he stands to leave I want to ask what the
birds told him about how they are doing and what news
there is from the river, because it seems he must know. But I
balk, and what comes out sounds banal. 'The ducks like your
whistling.'

'The ducks just think I mean food.' And though they
follow him as he walks downstream, I refuse to believe that
a man who makes private music for birds believes that for a
minute.

I pass several pollarded willows with explosive coiffes of
regrowth in fresh yellow-green leaf. Somewhere on this
stretch of river in a hollow willow trunk, there rested for a
time a terracotta head: a poor, troubling likeness of the
poet Sylvia Plath made by a student friend. She and Ted
Hughes, to whom she was (disastrously) married, both
wrote about her struggle to come up with an appropriate
way to dispose of it, and how they eventually came here
and consigned it to the willow.

I think of a toad in Calderdale, West Yorkshire, which I
always do when I think of Plath because, one day when I
walked to see her grave at Heptonstall near Hebden Bridge,
I met a man called Nick who told me a story. Walking up
Hebden Beck, we had fallen into conversation about the
River Calder, and the floods that had devastated the area
twice in recent years. The first time, he said, he had been
forced to abandon his car and walked for hours to get home.
Arriving after dark, exhausted and soaked to the skin, he
noticed that a toad had joined him on the doorstep. Realising
he had left his keys in the car, he knocked and waited. The
toad waited also, and when the door opened and warm light
flooded out into the night, it scrambled ahead of him, into
the house.

And then I think of another poet, Polly Aktin, who I've not met beyond social media, but hope to – in a lake, perhaps, where she has some release from pain and fatigue resulting from an inherited condition. I think of the frogs she writes of in her poem *Pond Life*, which migrate through her house as they do through ours from time to time: 'I count frogs to bring myself to the limits of sleep or mammalian life.' Those taxonomic limits, I think, only exist if we look out from the tips of our branch of the family tree. Follow the branch down, and up again and there is a perfect continuum from me to say, Polly, or to Plath and the unnamed student who sculpted her head; to the Woolfs, to Brooke or to anyone who has swum here; to the duck-whistling man and in fact, to the ducks, or the amphibians or any of the beings that swim or sip or trail branches or fronds in the water, or reach for it with root and filament, or whose cells swell with the same old stuff that has sustained a million before. There are no missing links on any journey from branch to branch of this strange, beautiful tree, just an unbroken line of relations, with a river flowing through them all.

Ted Hughes' poem *The Earthenware Head*, written long after Plath's suicide, suggests she had second thoughts about abandoning the sculpture and went back to the river to look but never found it. He envisioned it, deathless, in the river. Perhaps it is there still.

The biggest of the willows I encounter has an entirely hollow trunk. It's a bit like a sentry box, or actually, given that it is perched right on the water's edge, a changing cubicle. The opening that faces the river has a large burl at hand height, whose wood has been smoothed by touch, and the tree's roots form rungs which I think might allow me to get in and out of the water. The inner walls are charred, glossy black and scaly, and decked with cobwebs and the dry, gleaming slime trails of slugs. My own breathing sounds loud in there. It is both secret and public, and it reeks of something bodily and basic. As if my thoughts have formed a bubble outside, I hear a voice – older, male, chuckling. 'Whoa. The stories that tree could tell.'

The couple move on. I use the willow cubicle to change into my swimsuit and climb down the roots into the water. It's deep and weedy, the bottom silky soft. The mallards return with a bold enquiry about snacks, and I push a little bow wave with my hands to shoo them off. The male is magnificent. Plump, glossy, immaculate, his colours gleam like fresh enamel: inky blue, racing green, and his breast has the lustre and swell of polished walnut burr-wood. Only his tangerine feet don't fit – they are ridiculous compared to the rest of him. But they propel him swiftly and as he goes, he jettisons a squirt of excrement, which separates into a milky cloud and a darker pellet that sinks fast. There are worse things in the water than duck shit, I'm sure. More big flakes of that brown scum for starters. But fortunately, the current is entraining the surface flotsam down one side of the channel and it's easy enough to avoid. The water is chilly so I swim hard upstream for five minutes, feeling the weed stroke my legs, but making so little progress against the flow that it takes just a minute to skim back to the tree and haul out on the roots.

A few months later King's College, which owns Grantchester Meadows, makes an ill-advised attempt to ban swimming and paddling there – another knee-jerk reaction to the post-lockdown surge in public need for green and blue space. Twenty thousand people sign a petition, and the College backtracks within weeks. Meanwhile the Cam is regularly contaminated with farm pollution and sewage and the Nine Wells springs run at a fraction of their capacity. These are not problems created by the public: who would seriously think it might be a good idea to run out of water or poison a river? Water authorities propose augmenting the springs with water pumped from elsewhere in the already stressed aquifer and recharging what should be pristine groundwater with treated effluent. With things this bad, swimming bans are not part of any meaningful river protection. Actions that would help include reducing leakage, the use of treated grey water to irrigate crops rather than gold standard chalk river water, and for us all to use less of the good stuff. Massive public education is going to be crucial in an increasingly water-stressed future, and a good place to start would be by encouraging people to get to know their local river more, not banning them from it. Any action that increases public isolation from nature is potentially disastrous. How would a moth eking out its short life flickering at a window pane know or care if the world beyond the glass was poisoned?

A river released

Meander A sinuous mobile curve in a river channel, whose form and position changes through the dynamic processes of erosion on the faster-flowing outside of the bend and deposition on the slower-flowing inside.

Canalisation The process of artificially straightening, directing or restricting a river by modification of its banks and channel, usually as part of a flood management, irrigation or drainage scheme. Sometimes also referred to as channelisation.

Where rivers run on slight gradients, they like to wander. So much so that any you see running straight over broadly level plains for more than ten times their length have almost certainly been artificially straightened – usually to create space for farming or development, or to hasten water on its way. A straightened or canalised river is also a shortened one, so unless the channel also becomes bigger or deeper, water has less space, flows faster and flooding is more likely. Hence canalised rivers are often hemmed in by raised banks or levees. This treatment tends to increase the risk of flooding downstream. This is what happened on a relatively small scale in the small Lakeland valley of Swindale in Cumbria, part of the area now managed as both a reserve and working farmland by the RSPB. I visited with ecologist Lee Schofield in 2020, and he gave me a tour.

When he came to Swindale, Lee says, the beck was ruler straight and uniformly deep and the speed of its flow contributed to regular flooding downstream. Salmon were seen, but the river lacked suitable spawning sites. 'I don't judge the people that did it – life must have been incredibly tough here, farming is marginal and back then they were trying to grow and rear everything they needed. They did what made sense, and they couldn't afford flooding to wreck their hay meadows.'

But following the winter flooding of 2015/16, the reduced water capacity of catchments like Swindale made much less sense. Perhaps flooding here, the thinking went, should be considered an ecosystem service worth investing in. The solution was drastic – a wholesale remodelling of part of the valley – but faced with a £500-million regional bill for damage caused by Storm Desmond, so-called Natural Flood

Management schemes started to seem like good value. The plan was simple enough: to excavate a new re-wiggled channel based on geo-physical evidence for the route the beck might once have taken. The excavators encountered a problem at the lower end, however, when the reassuring deposits of gravel indicating a previous riverbed disappeared.

'We'd got it wrong. We were now forcing a completely new route and making a vast muddy mess in the process,' says Lee, 'but at that stage, we had little choice. We made the channel wider at that point to try and slow the flow and reduce the scouring effect, but that was all we could do.'

Fish were collected from the old straight channel, which was then dammed, forcing water into the new sinuous one. 'That happened on a Friday, and then that weekend a massive summer downpour caused the whole valley to flood. I was in a panic,' Lee told me. 'The channel was nowhere to be seen under the floodwater, and I was sure all the excavated soil we'd heaped up was going to be washed downstream. I fully expected a scene of devastation by the time we got back here on the Monday. But when I arrived, I couldn't believe it. Not only was the water running in the new channel, it was running clear. And even this awful mudbath section had a new bed of gleaming gravel, freshly delivered by the flood. New bars and riffles had formed, transforming the bland new channel into something that already resembled a natural river. A process we thought might take years had happened in a weekend. And you know what else? Salmon were spawning here within months.'

It was far from a *fait accompli* but that's the point. The beck is now free to change as it will, and Lee's wonder, even five years on, at the seasonal – sometimes daily – changes, wrought by the newly dynamic flow is infectious. We wade though areas of wet ground – recently collapsed banks, zones of active erosion and deposition. In time this river will writhe like a snake all over the plain, which is now thick with flowers; he points out melancholy thistle, globeflower and great burnet, bistort, knapweed, devil's bit scabious, eyebright, heath spotted orchids, ragged robin, yellow rattle – a joyous throng of colour and insect hum.

CHAPTER 19

The Mucky Beck

A small dale nestles in the eastern Pennines, riddled with springs that gather into more than a dozen becks that hurry downhill. In the valley bottom, where the largest flow once spread wide and shallow enough to cross with ease, a settlement developed in early medieval times. The town this settlement on the 'broad ford' became, Bradford, was well placed for processing wool, with good grazing land around and the flow of the beck to power mills and carry away waste. In 1530 a new channel or 'goit' was constructed to carry water along a contour, greatly increasing the number of mills it could power and the area over which industry could be carried out. And so it has been for almost 500 years – the beck repeatedly diverted and harnessed, channelised, canalised, culverted, imprisoned, dammed. Worse abuses have been visited on the water itself. The business of cleaning wool, known as fulling, is a mucky one – more than half the weight of unwashed fleece comprises mud, dust, faeces and lanolin, the grease that coats sheep hair. These are natural substances, but the process by which they decay in water devours oxygen and produces hydrogen sulphide, and as cottage industry gave way to factory-scale operations, the once sparkling, trout-filled stream became unliveable for anything but bacteria.

The population of Bradford boomed in the nineteenth century with an influx of low-paid mill workers, many of whom lived in conditions of scarcely imaginable squalor. Everything from increasingly diverse industrial effluents to human sewage went into what had by then become known as the Mucky Beck. But nowhere was filth more lucrative. By the 1860s Bradford claimed to be the richest town in the world, and was almost certainly also the most polluted. A public health official visiting in 1843 reported the filthiest town he had ever seen. If you were lucky enough to own a silver watch case, it would tarnish in your pocket if you spent too much time in the pall of hydrogen sulphide hovering over the coal-black water.

The first sewer in Bradford was built in 1862. While the installation of flushing toilets made some lives more sanitary, waste that had previously been collected from unplumbed privies for use as fertiliser was now flushed directly into watercourses. Within ten years there were more than 100 miles of sewers discharging two million gallons of waste into the beck every day. The problems were compounded by the routine diversion of beck water to feed a sluggish canal. Low flows resulted in stagnant conditions in which the water could be ignited with a match, and the flames would rise six feet high.

A sewage works was built at Frizinghall in 1873, but typically for Bradford, this was not a public or environmental health scheme, but a muck-and-brass commercial enterprise – an effort to extract lanolin from the water for making soap. This business collapsed within a year or two, but an industrial scale works built later at Esholt by Bradford Corporation did turn a profit out of lanolin and concentrated semi-solid waste known as sludge cake, which was sold as fertiliser. The liquid drained off was returned to the beck more or less untreated. Meanwhile local mineworks meant that several of the tributary becks often ran red with ochre. Some of them still do.

During the Industrial Revolution, when increasingly polluted water became a blight, the obvious solution was to wall it in, cover it up. Locations on the city's becks and the goit had become premium land, characterised by massive mill buildings and canyonlike streets, but with little evidence of a watercourse, except when it burst out of its culverts after heavy rain, which, having been robbed of floodplain, it regularly did until an underground flood relief channel was created in the early 1990s. This continues to divert high flows almost a mile around the worst pinch points.

Bradford's fortunes have fallen since its industrial boomtime, but building land is still too valuable for private owners to consider restoring any green or watery space. Even where land is publicly owned, there is the problem that often it is contaminated with undocumented industrial waste from mills, tanneries, dyeworks and chemical factories, some of it local, more still imported for backfill or simply dumped.

I take a spring walk with the Friends of Bradford Becks (FOBBs), led by Andrew Mindham of Bradford City Council, Nick Milsom of the Aire Rivers Trust and Rob Hellawell who glories in the title of Pollution Hunter. We cross busy roads, pass tyre shops, takeaways and discount supermarkets, and meet the beck under a railway bridge where a detailed graffito of a marbled white butterfly dances above a collection of discarded energy drink cans and burger boxes.

Upstream is an area of dereliction, where the banks are nonetheless green and lined with trees – cherry, horse chestnut, holly, oak, birch and hawthorn, the larger ones with ivy-clad trunks. There are grey wagtails, and Andrew tells me he has seen dippers, herons and kingfishers here too. And there are fish, thanks to modification works carried out on several barriers downstream. A recent electrofishing survey yielded trout, bullheads, minnows and an eel. A little further upstream, Andrew shows the group where bank restoration efforts are helping more plants become established at the water's edge.

Just below Briggate Bridge the river jinks around a bend with a lively little rapid made of mossy masonry that passes for boulders. The sun sparkles on the water, overhanging willows are coming into leaf and the bank is thick with rushes, forget-me-nots, cow parsley and red campion. Opposite on a high bank is a new housing development, where gardens back onto the water. They have high gravel-boarded fences but I can imagine gates in those panels and children swarming down to the water with nets or toy boats. The youngsters dabble, poke about, hop on stepping stones; older ones idle, laugh, show off.

But in the real world, a few metres upstream is what looks like a concrete bunker with narrow horizontal slots for windows. This is what is known as a combined sewer overflow or CSO. Next to it is another concrete slab with a manhole cover. The cover has buckled. And sprayed like vomit down the bank from both the CSO and the manhole are two fans of stinking debris – sanitary products and wet wipes, condoms, clumps of toilet papier-mâché. A fiesta of flushed unmentionables; the stuff we'd rather not deal with because we can't stand the emissions of our own bodies.

Life as we know it is, dare I write it, *moist.* A survey by the *New Yorker* suggests this to be one of the most hated words in the English language, and a follow-up study suggested the aversion relates not to the sound of the word, as some respondents claimed, but to an association with body fluids. No matter that it is our very moistness that allows us to function: we just can't abide those slick, slimy, essential fluids. And because muck means money to be made, our aversion has been exploited and amplified by an entire industry devoted to obsessive personal hygiene. *Look at the purity of this airbrushed skin,* coo a thousand advertisements. *See, this squeaky-clean baby, this pristine child, this odourless body, this whiter-than-white underwear! Imagine this safe and sanitary easy-wipe life! And best of all, flushable! All evidence of your disgusting leaks, your unacceptable moistness, gone, just like that!*

Our house is Regency in age, if not architecture, and has no mains drainage. When we moved in we had to adjust to the dubious novelty of a septic tank and wonky old pipes. One carelessly disposed wet wipe or sanitary pad is enough to have the downstairs toilet backing up or waste bubbling into the back yard. This kind of thing changes your idea of what's flushable pretty fast, but most households don't have to deal with such things. Press the lever – it's gone. Except it isn't, not really. The consequences still exist, but they are elsewhere: sanitary products and condoms swirling in eddies and festooning tree branches, wet wipes forming huge microfibre reefs in larger rivers like the Thames.

There are two main types of sewerage in the UK. Modern 'separate' systems send foul (toilet) waste and grey water (from baths and washing machines) into one set of pipes for treatment and discharge into a river or the sea, while surface water (rain from gutters and drains) goes into a separate system, discharging directly into the nearest watercourse. In older 'combined' systems, like those under much of Bradford, one set of pipes takes everything: foul, grey and surface water. Because rain falls in pulses, the volume of surface water varies vastly over time, and heavy rain can result in bottlenecks at treatment plants. The increased runoff as more land is built on, and more gardens and amenity areas are paved or plastic-turfed for parking or ease of maintenance, means there is ever more surface water to deal with. To avoid the risk of raw sewage bubbling up in streets or houses, water treatment companies have special permission to divert untreated combined discharges, including rain, runoff, bathwater, kitchen wastes, laundry water, toilet flushings and commercial effluent directly into rivers, under extreme circumstances. These emergency outlets are CSOs, and there are tens of thousands of them around the country. Rob Hellawell thinks there are 50 or 60 on Bradford Beck, but no one knows exactly because many are old and even the water company don't claim to know the full anatomy of the system under the city.

Exactly what constitutes the kind of extreme circumstances under which CSO releases are permissible is not written down. And in a privatised system where it is undeniably cheaper to release raw sewage than treat it, this is a problem. In many places across the country the releases might be continuous for weeks on end – come rain or shine. Water companies are obliged to report these releases, and figures released by the Environment Agency state that in 2020 raw sewage had flowed from CSOs into England's rivers and seas on 403,171 occasions, amounting to 3.1 million hours of free-flowing filth. The reality was probably worse still, as not all CSOs are monitored and some outfalls filmed and photographed by activists do not appear in official reports. In 2021 the official figures were 372,533 releases over 2.7 million hours. While it is clearly impossible to fix the problem of 30 years' underinvestment in infrastructure overnight (the line trotted out by my MP in lieu of useful comment when I emailed him in 2021), the financial incentive for companies to release sewage unnecessarily could be addressed by a respected, empowered and well-funded regulator, and the fact that we currently have no such thing is entirely a political choice.

A little way downstream of the CSO, debris festoons the branches of alder, sycamore and ash that overhang the water: 'Bradford blossom', Rob calls it, almost affectionately. All the vegetation over which discharge has run has a dull blue-grey fibrous patina, and the spring air hums with the aroma of raw sewage. The height of this grotesque decoration gives a clear indication of how flashy the beck is – its average flow of $0.6m^3$ per second rises more than a hundredfold in peak conditions. Rob says he has seen it come up half a metre in minutes.

'It goes black and brings plastic rubbish, rubble, debris, bits of mill, children's toys – but it runs clear again relatively fast and then you're just left with the telltale tint of routine domestic discharge.' He points to the water.

'See that blue colour? It's a result of two things that shouldn't be there: optical brighteners from cleaning products – washing powder and the like – and the amino acid tryptophan, which is a breakdown product of faecal matter. Both fluoresce blue so you can see them in strong sunlight.' He goes on to describe a test that volunteer water quality monitors are using to help detect waste from domestic sources, in which a tampon is dunked and examined under UV light.

Later in the day I visit Professor David Lerner, known as Barney, formerly of the University of Sheffield and a driving force behind FOBBs. He explains that while there is often little that can be done about antiquated combined sewerage systems embedded into the infrastructure of older towns and cities without colossal disruption and expense, new-builds are a different matter. Since the 1950s, we've been building separate systems for domestic drainage. This is sensible, because it reduces the overall volume to be treated, and eliminates the pressure from pulses of storm water. What is less sensible is that the pipes used for the different flows are identical, and often laid side by side in the same trench. So as soon as someone decides to move their washing machine or build an extension or an ensuite, there's an opportunity for things to go wrong. 'Builders dig down, find a pipe, connect to it and hey presto, a family's waste is suddenly in the system meant for rainwater,' says Barney. 'Once a misconnection like that is made it can be almost impossible to trace, and yet it could so easily be avoided. Despite the housebuilding boom that has been going on most of the last seventy years, no government has instigated the simple, cost-neutral measure of using pipes of different colours so that builders and plumbers can tell the difference, or the inexpensive one of ensuring plumbers and builders understand the consequences of misconnection.'

Faced with such failure of legislation and regulation, grassroots community activists like FOBBs are doing work the Environment Agency cannot. Some are using timelapse cameras to monitor CSOs. On the River Wharfe, Mark Barrow, an underwater photographer whose passion is fish, spends at least as much time filming sewage. Also on the Wharfe, the Ilkley Clean River Group (ICRG) and their partners began testing water downstream of sewage treatment works for pathogens associated with sewage. According to UK recommendations, in order to be considered safe for bathing, water should contain fewer than 1,000 colony-forming units (cfu) per millilitre of the gut bacterium *E. coli*. This already sounds like a lot, and river users weren't comforted to discover that during high water in Ilkley in 2019, levels reached 48,000 cfu per millilitre. Even in low flows, when there was no possible excuse for untreated sewage to be discharged, values sometimes exceeded 35,000 cfu per millilitre. In a landmark action that places much greater statutory pressure on the water company to clean up their act, the ICRG volunteers secured bathing water status for their section of the Wharfe – the first river to be thus designated in the country. Other groups are taking another approach, exploring and in some cases actively campaigning for the concept of legal personhood to be applied to UK rivers including the Thames, the Frome, the Cam and the Findhorn. It's already well established in law for non-human entities to be granted the rights of personhood – companies have been able to claim such for decades. And personhood would bring rights that have already been extended to rivers in India, Canada and New Zealand. A right to be, at the very least.

It's going to be a big ask here. In October 2021, as the new Environment Bill passed though parliament, the Conservative government recommended MPs reject amendments that would have obliged water companies to stop adulterating natural waterways in all but genuinely extreme circumstances. The wording of the Bill was watered down from an ambition to 'cease' raw sewage outflows to an entirely unspecified one to 'reduce their impact'. There was thus no requirement for these reductions to be meaningful in any way. A few months later, in March 2022, the government sought to assuage public outcry by announcing what it called a new Storm Overflows Discharge Reduction Plan. This plan would, it said, oblige water companies to reduce sewage overflows into rivers by 40 per cent by 2040. According to this vision, 18 years from now when I am turning 70, we could still be seeing filth emptied freely and deliberately into our natural watercourses for up to 1.6 million hours a year by profit-making corporations, without anyone being in trouble for it. You bet I'm angry, and I'm far from the only one.

Unlike the executives of some private companies, most of us aren't trashing rivers deliberately, but there are things we can all do to reduce the problem. There is no need to flush anything other than human waste and toilet paper – everything else can be paper-wrapped and disposed of in a sanitary manner. There is also a lot more water and chemical waste going into the system than is strictly necessary. Choosing a low-volume flush wherever possible, not flushing every little wee can make a difference. And we can massively reduce grey water discharge by washing clothes and bedding less (most items of daywear can serve several days' use, and jeans can go for months before they actually need washing). You can, if you want to help, shower instead of bathe, share bathwater with family and resist the everyday extravagance of spa-style monsoon showers. You might also change washing powder or switch to washing balls to keep harmful substances out of rivers. Where possible, use grey and rainwater on the garden instead of sending it down a drain. Consider harvesting grey water for toilet flushing. Pee outside sometimes (a compost heap will benefit from a bit of urine). Reduce runoff by not decking or paving outside areas more than necessary and for pity's sake, a lawn should be grass, not a synthetic facsimile, which apart from shedding microplastics and excluding almost all biodiversity cannot suck up water. None of this is hard.

Unfortunately, it's not just domestic and industrial inputs of cities and towns, factories and mines that end up in our rivers. Rural areas produce their own assault on the arteries of the land.

The Yorkshire Derwent runs almost exclusively through farmland. Thousands of tonnes of silt a year are dredged out of the lower, navigable section, and virtually all of this comes from fields — it is the soil in which our food should be growing. There's an often-repeated warning that at current rates of loss the UK will run out of cultivatable soil in less than a century, and while these calculations are disputed, on days of heavy rain around here, I can believe it. Roads, ditches and becks are thick with mud, the river soupy with it. Maize crops seem to be particularly bad for this, and potatoes are the worst — harvesting them causes huge upheaval in the soil, loosening it to a greater depth than other root crops. If heavy rain falls in the following weeks, the potential for wash-off is huge. Of course it's very much in a farmer's interest to preserve soil, but potato farming around here tends to be a corporate business — fields are rented by contractors for just a season or two at a time; they take one crop and move on. The worst offenders, I am told, are those supplying a maker of oven chips — a company that could make a massive difference by insisting on, and paying for, better practice.

Animal farming produces vast quantities of waste. There's value in these nitrogen-rich effluents, and some of it can be used as fertiliser, but the sheer volume of excrement produced by industrial-scale operations makes safe storage and disposal hugely challenging. If muck is spread at the wrong time, such as before heavy rain, the nutrient ends up not in the soil but in runoff, and in rivers. When a body of water contains too much nutrient (a condition described as hypereutrophic) it tends to become green and opaque as a result of algal and bacterial blooms. These organisms are natural, but where they occur in unnaturally high densities they become problematic because they are short-lived, and when they die the process of decay results in oxygen depletion and makes the water unliveable for more complex forms and communities of life.

The River Wye is the fourth longest river in Britain, and has long been considered ecologically, aesthetically and culturally superlative. Like the Yorkshire Derwent, it has a plethora of protective designations: SSSIs, a Special Area of Conservation (SAC), an Environmentally Sensitive Area and an Area of Outstanding Natural Beauty. However, in the space of astonishingly few years, it has become one of the most appallingly polluted rivers in the nation. In summer, its waters turn bright green with algal blooms, its gravels and pebbles are thick with slime, the water smells and tastes of ammonia and mass die-offs of fish happen almost routinely. Most of the pollution is agricultural – slurry from dairy farms and intensive poultry units (IPUs), of which there are now more than 110 in the central Welsh county of Powys alone. These, and similar units in Herefordshire on the English bank of the Wye, are 'home' to as many as 20 million birds on any given day, producing prodigious quantities of shit. There are rules about how much chicken muck and other farm slurry can be spread and when. Farmers who break these rules are also likely to be breaching the conditions of various subsidy payments. But as with sewage, inadequate monitoring and enforcement means that rules are flaunted routinely and almost always without consequence. Farm inspections average once in 263 years according to the Environment Agency's own pre-pandemic figures for 2018–2019, so financially at least, it is worth the risk to save money on the storage and disposal of waste.

Rearing birds like this is how you make them cheap. The real cost of a whole chicken offered for £3 in a UK supermarket is hard to calculate, but it includes a dying river.

As of 2022, licences for new IPUs are still being issued in Powys, and smaller units (containing fewer than 40,000 birds) do not need to apply for an environmental permit and thus operate almost entirely unregulated in terms of their ecological impact.

The alternative to proactive state regulation of the water industry, agriculture or any other sector is a system reliant on public reporting, and for that to be effective we need a public clued up enough to know when something is wrong, and motivated enough to act. An increasing number of people are willing and able to do so, but reports are seldom followed up by an emaciated Environment Agency, and prosecutions are limited to breaches so heinous and public that they cannot be ignored. When Herefordshire farmer John Price took it upon himself to fell trees, dredge and reprofile the bank along 1.5km of the River Lugg (another SSSI and SAC-designated river) in December 2020, the images went viral on social media. Price, initially bullish, claimed he was acting to protect his land and local houses from flooding and reportedly said he would 'tear the authorities apart' if they tried to prosecute. However, when he was brought to court by Natural England and the Environment Agency in May 2022, he pleaded guilty to seven charges of unauthorised operations and environmental damage. He was convicted and sentenced in April 2023 to 12 months in prison and required to pay £1.2 million for court costs and ecological restoration work. In a world changing so fast it is difficult even for specialists to keep up, it has never been more important for farmers, river managers and conservationists to actively bridge one of the most stubborn divisions in British society: that between so-called 'town' and 'country'. The failures in our current system of land and water management and protection are systemic and endemic, and utterly depressing. At the time of this book's printing, not a single river in England meets the Environment Agency's own criteria for good chemical and ecological condition, and that is a problem for us all.

But somehow, sometimes, in some places, healing is happening. Our walk on Bradford Beck brings us to Valley Road, where a broad swathe of mown grass lies alongside a steep wooded slope. Beneath a canopy of oak and sycamore is an understory of rowan and hawthorn in flower and a blackcap is belting out a torrent of song. Huge wrinkled black rocks rear out of a shimmering ground-fog of cow parsley. It's so unexpectedly lovely, it takes me a minute to realise the beck is missing. Covered over about 100 years ago, perhaps in preparation for a bypass to the east of Shipley that was never built, it runs pointlessly underground for about 80m. The culvert where it disappears is fenced off with spiked railings, having been structurally condemned thirty years ago. The plan formulated by the city council, with Barney's help, is to create a new, broad channel, meandering through a wetland habitat in a natural looking reprofiled valley, then divert the river into it and demolish the culvert. Both Andrew and Barney describe this as an environmental project, with bonuses for public access and amenity, but these are hard things to find funding for, so they've had to be patient, creative and opportunistic. Under new flood projections the culvert poses a theoretical risk to the road and local homes and businesses, and it is this that has provided the justification, while a widening scheme on the road provides both the opportunity and a big chunk of the money. The rest is coming from an EU grant squeaked in under the Brexit wire. This costly work will only be the start. Once exposed and accessible, the chemical condition of the river will be more apparent to all, and the team hope this will help boost public support for better regulation. More love can only be a good thing.

Daylighting schemes like these are becoming de rigueur in urban planning. In Sheffield, city of seven hills and many rivers, all have been exploited by industry. Being steep, their energy was ideal for mills powering the city's gigantic steelworks. All were severely polluted throughout most of the nineteenth and twentieth centuries. By the early 1970s, the Don in particular was almost as contaminated as Bradford Beck in the Industrial Revolution – its waters black and with a similar propensity to catch fire. Things have improved since then, chemically and structurally. For example the Porter Brook was once dammed in at least 20 places and extensively culverted in the city centre, but some of this infrastructure is being reversed, with daylighting projects beginning to open the culverts and provide the brook with floodable areas in parks, which in normal flows provide much-needed green space to city residents. Meanwhile a long suburban stretch of the Rivelin is now a linear oasis of wooded, rushy and ferny banks, and rapids where chunks of masonry clad in mosses are almost indistinguishable from natural rock. There are inviting spots to paddle and picnic, pieces of public art, cafes. The Rivelin Valley Nature Trail is community maintained and genuinely remarkable for the lack of litter and dog shit. It feels loved. It *is* loved, and it is returning the love in spades. Every city should have this. Every city could have this.

My walk with FOBBs ends at the beginning of a brick-lined channel that leads to and under the city – this, says Andrew, is as far as any of the good stuff can go. After that, the water goes dark and for several kilometres the beck runs entirely below ground, under streets and buildings. In some basements it can be heard gurgling in the walls like a trapped but restless spirit. Amazingly, urban explorers who venture into these labyrinthine networks report having seen trout there – the fish don't make it all the way through, but they keep trying, driven perhaps by something we are in danger of forgetting. A memory not their own, of sparkling water, oxygen-rich riffles and pools, clean gravel. A place of promise.

Withow Gap

Mere *A shallow body of water or wetland, usually glacial in origin.*

The cliff road from Skipsea terminates abruptly just beyond a concrete blockade placed to stop cars plunging off the edge of England. Beyond the lip of broken tarmac is a three-metre drop to a narrow strip of beach, then the North Sea, restless today under wintry drizzle and bloated with land already consumed, lending it the greige hue of day-old milky tea.

You'd be forgiven for assuming Skipsea is and must always have been a coastal settlement. In fact it is set a kilometre from the sea, and back when it was named, it was considerably further inland. The 'sea' in the name, like *See* in Dutch or German, referred not to a body of brine but to a lake – in this case one of myriad shallow meres that once existed across the area of East Yorkshire now known as Holderness. In addition to a brackish etymology shared with *mer, mare* and marine, these meres also have geological origins in common with other small landlocked waterbodies across the Low Countries of Belgium and the Netherlands. They formed in the depressions created by vast blocks of slowly melting glacial ice between 12,000 and 13,000 years ago, and were a defining feature of the low-lying landscape that once linked Britain with mainland Europe. Now completely submerged, the land is named after Dogger Bank, its highest point, and the last to be inundated.

Of these once uncountable pools, only one remains as open water on the Holderness side, at Hornsea, five miles south of here. Others filled with sediment or peat and succeeded to reed bed, marsh, woodland, grassland or heath, or were deliberately drained or filled for settlement or agriculture.

I peer off the cliff edge. The slope is steep but nowhere near vertical, and there's an orange and blue-flecked rope hanging down it, knotted at regular intervals to aid grip. The cliff face looks uneven and bulgy enough to provide footholds, and I know it's only a few hundred metres along the beach to my destination. I figure walking that way I will be much less exposed to the wind, and so I half jump, half step down from the lip.

I realise in a second I've made a mistake. The bulges are not firm, but porridgy, and my right foot sinks to the ankle. I hurriedly adjust my stride, aiming for what looks like a firmer area just below. This time I sink shin-deep and lose my balance, sliding onto one hip in fudgy slop. I grab the rope with one hand, then the other. Mud gloops into my coat sleeves. I paddle my feet, finding firmer footing beneath the false surface, haul myself back up the cliff, and crawl onto the straggly grass, filthy and chastened.

I knew these cliffs were eroding — Holderness has the fastest receding coastline in Europe. But I had imagined that material was being scrubbed with each spring tide, and the odd more dramatic landslip. The liquification is shocking: as though the land is barely putting up a fight. It's not only waves and tide doing damage here, I realise, but rain. A single drop may be the tiniest of flows, but by insinuating between grains of silt and clay and other glacial spoil, each one is helping to loosen the fabric of the land from itself. The sea just cleans up the mess.

I give up on accessing the beach and cut along the edge of a field behind a row of eclectic and shabby huts, caravans and mobile homes. One hut is tightly swaddled in plastic mesh, perhaps to stop bits of it blowing away, and as I pass a kestrel emerges from a hole in the netting and swoops ahead, making slow, rowing progress into the wind. I follow its line and eventually, past the last hut, the ground drops to the channel of a tiny watercourse. A drain, little more. It flows into a pipe and emerges in the cliff face, where slippery — but this time mercifully firm — footholds lead down to the beach. I walk the few metres to the sea, wade knee deep and try to wash off the worst of the mud, then when my hands are burning with cold turn back to the cliff, and survey the reason I've come. A dark band in the cliff-face, fifty metres long and two or more deep in the middle. At either end the band tapers upwards, so that the whole feature has the form of a wide smile. From a distance the material in this band appears fine-textured compared to the chalk-studded clay in the layer below and the rooty topsoil above. I'm looking at the remains of Withow Mere, with the tiny flow that once kept it topped up rushing out of the plastic pipe. The mere was drained by Skipsea farmers in the seventeenth century to create more land for cultivation. Land that is now being taken back by rain and tide. It's strange to imagine this dark, interred space as a lens of water, hovering above my head. But there's more wonder to come. All through the northern end of the feature, jutting at every angle, are pieces of wood. The anaerobic, slightly acidic conditions that existed in this ground until it was exposed by erosion mean that trees felled three thousand years ago are still here. I work my away along the face, unable to resist touching the timbers in turn. They range in size from twigs to trunks 35cm across, and the wood is saturated and spongy. Water and air bubble out between fibres when I press hard.

The preservation is astonishing. Clearly visible are growth rings in trunks and branches and healed scars where smaller twigs fell off when the trees were still alive. The outer surfaces are dark chocolate coloured, while the insides, exposed by fresh breaks, are the rich brown of tanned leather. Some have been snapped cleanly, others are disintegrating in chunks, while a few appear to taper, like fat blunt pencils, and surely, those are gouge-marks in the cut ends, overlapping chisellings about the width of a little fingernail?

I've seen the same marks on several sites around Britain in recent years, and I've seen the razor-edged tools, and the stout, workmanlike operatives that wielded them. And if there was ever any doubt, further proof came in the form of a great wad of preserved hair pulled out of this very cliff by a sharp-eyed local called Sheila Cadman in 2017, and later identified unequivocally as belonging to a Eurasian beaver.

These timbers were felled and dragged into the water, and wedged in place where immersion kept them fresh. Each one added to the massive accumulation of debris that ensured water in the mere remained deep enough for beavers to be able to dive down to the underwater entrances of burrow lodges where they could rear their young safe from wolves, lynx and bears. All were subsequently hunted to extinction in the British Isles – some doubtless by my ancestors – but their ghosts are here, a shadow ecology, so close that I can touch what they touched.

I pick up a few pieces of washed-out wood lying at the foot of the cliff, and notice other debris there – masonry, chunks of weathered concrete and dozens of what look like small loaves of terracotta-crusted bread: house bricks, rounded off and juggled up by the tide. I pick one up and wonder about the building it was once part of and the people who might have worked or resided there, day in day out, perhaps for whole lifetimes. Did they ever glimpse a future in which those familiar walls would be reduced to wave-worn debris? Or that it may come to rest alongside rodent architecture many times older and, in their time, already forgotten? This is a place where timelines jumble, where cycles bigger than I can see intersect and where the partitions and facades around my own life feel tissue thin.

CHAPTER 20

Rodents of unusual size

Somewhere close by, under cover of darkness, a tree is being felled. A woodcutter is working covertly, using razor-edged blades to hack at the wood as they have night after night in this small Cornish valley, leaving tell-tale stumps and heaps of chippings. By day, the extent of the disruption is startling. Over the last few years it's started happening all over Britain. Trees down, woodlands unrecognisable, swathes of saturated ground becoming ever more difficult to navigate.

I'm about to catch one of the perpetrators in the act, following a sound that is both strange and familiar: rapid bursts of a low-pitched, soft-round-the-edges judder. We hear something similar on November nights at home when wood mice find their way into the eaves and roof spaces and attempt to dismantle the house. Only this is very much louder.

G-g-g-g-g-g-g-g-g-g-g.

I've never heard a beaver gnawing before, but it's unmistakeable. I grin in the dark. The sound comes in furtive bursts, and I realise that the animal is probably using the breaks to listen. Mid-gnaw, the volume reverberating around its own skull must render it effectively deaf to other sounds, so I time my approach to the bouts. *G-g-g-g-g-g-g-g-g-g-g.* Three steps, and wait out the silence. *G-g-g-g-g-g-g-g-g.* Two more. It's close, I think. Possibly in a tight cluster of alder just ahead. I wait, holding my breath into a long, elastic silence.

Ker-PLOSH!

I jump half out of my skin. The splash seemed enormous and so close, the animal must have been crouched against the bank less than a metre from my boots.

A surge of laughter almost bursts my lungs and I convulse with the effort of keeping silent. When I've composed myself enough to hold my borrowed redlight torch steady, I scan the water, and there, gliding parallel with the bank, is a low, humped form, an island on the move.

It seems huge, but I realise it looks big because it's incredibly close. The strange light and the unfamiliar surroundings are playing with my perception of distance, but once I've adjusted and gathered my wits the thought booms in my mind like a cathedral organ: *An English beaver – a creature whose kind I've awaited so long they began to seem almost mythical – is swimming past me, no more than two metres away.*

That these long-absent natives are back in Britain at all is disproportionately the work of one person. The ubiquitous Derek Gow is part Scotsman, part bulldozer, and, as has often been observed, not entirely unlike a beaver in physical appearance. I've encountered him many times over the past 20 years: reading, hearing and reporting on his varied adventures in conservation and animal husbandry, including captive breeding and, in some cases, reintroductions of species from water voles to wildcats to white storks. But it's likely to be beavers that he'll be most remembered for – not least because of his steadfast refusal to give up on a process that has taken a preposterously long time.

It was 1992 when the EU Habitats and Species Directive obliged member states to consider reintroductions of extinct native species. The Eurasian beaver – a large herbivorous rodent hunted to the brink of extinction by humans – was an obvious, and in most places relatively uncontentious, candidate for restoration. In fact reintroductions had begun in Sweden as early as the 1920s, and by the early 2000s a further 22 EU countries had joined in. Anticipating a UK reintroduction programme, Derek arranged for the import of Polish beavers in the mid 1990s, and in 2001 released a small colony into semi-wildness on Ham Fen nature reserve in Kent. But political procrastination and obstruction bogged further progress for years after that, and by the time a trial was finally approved in Knapdale Forest, Argyll, by the Scottish government in 2008, beavers had already been living free on the River Tay for some years. Whether they came by accident or design borne of sheer frustration, no one is telling.

The official Scottish Beaver Trial was a partnership between the Scottish Wildlife Trust, the Forestry Commission, and the Royal Zoological Society of Scotland, led in the field by another dogged beaver advocate, Roisin Campbell-Palmer, and supplied with beavers imported by Derek. Once released to do their thing, the animals and their habitat were closely monitored by a small army of ecologists. The trial was judged successful in 2017, and additional animals were released. In 2018 the beaver was officially reinstated on the list of British native species, then almost immediately NatureScot, the public agency responsible for Scotland's natural heritage, granted permission for lethal control of beavers on the Tay, where the population had continued rising steadily. Meanwhile, a not dissimilar dual situation had arisen in Devon, where free-living beavers were reported on the River Otter in 2013, not long after an enclosed trial managed by the Devon Wildlife Trust had got underway.

Locals took the free-living Otter beavers* to their hearts, and objected loudly when Defra suggested that as unofficial introductions they may have to be trapped and even destroyed. A compromise was reached in 2015, in which the free-living animals were incorporated into a wider trial, after tests showed them to be the 'right' species (Eurasian, rather than Canadian) and free of infections including *Echinococcus multilocularis* and bovine TB, which were deemed

---

*That beavers appeared on a river named after our other large semi-aquatic riverine mammal is as apt as it is confusing, as detractors often confuse the two species and mistakenly assume beavers will eat fish.

an unacceptable risk in beavers despite already being present in domestic pets, livestock and other wildlife. In addition to ecological and hydrological studies, this unplanned trial has allowed researchers to conduct detailed cost-benefit analyses on the impact of beavers at catchment scale, and sociological studies into public opinion.

These various trials have yielded huge volumes of information. At the enclosed sites, rigorous monitoring recorded everything from flow rates to water quality (including levels of nitrogen, phosphorus and sediment) and trends in biodiversity before and after the introduction of beavers. By the time I visited the enclosed Devon trial in 2014, three years after a single pair of beavers was introduced, that small woodland had already been transformed into an organic clutterscape of interconnecting pools, dams, canals – with some abrupt level changes and some so subtle they fooled the eye. It's not hard to see why people might object at first, because if you're used to tidiness, to orderly verticals and horizontals, a beaver-worked landscape is challenging, chaotic, even. But after a couple of hours exploring with project officer Mark Elliot, I saw differently. Much of the ground Mark guided me over was actually a matrix of mossy fallen timbers, with treacherous, knee-wrenching gaps to humble anyone trying to move too fast. He explained how the pools store water temporarily when it rains and release it slowly through leaky dams, thus flattening the curve of peak flows after heavy rain. A delay of just a few hours can make all the difference between a river that swells manageably downstream and one that bursts its banks, causing serious flooding. The pools also act as settling basins in which particles can be trapped, and even dissolved materials can be fixed and removed from the water. Levels of pollutants were significantly lower in water flowing out of the trial site than water flowing in. Meanwhile, Mark said, careful biological surveys of the site before and during the trial showed dramatic upticks in both abundance and diversity. Light reaching the woodland floor after trees were felled was a boost to low-growing flowering plants, and thus to insects, and in turn for the birds and bats that feed on them. The abundant dead wood of such places makes good eating for various wood-boring invertebrates and for grub-eaters like woodpeckers. Amphibian numbers boomed. Many beaver trials also report a boost to fish populations, including those of commercially and recreationally valuable species.

The sheer range of ecological benefits of beaver presence are the reason they are considered a keystone species. If a tiny site of a handful of acres can achieve so much, the potential at landscape scale is enough to make hydrologists and ecologists dance, and even economists might feel their feet tap at the sheer affordability of letting nature do its thing. The estimated cost of winter flooding in 2015/16 to the UK economy was estimated by the government at £1.6 billion, and every year much smaller floods take a toll on local economies, not to mention the wellbeing and mental health of householders and business owners. Human-engineered flood defences that might reduce the risk tend to be colossally expensive. Beavers are astonishingly cheap.

But not everyone is convinced, and some remain outright hostile to the idea. Farmers are often dubious, especially in low-lying areas where drainage has been central to land management for centuries. The noises coming out of the angling community as a whole have been far from welcoming. It's true that barriers can be a problem for fish, in particular migratory species. The Angling Trust has recorded more than 26,000 humanmade barriers on UK rivers, and with many fish stocks in dire decline, they're keen to see these reduced, and thus opposed to the installation of any new ones, be it by humans or beavers. But beaver dams are porous, and even the tallest are at best temporary obstacles, provided rivers are allowed to behave naturally – pulses of water mean that fish only have to bide their time. I've watched little trout waiting at small drops for levels to rise – seen them wriggle over and through accumulations of woody debris. Eels have no trouble doing the same. And the other benefits to fish from improved habitat and water quality are undeniable. In the River Otter catchment, the impoundments created by beaver dams contain significantly more fish than similar reaches without dams. Another study, by researchers at the University of Southampton, revealed that not only were brown trout more numerous in Scottish rivers into which beavers had been re-established, they were also bigger. The fact that this work was co-funded by NatureScot and two major pro-angling organisations, the Game and Wildlife Conservation Trust and Salmon and Trout Conservation, may help the results gain traction even in beaver-sceptic sections of the fishing community.

It is usually reported that beavers went extinct in Britain in the late sixteenth century, although odd records exist as late as the 1780s, notably in Yorkshire on the catchment of the Wharfe. That county got its first new beavers in the spring of 2019, and I was thrilled to be there as an observer when a magnificent female, pregnant and furious, and a small, placid male were released into an enclosure in Cropton Forest on the edge of the North York Moors. Their new home is a pool on a tiny beck, whose waters flow into the Seven, the Rye and then the Derwent. Both had been trapped from the Tay population, having made an unwelcome appearance on private land, and had been driven south by Roisin Campbell-Palmer. When the moment came to open the crates, the male made an unhurried exit, ambled around in the sunshine for a minute before slipping into the water and cruising back and forth, emerging on a log to groom himself and watch us with calm indifference. The female, however, was wildness itself. A hissing, growling fury, she barrelled from the crate, straight into the water where she swam straight to the far side of the pool and wasn't seen again that day. While I was grateful for a chance to watch the male – a beaver, in Yorkshire! – my heart exploded for that mother-to-be and her seething contempt for humanity. A beaver is not a bear, or a wolf, or a lynx, but is a personality to be reckoned with, all the same.

That little family has thrived and grown, and I think of them often, doing their work upstream on my own river. All that lies between them and the possibility of my one day meeting their descendants on my patch is a sturdy fence. Like almost all English beavers they remain enclosed – reintroduced but not free. I wonder how long it will take, when the fences come down as they surely soon must, for a pair of prospecting youngsters to negotiate the few dozen kilometres of winding flow to my doorstep.

Those two Scottish arrivals in Yorkshire were the first beavers I saw in Britain, but that was a release day – busy with people and travel arrangements and press photo opportunities – and nothing like a natural encounter. Now, though, on this damp Cornish spring night, it's just the two of us, and though we're fenced in, there is no doubt who is the interloper. I'm not sure if the beaver sees me, or some hint of the red light beaming from the torch. More likely it smells me. At any rate, my presence continues to irritate. The paddle tail smacks the water again and the animal submerges.

I crouch on the bank and wait, and a few minutes later the beaver slides into view again – this time a little further out. The smoothness of the movement is almost supernatural. There is no swish, none of the rise and fall of gaited locomotion, the chugging hurry of a water vole or even the flick and flex of a swimming fish: just a glide as flat as the water. It dives again, the movement just as sudden as before, but this time splashless and silent: the rolling of a perfectly oiled wheel.

On the next pass, the torchlight catches in one small eye and I realise the beaver is watching me too, and waiting. It has business on the bank where the nuisance human is loitering. When it slides out of sight again, I rise as quietly as I can, and move on. It's not easy. What remains of this five acres of woodland is thick with vegetation responding to beaver-browsing by putting out vigorous new growth. It is strewn with fallen trees and above all, it is wet: a boot-sucking, trouser-soaking, toe-squelching mire. It's hard enough to move around by day. At night, even more so.

Like the enclosure in Devon, this one feels primordial, but it is very new. I think of the wood-choked remains of Withow Mere, and of the tree debris being so carefully, cautiously introduced to those Scottish salmon rivers. The sight of waterways full of timber has been anathema for centuries. But that's the shifting baseline – a perspective born from obsessive tidiness, risk aversion and the absence of this one critically important species. Ecologists also describe beavers as ecosystem engineers – an easier sell to nervous landowners than to say they are wreakers of essential havoc. Almost everything about a beaver-worked landscape is challenging to the uninitiated. The area around this pond, like every other beaver reintroduction area I've visited, grates on our warped aesthetic of how a landscape should look. Just as our idea of human beauty has been narrowed to a set of mathematical ratios and airbrushed skin tones, our idealised expectation of land has been simplified, with a marked absence of disarray, filth and decay. But it is complexity that stabilises and sustains a functioning ecology. We need to embrace the mess. Reject nothing, select nothing, scorn nothing.

I locate another viewpoint further around the irregular margin of the pool. There's a rough bench, and I sit and stare at the glassy expanse of water, looking for ripples. On the other side of the pond, pale in the red torchglow, a long log rises at a shallow angle and begins twirling on its end. Holding the torch in one hand and binoculars in the other, I can see the humped outline of another beaver squatting on the bank, manipulating one end of the branch with capable paws, while the other end is supported by water.

This Cornish trial is taking place at Woodland Valley Farm, 70 hectares of verdant hummocky terrain, where no two gates are fastened in the same way, and organic pasture-fed beef cattle are reared by the stout and smiley Chris Jones. There's something of the hobbit about Chris, but spend a day in his company and you soon discover an intellect that is more Gandalf than Baggins – polymathic and enormous fun, and one of these people who seem to get twice as much value from a twenty-four-hour day as most mortals.

The farm also now incorporates a bunk barn, event venue and study centre. The outbuildings are stacked with educational materials, wedding props and farmyard paraphernalia – a jumble in which I suspect only Chris can find anything. Amongst all this I come across a stuffed beaver from Bavaria, where perhaps he once had a Germanic name, but on arrival in Cornwall he was dubbed Trevor. Trevor has orange incisors, tiny orange glass eyes, and at first glance his sun-bleached, strawberry blonde fur looks dry and wiry. But up close the hairs gleam, and when stroked they feel so lusciously sleek that it is hard to stop. My fingers disappear into an underfur of extraordinary depth and softness. The majority of hairs in beaver pelage are underfur: short and fine, sprouting at a density of up to 20,000 per square centimetre and matting into a felt that traps warm air and prevents water making contact with the skin. Growing through this undercoat are longer guard hairs, a few hundred per square centimetre, and these are glossy and water repellent, thanks to regular anointing with oil from a modified anal gland, which is combed through the fur as part of an assiduous grooming routine. It's little wonder this fur was so prized, but it is to humanity's shame that commercial hunting reduced a Eurasian population of 100,000,000 to around 1,000 animals by the early 1900s: a 99.999 per cent extermination.

It wasn't only for their coats that beavers were killed, but also for meat and for castoreum – a greasy scent produced by twin sacs under the tail, which often contains high concentrations of salicylic acid, originating in the stems and leaves of the willows that beavers like to eat. Salicylic acid is a precursor of aspirin, and castoreum has been used medicinally for centuries, possibly millennia. It is also valued by the perfume industry. On the day of the Yorkshire reintroduction, I asked about castoreum when I rode to the release site with local project officer for the Forestry Commission, Cath Bashforth. She mentioned there was some tincture in a plastic vial in the central compartment between our seats.

'You can have a sniff but for God's sake don't spill it in here.' She slowed to a crawl to avoid jolting me and wrinkled her nose as I cautiously uncapped the tube. The scent made me think of very old furniture: a slight fustiness. Not unpleasant to my nose at all – but then I'm not easily offended by odours and can barely even detect the infamous stink of fox, so perhaps some of the more volatile beaver notes are also lost on me.

Chris took me on a guided tour of Woodland Valley soon after I arrived, and we stood with our backs to a chilly wind while two ponies in mud-caked coats gambolled around us and Tandy, a white terrier with a blur of tail, raced further spirals around them. In the sweep of an arm Chris showed me where a small watercourse, the Nankilly Water, rises just a few hundred metres upstream of the farm, and explained that it was canalised in Victorian times, when landowners were given interest-free loans for drainage projects. After the farm it joins the Tresillian River, and ultimately discharges into the Fal estuary about four miles away. A few years ago the Tresillian flooded the small village of Ladock, just downstream of Woodland Valley. Chris had been reading about beavers since Derek Gow introduced them in Kent in

2001, admiring the biodiversity benefits they brought, but it was the flooding that provided the final motivation.

'It really focussed us. The Nankilly is small but very flashy, and the rain that caused that flood will happen again. We had to do something.'

Compared with the changes wrought by the species' disappearance – infilling, succession to forest, heath or grassland and the development of farmland – the impact of beaver restoration is staggeringly swift. Remodelling often begins within a day or two of their arrival in a new habitat, and so it proved here. After three years Chris's woodland was completely transformed, and much like the Devon enclosure, it now looks chaotic. But amongst the disarray are a series of dams so precisely constructed it's hard not to credit the makers with calculating intelligence. I said as much, and Chris grinned. 'You're not the only one to think that! I had a couple of engineers here the other day – they've been building and designing leaky dams for other projects and when I showed them this, they almost cried!'

Is this pure instinct, or are beavers genuinely smart, I wondered?

'They're definitely smart – on a par with rats I'd say – with an ability to experiment and puzzle things out. Their engineering isn't the kind that requires reasoning or planning, but they seem to have some way to rattle through the options, make decisions, and flex their behaviour to achieve particular ends.'

'What motivates them?' I asked. 'Why and how do they build like that, if not through understanding of consequences?' Chris leant on his stick and pondered for a moment.

'Something about running water seems to rankle with them. It's like they feel a compulsion to fix every leak, staunch every trickle, using whatever materials are available – wood, mud, leaves. They don't need to understand what they're doing – what matters in evolutionary terms is that doing it creates a habitat in which they and their offspring

are better able to thrive. Actually,' he added, cheekily, 'I think
beavers look at water like money – a dam is their bank
account, and like good Yorkshiremen they don't like to leak.'

Having splodged though squelching ground and rivulets of
moonlit water running over grass between trees, I have to
let myself out of the kind of enclosure you might expect to
see around a zoo exhibit: a fence sunk well into the ground
then folded inwards so that any attempt to burrow soon
encounters heavy-gauge galvanised mesh. There are several
electrified strands, including a sturdy one at the bottom on
which, during a later visit, Lochy will catch an ankle. He's
used to the kind of shock given by the electric mesh fence
our neighbour uses to pen his pet sheep – no more than a
ticking tickle. This one, he will sob into my tight hug, makes
his heart hurt. For all the good these animals are doing, they
are still treated as though they pose a high risk.

Over dinner and local wine, we talk about floods. I tell
Chris about recent inundations closer to home in York and
Hebden Bridge, in Leeds and Sheffield, and Pickering,
Helmsley and Malton. About Tadcaster Bridge, and how
there is still only one enclosed beaver trial in Yorkshire. He
sighs. 'The trials now are just repetitive, and completely
unnecessary. All they're doing now is keeping researchers
busy and mollifying some benighted landowners. We need
government to say very clearly what actually needs to
happen, which is for the blasted fences to go and beavers to
be part of the fauna almost everywhere, and then for
policymakers to follow that up. Until then, disasters like
those, coming ever thicker and faster, will continue
destroying livelihoods, rendering property uninsurable and
probably costing human lives.'

The next evening we drive south-west almost as far as it's
possible to go, to the tiny village of Morvah, where we meet
farmers Lisa and Piers Guy. We take a walk around parts of

the farm where over recent years they have been planting, sowing wildflowers and allowing a little spring running through a corridor of access land to renaturalise. They seem as keen to feed insects and birds as they are to supply organic Dexter beef to market.

It's a big night for Lisa. After farming here for 25 years, the family is deeply invested in the local community as well as the landscape, and they are among a handful of land managers collaborating in a catchment rewilding project called Cliff to Carn. The logical next step, as Lisa sees it, is beavers, and there is at least the possibility for this to be one of the first officially sanctioned unfenced introductions. The catchment is just three miles long from source to sea, with high ground around, making it unlikely that animals will disperse – though a population would fairly soon outgrow the available territories, creating a surplus that could serve to supply other reintroduction schemes.

Lisa has invited Chris to talk to the neighbours, in the hope of winning support for her plan. The event is held in a barn smartened up to serve as a wedding venue, and Chris gives a detailed account of the benefits and challenges the project might bring. As a farmer himself he makes a different case to those I've heard before: largely skipping the big picture he speaks about so passionately at other times. He's exactly the right person to sell the idea here – no flannel, no grand claims, just pragmatic, warts-and-all detail. Afterwards there are questions.

'How can they be controlled if they become a problem?' asks one woman. 'You can't know the outcome of just letting them go after so long.'

'Well, yes we can,' says Chris calmly. 'The outcome is they will fell trees. They will cause small-scale flooding. They might block culverts, they might raid crops. They might burrow into banks. And there are places in the country where any of that could be catastrophic – the perched rivers of the Fens for example. But here, all those challenges can be addressed. Trees and culverts can be protected. We can use beaver deceiver flow devices to drain dams where necessary. And again, if need be, there are the options of trapping or shooting. We have to be utterly unsentimental.'

In response to a question about how many beavers might one day be on the land and what would happen if they became too many, he's startlingly practical.

'When every Cornish schoolchild goes to school in a beaverskin gilet, then perhaps we might say there are enough.' There's a ripple of laughter, but he's not joking. 'Look, firstly, they're unlikely to build up very fast because they are predated by foxes, killed by cars, they drown in burrows. Plus they're territorial, so there's a natural limit to how many remain in an area. But if they do fill all the available space, then there may come a point where they become a resource.'

The thought of fashion fur revolts me. But, remembering the lustre of Trevor's flanks, I can imagine that garment. Warm in the most ferocious weather, hardwearing enough to last a lifetime, free of plastic microfibres and toxic dyes, locally made without sweatshop labour. I find myself wondering if after all, I could one day wear such a thing myself.

'What about TB?' another woman asks. 'Can they carry that?'

Chris shakes his head and starts to reply, but the questioner is on a roll, and talks over him, implicating a badger vaccination programme run by the Cornwall Wildlife Trust in a recent herd breakdown. Later in conversation with Lisa, the same woman seems resigned.

'Well, we'll see, I suppose. But not wolves, Lisa. I draw the line at wolves.'

This kind of paranoia is the joint responsibility of extreme rewilders insisting that nothing short of restoring all the missing components of our postglacial fauna is worthy of the name, and equally extreme opponents who miss no opportunity for scaremongering. But wilding does not have to be an absolute. It is a spectrum of opportunities for ecological restoration, including habitat creation, species reintroduction, lighter-touch management and regenerative farming, all of which create space for natural processes to play out, and the importance of community engagement and decision making is impossible to overstate. On that score, Lisa seems to be doing well.

Considering all the ecological and hydrological evidence and mostly positive public opinion, there is little doubt that Britain will be better with beavers. But rivers run long, threading together many different communities, and often they are also the boundary between land owned by different people. So there has to be collaboration, communication and consent. Even now, projects might be lobbied against by minorities including large landowners and angling organisations, who exert significant influence and privilege. According to Derek Gow, these objections are based on an assumption that any beaver release, anywhere, would be the thin end of the wedge, leading to an unacceptable loss of control. And yet when a social-science approach was taken to appraising the opinions of recreational anglers and fishery managers on the Otter, the only river in England where anglers currently have actual experience of free-living beavers and their effects, the results suggest a range of nuanced opinion: some welcoming, an equal number apprehensive, and a slightly greater number in favour of wider releases with a proviso that contingencies are set in place to manage the animals should they become a problem. As such, a majority were pro-beaver restoration.

This diversity does not yet appear to be reflected in the stance of bodies like the Angling Trust. It's strikingly similar to what Arran told me about attitudes among anglers to access for kayakers, paddleboarders and swimmers, and chimes with my experience in the supposedly tribal conflict between farming or estate management and landscape restoration, where a minority in positions of significant influence continue stoking an 'us and them' narrative. I see them increasingly as an old guard of noisy ghosts, reliant on friends in high places, and determined never to be part of a compromise solution. And I also think that perhaps this little gathering in a wedding barn on the very tip of England is how it will be done instead. Not by outsiders, or policymakers. Not by unions or governing bodies or boards of trustees, but by individuals: nervous, faltering, hilarious, obsessive, furious, generous people with the patience, integrity, humility and resilience to bring an entire community cautiously with them.

The narrow bridge

Floodplain Low-lying land alongside a river, over which water spills naturally during flood events. Floodplains tend to be both fertile and level – making them a tempting prospect for both agriculture and development, with consequences for water quality and hydrology.

Ings A Norse word for areas of floodplain, water meadow and wetland in the north of England, especially Yorkshire and Humberside.

I don't believe we ever meant to wreck the place. Changes happened incrementally. The digging of a ditch to irrigate crops or to drain a small patch of land for cultivation to feed a community. A small weir to create a head of water to power a village mill. A sewer to provide life- and health-saving sanitation. Then a little bit more and suddenly a *lot* more. Those early steps were small and probably felt like essential progress, environmentally innocuous, if they were thought about at all. The river would take care of it. But eventually over time the decisions began to be made not by people, but by a system. And for those benefiting most from the system, natural thirsts and hungers, and basic comfort needs have been replaced by other cravings; power and profit, or luxuries that serve as proxies for both. At the behest of the system, we've dammed whole valleys and flooded homes, heartlands and ecosystems, drowned some rivers, drained others and buried still more in the dark. We've pumped them with toxins, leaked silt, fertilisers and pesticides into them, choked them with plastic. We have excluded people from the right to access clean flowing water to gaze upon, bathe in, or travel along, to the extent that millions of us no longer have any idea what we're missing.

The implications of food production for climate and biodiversity weigh heavy on my conscience, and my diet now includes hardly any meat. I try to avoid dietary labels that seem to evoke tribalism and lack the kind of nuance that is needed when there are so many variables to weigh up – health, food miles, sustainability, animal welfare, use of agrochemicals and antibiotics, politics, human rights, packaging, allergies, not to mention price and the likes, dislikes and intolerances of a whole family. Saying 'not today' to meat means I have no difficulty in declining the cheap, intensively reared or imported stuff for months, sometimes years on end, but I can avoid offending people who have gone to trouble on my behalf, I can eat food that might otherwise go to waste, and I can serve meals that feel auspicious. In practice this means I almost always eat vegetarian or vegan food but occasionally enjoy a plate of mussels or culled venison.

Food politics has got me into some intense debates on social media, especially with farmers. Of the latter, one of the most thoughtful and constructive is Rob Rose, who regards his Dexter beef as a by-product of conservation. He farms on the floodplain of the Lower Derwent, and so along with concern for the environment, we are also connected by a river.

The problem with any reducetarian approach to meat, says Rob, is that well-meaning people might decide to go vegetarian or vegan one or more days a week, but if the animal produce they do buy and consume is still intensively reared or imported, the big players easily maintain their market share by intensifying further and selling more, worse and cheaper to everyone else – at the expense of health, animal welfare and the planet. The timing of the annual Veganuary campaign drives him to despair, because dairy cows don't have an off switch. If thousands of gallons of milk get tipped down the drains by farmers who can't sell the stuff, that won't help farming become more sustainable. He says that eating less meat and dairy won't help unless there's a simultaneous switch to local, organic and regenerative suppliers to provide what we do consume – made by enough people to maintain thousands of small businesses like his. Until then, his way of doing things is so marginal it is little wonder few are willing to try.

The upshot of all this was a promise that the next time I ate meat, it would be Rosewood Farm beef. I made good on this and ordered a joint for Christmas, and said I'd go to collect it in person.

On the drive I realise I'm nervous, because I'm not sure Rob trusts me, and I want him to. But he's shyly welcoming and immediately takes me to meet his herd of black and auburn cattle, shoving gently along the open side of a shed, exhaling the odd conversational *muuurh*. Dexters are very little – their heads are level with my midriff, and they gaze from under adorably long lashes – but Rob scotches any impression of docility. 'Don't believe it,' he says. 'Riled up they'd easily kill a dog, even a human. They're a domestic breed, but have retained strong wild instincts that allow them to survive independently of our care.' In an adjacent pen, Whiskey, an eight-year-old home-bred bull with a mop of Adonis curls and a neck almost as deep as his chest, flares his nostrils and rolls his eyes as if to emphasize the point. Rob chose Dexters after reading about a man named Michael F. Twist who kept one as a childhood pet in the 1920s, which was collected off a train and transported in the back of a car. Small stature makes them lighter on the land. 'It also helped that they cost less than big breeds and that was important when we were starting out. But mainly it came down to the meat. They taste great.'

They're hardy too. Rob's herd is under cover for the winter, not because they can't cope with cold and wet, but because their grazing land is now needed for something else. Rob gives me directions so I can see for myself. It's a short drive, and I park up near what has been a crossing place over the Derwent for 700 years. The current bridge, built in 1798, originally had three arches, one over the main channel and smaller ones either side to accommodate high flows. But these plainly weren't capacious enough, and on the western bank there are now a further seven brick arches, and today the river is in full spate, running through every one of them. It's slightly unnerving, standing close above so much water, flowing so fast.

The bridge is only wide enough for one vehicle to cross at a time, and a pair of massive, brutally ugly blue crash barriers have been installed to protect the old stone parapets. I can't help thinking that if this was the Dales, the Moors, or York, and not the edge of the South Yorkshire Coalfield, the modifications might have been more sensitively done.

Upstream of the bridge, the crest of a grassy bank shows just a few centimetres above the water level. In the main river channel, its turbid grey-brown flow is chugging faster than I could run. Beyond the bank, a public footpath sign points directly into a huge pewtery lake. This is part of the long swathe of floodplain known as Derwent Ings, and it is currently at least a metre under water. It is also Rob's grazing land. In summer it is first hay meadow, then pasture, and in winter it becomes this water world. And as far as I can see, on and around and above the silvered surface, there are birds. Huge flocks of pochard and wigeon, interspersed with smaller groups of gulls and gangs of cormorants. A few dozen swans are gliding between half-submerged hawthorns, and beyond them is a grassy slope teeming with hundreds of lapwings, blending so well with the background it's only their movement that makes them visible, even through binoculars. Further away still I can see the flickering beige and white of scores of golden plover. It's easy to see why these watery pastures are due to become part of the extensive patchwork of floodplain already designated as the Lower Derwent Valley National Nature Reserve, a Site of Special Scientific Interest and a Wetland of International Importance under the Ramsar Convention. Easy to see too, why Rob regards his tenancy as a sort of timeshare, with the river in charge. He's walking a line between tradition and subversion that feels ... fluid.

I turn and face the other way, south and downstream. The wind gusts drizzle into my face as I lean on the ugly blue barrier. The skyline here is dominated by the cooling towers of Drax power station, one of three built in the 1960s in this part of Yorkshire. Drax, Eggborough and Ferrybridge were visible from high ground 50 miles away, and some days it seemed that all the grey of the sky above the Vale of York was a product of their relentless exhalations. Drax alone supplied 6 per cent of UK electricity, and in 2007 was the largest source of carbon dioxide emissions in the country. But times are changing. Ferrybridge closed in 2016, Eggborough in 2018, and their cooling towers are being demolished. Drax has burned its last coal and now runs mostly on wood pellets shipped from the US in 50,000-tonne consignments. The government has also given the green light for four new gas-fired turbines within the facility. Our compulsion to burn dies so hard.

But from where I'm standing, by doing no more than swivelling my eyes over the trees on the other side of the swollen river, I can also see the sweeping vanes of three huge wind turbines. More lapwings appear overhead; a flock of sixty or seventy flying in close formation then exploding apart as though each bird were suddenly overwhelmed with an urge to freestyle. They slew and tumble, scattering across the sky like the shortest of shorthand glyphs.

These are truly bridge years we're living. Water is rising, the crossing is narrow and precarious, and I'm afraid. But we have no choice, we have to try.

CHAPTER 21

Heartland

It's Midsummer's Day. Lochy and I leave home early to reach the Dales before nine. With a planned solstice trip to Scotland cancelled because of the pandemic, coming here on this auspicious date has become almost an obsession. But now I'm not sure it's a good idea. This little pilgrimage has been on my mind for years, but I'd planned to come alone, and to linger in the place as long as I wanted. To find something of what Roger Deakin's legacy has come to symbolise for me – a freedom to be diverted, distracted, to slip the leash. This is going to be an off-piste excursion, on potentially very steep ground, in search of a place I know others have failed to find. Writer and blogger Joe Minihane took two goes in his attempt to retrace Deakin's amphibious wanderings here. Attempting it with a child in tow might not be wise, but Roy's post-lockdown schedule demands he work today, so short of postponing I have no choice but to make it a two-handed expedition, mum and boy. You never quite know how such things are going to work out – children have their own ideas about what is fun and if they're not happy, it's hard for anyone else to be.

But the day is magic from the start. It is still a novelty to be away from home. We're not leaving the county but North Yorkshire is big. Today it feels vast. We bypass York – then Harrogate, drive though Pateley Bridge and Grassington, under the dramatic overhanging crag at Kilnsey and eventually up into Littondale. Roy and I got married a little further up on the banks of the Skirfare at Halton Gill – our wedding pictures were taken with us in the almost dry bed of the river, with our loved ones crowded along the bridge above. Lochy listens to my

stories of before he was born. The memories are still fresh
in my head, but I recall the way my own parents' tales of
life before me seemed like ancient lore. So I give him his
own prehistory, with as much flourish and colour as truth
will allow.

We park near the Falcon Hotel in Arncliffe and just
outside the village we find the beck and I settle the boy on
a flowery bank and tell him another story, about Roger
Deakin and his book. I pull a battered copy of *Waterlog* out
of my pack and read Chapter 19, 'An Encounter with
Naiads', which tells how Roger heard of a special place
from the botanist Richard Mabey, who cautioned that
abseiling might be necessary. I read aloud about the swifts
in Arncliffe and the steep 'cruel road' to Malham, the
mysterious vertical forest growing on Yew Cogar Scar; the
black rabbit and finally about the pool with water so clear
you could see the deep bottom and so cold it burned, and
which might still be home to fairies and sprites whom one
must never try to kiss.

Lochy homes in on practicalities right away.

'I'll need a wetsuit and a rope.'

'I have your wetsuit in my pack. We don't have a rope, but
I think I've found another way so we won't have to abseil.' I
show him the map, on which I've identified the approximate
location of the pool and the route I have in mind to get to
the bottom of Yew Cogar Scar. 'Then, we just stick to the
river and keep going until we find the pool. That way we
can't miss it – as long as it's still there – we have to remember
rivers can change.'

We walk, dropping down to the beck before the valley
sides close in and become too steep, and picking our way,
discussing route options. There are a couple of drystone
walls to negotiate, and some crags – some we can avoid by
crossing the water. Others we climb, carefully. At the points
where we need to scramble, he goes first, nimble and
confident. He makes me feel… not old, but cautious, as I

favour a hip that has been giving me gip. Where the scrambling is steep, he peers to inspect each move, calling back, making good choices.

'This looks OK, I can jump down here,' or 'This looks too difficult, I'm coming back,' and then 'Mummy, pass your rucksack to me for this bit, it's heavy and you need to balance carefully.' For the first time, it seems I am walking with my son as an equal and it's like a little glimpse of a man I hope to know one day.

A few early clouds have cleared away, and sunlight seems to pervade all our senses. Long grasses patter the skin of our legs; our nostrils fill with the scents of water and sun-baked rock, and the pink smoulder of trodden thyme; skylarks and curlews pour out liquid notes as though trying to fill the beck with music.

We talk about flowers and birds and Minecraft. At the next crossing, he weighs up the options. The stepping-stones are all natural ones – unevenly spaced, some mossy, others slick with water flowing over them. He wobbles on one, slips and steps into the water, keeps his balance. This might be where it all begins to go wrong, where the excursion becomes one long ordeal of coaxing and complaint. But he laughs. 'Oh well. My socks are wet now, so it won't matter if it happens again.'

There is no mistaking Yew Cogar Scar as it comes into sight. It is a long crag, on which trees rooted between bedding planes of ancient rock eke out a living from water trickling down to dampen crevices. There are a few twisted and dwarven ash trees clinging on too, but yew dominates. There can't be much soil there – not much of anything in fact. I wonder briefly if there might be a spring inside the crag, but it's north-facing and overhanging and so a large part remains in deep shade – even now, close to midday on the summer solstice. More likely it is this topography that makes life just possible for the trees. A spring would make things too easy perhaps – tempt them to grow fatally fast. As it is, their existence is not measured in size. They have forgone growth in favour of an arboreal asceticism, becoming natural bonsais. Most have small trunks and are no more than five or six feet tall. Their wood must be extraordinarily dense – are the rings even countable, I wonder? Those at the top of the crag are wind-sculpted, while those below the overhang have a cantilevered form, growing out from the cliff then making an abrupt ninety-degree turn upwards, rising parallel with the rock face. It looks like a scene painted on an oriental scroll.

The name of this place has the allure of one for which there is no obvious explanation. The 'yew' part is straightforward enough, but 'cogar'? What is that? An internet search yields little information other than on how to climb it. The entry on the British Mountaineering Council website: 'Sheltered crimpy steepness, first climbed out of necessity to retrieve Yew wood for weapons with which to fight the Scots,' feels as fanciful as it is intriguing and perfunctory. And it doesn't help locate the name in time. People from these parts have been squabbling with their northern neighbours for a fair wee while. But, considering the strangeness of the name and the drama of the place, the dearth of etymological information seems surprising. There are some Celtic words I feel might shed light, including the Welsh *cogan* and *cwgan* – which refer to bowl shapes and might be used to describe landscape features, and the Irish *cogair* or *cocur*: words for whispers, or secret discussions. The Dales were once part of the huge territory of the Celtic Old North and there are, I know, the remains of a prehistoric settlement up above the crag – now visible as collapsed stone walls in circles and squares. Could the name be Cumbric – a version of Brythonic related to Old Welsh? The crag has probably changed little in three thousand years and, as a location with little economic or strategic value, may have escaped renaming

by subsequent invaders. Wary of clutching at straws, but
curious, I have asked around. Dales historian Tom Lord
agrees the name is likely pre-Saxon in origin, and revealed
that a parcel of land close to Arncliffe is referred to as
Yuden or Yueden in the chartulary of Fountains Abbey,
which once owned it. Meanwhile linguist and dalesman
Kester Clegg points to other Celtic placenames that survive
locally, including Pen-y-Ghent and Pen Hill. Indeed
Yorkshire itself can claim a Brythonic root. Before the
Roman occupation, the settlement of York was known as
Eburakon, meaning 'place of yews'. It evolved via Latinisation
to *Eboracum*, which was anglicised to *Eoforwic*, which under
the Danelaw became *Jorvik*. The Normans called it *Everwic*,
and *Eborienc*, but the Old Norse version stuck better and
Jorvik was gradually compressed into York, though it took
the invention of the printing press to standardise this
spelling. It could be argued that the real symbol of Yorkshire
is not the white rose, but the yew. This grand but mysterious
shadowed crag, with its exposed bedrock and its ancient,
cautious trees, feels like a heartland in more ways than one.

'*Yew Cogar. Yeeeeoooo Co-GAR.*'

I find myself repeating it, feeling my lips purse and stretch,
my cheeks hollow and my jaw rock, my tongue damming
and releasing the flow of air. A sound for an idea of a place
far older than England. To hold a prehistoric hand axe you
must settle it into your palm and grasp it with your fingers,
and if it was not the right shape you would know. To be in a
place and speak its old name is to fit yourself into and
around the idea of it in a similar way. And to speak this idea
you must shape your lips, tongue, cheeks and glottis. Whether
they sit like an axe in the hand or a name in the mouth,
ideas have postural connotations that endure through time.

We speak languages with many tributaries, but follow
them back far enough and the tributaries begin to converge
again, becoming branches on a tree that lead to a shared
trunk and root system.

A tree is a river, and a river is a tree.

River names tend to be old, and often they are shared. For example in Britain there are multiple Derwents, Dons, Tames, Avons, Usk/Esks and Dees, among others. There are three rivers bearing the name Ouse in England – the Sussex Ouse, the East Anglian Great Ouse and the Yorkshire Ouse, into which these waters of Cowside Beck will eventually flow via the Skirfare and the Wharfe. The French River Oussa is the alleged site of the miracle of Lourdes. The etymology of the name is ancient, pre-Roman, and thus somewhat obscure, but it seems that the common pursed-lip *ooo* sound in 'Ouse' and 'water' are not a coincidence. The sound *oooa* and the expression that goes with it have been part of the idea of water here and across Europe for millennia. *Water*, English; *Uisge*, Scots Gaelic; *Dŵr*, Welsh; *Aqua, Acqua, Agua,* Latin, Italian, Spanish and Portuguese. *Woda*, Polish; *Ur*, Basque; *Eau*, French. It's there too in weir, in wet and well, and in the names we give our most potent spirits: *whisky* and *vodka* come from words for water. As Samantha Walton notes in *Everybody Needs Beauty,* even the concept of wellness comes from *wiellan,* to rise with the abundance of a spring: To say we are well expresses health as a state of being like, or with, water. It's striking, when you start looking, how many rivers have names that probably once meant simply 'water': Wear, -went, Ure and Ouse. As we have forgotten the meaning of *oooa,* we've separated water from river – piped it and bottled it, sprinkled and flushed it.

The scale of Yew Cogar Scar only becomes apparent when we hear voices and spot a handful of climbers in the heavy shade at its base. Lochy is keen to watch, but after 15 minutes in which they appear to do nothing but stand about fiddling with ropes and pointing upwards, he gets bored and we continue.

I'm keeping up a commentary on the flowers – those I know, at least. My names are generic: silverweed, lady's bedstraw, bugle, chickweed, lady's mantle, speedwell. I'm not a botanist, and someone like Richard Mabey would be a handy companion now, though it would be a slow walk with a true plant lover. Walking with botanists is like walking with toddlers; they tend to stop to look at something every few paces. The next plant I spot is a clump of garish yellow trumpets at the water's edge: monkeyflower, so called because you can supposedly see a monkey face in the pattern of the red spots in the trumpet. It's not native and can be invasive, but thus far doesn't seem to be doing much harm here. In fact, this is becoming one of the world's best-studied wild plants, thanks to its fecundity and ease of culture, and its variability. It is the subject of intensive research into genetics, mutation, evolution and the formation of so-called Turing patterns in nature (anything from leopard spots to the way stars cluster into galaxies).

There are saplings of hawthorn and oak on the dalesides, replacements for the sparse and ancient contorted trees that dot the slopes. It's good to see some thoughtful planting in a landscape where trees have been forgotten about for generations.

The valley steepens; we're climbing now, past tributaries that cascade from the steep sides, falling almost vertically in places. Roger came down that way. The beck narrows to half its width, develops a pool-drop structure, hurrying and tumbling over ledges and becoming prettier with every step. There are limestone outcrops on either side, and in its bed, large moss-topped boulders. We also start to see deposits of calcite coating the rocks around each little fall, much thicker than that around the springs at home, and caramel coloured rather than off-white. This is tufa, a variety of limestone that precipitates out of water with a heavy load of dissolved calcite. Water that is slightly acidic can carry more calcite than that which is neutral or alkaline – but one of the things that happens when groundwater emerges into the air is that dissolved carbon dioxide (which results in mild acidity) is released. The pH increases, reducing the calcite-carrying capacity of the water. The agitation and mixing with air that happens as the water is chivvied over a cascade releases more CO_2 and hence more tufa, so deposits tend to accumulate around springs and waterfalls.

The pools are getting deeper. Lochy senses our destination must be close and scrambles ahead.

I disturb a half-dozen chimney sweeper moths – sooty black with white wing tips – from a clump of meadowsweet, then pause again to try and locate a stonechat I can hear clinking somewhere above us on the hillside. A shout comes from over the next outcrop.

'I've found it! And there's a cave!'

And there it is. The pool is smaller than we expected, less round than described, but otherwise unmistakeably, dreamily right. It is fed by a cascade; it has broad tufa steps at its downstream edge and a little cave from which a small ash tree is sprouting. Its rocky rim is festooned with mosses, thyme and rock-rose, and the banks are of short, sweet turf, busy with tiny emerald grasshoppers. Close by, but not quite overhanging, is a small cluster of mature ash – just a few trees. There are two kinds of wagtails – grey and pied – skimming and hopping on the cascade.

'Let's see how cold it is…' he kneels and plunges his arms in. 'Yow! *Freezing!*'

We swim – it's cold but the burn isn't as fierce as I expected. In neoprene the boy manages much longer than I do in just a swimsuit. He swims hard against the current then lets it whoosh him back across the pool. We explore the pools above, shallower and linked by smooth chutes.

He stays in until his lips turn blue and comes out shuddering, but we eat sandwiches and boiled eggs and watch the wagtails until he starts to look pink again.

There's a few minutes of drizzle as we continue walking, uphill, passing a farm where house martins hurtle through a mixed herd of cattle, then on up the steep flank of Cowside, where grasshoppers, moths, beetles and flies jump and flit amongst yellow mountain pansies and bedstraws, bird's eye primrose, bugle and thyme. The old cowpats look like giant burned crumpets, so riddled are they with the exit holes of hatched insects and the probings of long beaks – a good sign they are free of ivermectins.

We rest near the top, looking down on the toy farm below. The air has become sultry. I lie back on the turf – it's barely even damp after that lightest of rain showers. The insects hum, skylarks sing on.

I'm woken by something tickling my nose – a buttercup, with Lochy on the end of it.

'Mummy, I think we should get going.' I have that drunk feeling that comes from sleeping in the sun. For how long? He says half an hour at least. The realisation that he's been watching over me while I sleep chokes me up a little.

He's soon ahead again, shouting back, 'Mummy, what's this?' I find him hopping along a series of strangely shaped rocks, laid in a row that looks deliberate.

'It's called limestone pavement. This is just the start of it. There's lots more over there, look.'

He runs and climbs up onto a row of blocks near the break of the slope and surveys the ground ahead. 'Whoa.'

'It's cool, huh?'

'Did someone build it?'

I try to explain that no, the blocks are natural – the result of weathering. It's just water and plants – freeze and thaw, rooting and rotting, over and over. The blocks are called clints – the gaps between them are grykes. The latter are sheltered from frost and the drying effects of wind and direct sun but fed with trickles of moisture, are crammed with delicate and damp-loving cranesbills, hart's-tongue fern and spleenwort, herb Robert and even tiny trees. If you lie down on your front and lean your face into a gryke on a warm day, you can inhale the muggy aroma of a greenhouse.

'There's loads more – just *loads* of it.'

There is – from here it runs to Malham and beyond, with more on the flanks of Ingleborough and Whernside. On a satellite image of the Dales you can zoom in on it and see a pattern like the fine creases and crosshatchings in dry skin. Limestone pavement is an exposed version of a group of landforms know as alvars – areas of limestone with little or no soil. Limestone is relatively common, accounting for about a fifth of all the sedimentary rock on Earth. But pavements of the kind we're standing on are a speciality of Britain and Ireland, and globally rather rare because it takes a particular set of circumstances to make them. Like chalk, a lot of limestone is calcium carbonate derived from the remains of marine organisms. It is slightly soluble in water, and exposed limestone landscapes (karst) tend to be riddled with caves and potholes, which form along the slight weaknesses between layers of rock laid down at different times – the bedding planes. The gaps between the planes channel water. And the water freezes and thaws and flows, subjecting the rock to mechanical and chemical weathering in which the cracks become larger – eventually large enough for plants to take root in them. Plants speed up the process by adding both the mechanical pressure of roots driving into cracks and the gentle acidity of decay. Here, at the edges, the clints are so weathered they no longer look like blocks. They are all curves: knuckles and knobbles, hollows and flutings.

'You've seen some of it before – at Malham Cove and Ingleborough. Don't you remember?' He doesn't. I've forgotten that two years is an eternity to him – that the way he sees and interrogates the world is changing so fast. Back then he just took the extraordinary landscape at face value. Now, he recognises it as something unusual.

'This one is like the skeleton of a whale.' He runs along a series of blocks flanged like vertebrae. Perhaps it once was, I think. Not a fossil – but this rock was made under an ancient sea, and while it is too old to have been the bones of a mammal like a whale, it could have been part of some other life.

I try to articulate my vague understanding of the process – as much for my own benefit as his. 'You saw the tufa around the pool? It's like the calcite in the spring at home. And the gaps and holes in these blocks could be where it's come from. The rock that was once in the gaps dissolved and now it's probably been deposited again down the hill there, or much further away, depending where the water took it.'

'It looks like a ruin,' he says, clambering and jumping.

'I know what you mean. But it's not. It's just one of the ways the planet sort of rearranges things and renews herself. It's why this wise old Earth of ours still feels young and beautiful.'

It's striking how attempting to explain something can settle it in one's own mind. He's accepting rather than astonished, but I'm experiencing one of those surges of comprehension that feels like vertigo. It takes me out of myself – out of this mind, out of this body standing on a jutting bone of rock – far enough out that for a moment I grasp a bigger picture. This weird formation isn't just on the surface. We're standing on millions of cubic metres of it – a structure that is both skeleton and shell, as much conduit as barrier – and all of it potentially subject to the influence of running water. There are rivulets and rivers down there. Some of that drizzle we walked though earlier – freshly condensed in the air above us – has already gone on below, on its way to becoming something else. Seeping, washing, leaching, dissolving, depositing, freezing or vaporising. It has no destination, only spaces and forms it passes through, and occasional organic or mineral partners, any of which might sit out the dance for a matter of hours or billions of years, before the water whisks them back into play. Into re-creation. Nothing is new. It is all recycled in an endless process of wearing and mending and making do.

And then I'm back in my body looking at the boy who came to life inside me, whose molecules assembled from mine but which really came from rock and water and sunlight and air. And I run out of words.

CHAPTER 22

A descent into Hell Gill
(and out the other side)

But oh! that deep romantic chasm which slanted
Down the green hill athwart a cedarn cover!

Samuel Taylor Coleridge, *Kubla Khan*

There's one other place on Roger Deakin's Yorkshire odyssey where I've yet to go. It's been on the list for so long – too long, perhaps, because it's grown larger than life in my imagination. Roger first heard of it in Bernie's cafe, the famous cavers' hangout in Ingleton. I've done a little bit of caving – enough to know there are wonders to see down there, but also to know that hours of being squeezed like so many kilos of sausage meat isn't really my bag. I don't mind the dark and I'm not unduly claustrophobic, but I don't have a body built for tight spaces and I'm just not a fan of the sheer discomfort of it all. But this place isn't a cave. Not quite. It's a space between places, a space made by water. Deakin went there, but only got so far. Dressed only in Speedos® and wetsuit boots, he reached a place intimidating enough to turn him back, and as far as I know, he never got another chance.

I bought Orna a copy of *Waterlog* for her last birthday with the express motive of luring her here. Orna is my slightly younger, much funnier and far, far fitter friend. We've kayaked scores of rivers together, run mountain marathons together, watched phosphorescent waves breaking on a New Zealand beach at midnight. She can drink me under any table and run a marathon next day. Like Kate, she came to the hospital when Lochy was born, despite losing her own mum to cancer in those same days. And she indulges Lochy like a pet while reading the riot act to her own two boys, when I'm pretty sure he's just as guilty of whatever misdemeanour has been committed as they. Orna is one awesome woman. She was with Kate on her last trip. And it will never sit right that I can't help to shoulder that for her.

There are no two ways about it: losing friends to an adventure sport sucks, and part of the torment is that non-participants often fail to see accidents for what they are. Soon after Kate died, I had a routine appointment with my GP, in a practice where Kate had occasionally worked with geriatric patients. On discovering I was a friend of Kate's, the doctor gave a hollow laugh and said, 'Well, she was always trying to kill herself.' I couldn't trust myself to speak. On the way out I went to the toilet and retched.

Statistically speaking, neither kayaking, nor sailing, which Kate was equally committed to, are particularly dangerous sports. My GP was apparently an avid horsewoman, with pictures of horses all over her consulting room wall. On average horse riding is around four times more lethal than canoeing or kayaking, and also knocks recreational rock climbing and scuba diving into a cocked hat. In a league table compiled by the healthcare journal *Bandolier*, the sports with the highest risk of death are base-jumping (no surprise), swimming, running and cycling. Horse riding was tenth, canoeing fifteenth. The perceived risk of so-called adventure sports has much more to do with the fact that accidents tend to take place outside the realms of daily life and are therefore seen as newsworthy. Almost by definition, most participants are risk-aware and trained. While it is theoretically possible for a complete novice to buy a boat and leap onto a white-water river, it seldom happens. To anyone getting on even slightly lively water for the first time, the jeopardy is so very apparent that doing so uninitiated would require genuine recklessness. Wherever you learn to paddle, safety and risk management are part of the process. Respect for the water governs every decision. When accidents happen in recreational adventure sports, they are almost always just that. But even so, they force questions that it can be easier not to face. The more committed the adventurer, the more obvious the psychological workarounds become: dark humour, fatalist acceptance and extreme goal-orientation. I find them all troubling. All are deferrals, and all, to my mind, are a recipe for post-traumatic breakdown, somewhere along the line. If hurts of this complicated kind can't be processed when they happen, they will come back to bite later, and survivor PTSD only compounds a tragedy.

To a stranger we encounter today, Orna and I will look like a pair of (wince) middle-aged mums eccentrically dressed for fellwalking. But we're younger than Deakin when he attempted Hell Gill, we're considerably more experienced in white-water environments and we're better equipped, with neoprene tops and leggings with reinforced bums and knees, a floating drybag to carry food and water and a couple of lengths of climbing tape and karabiners. Neither of us feels any purist need to make the descent in just our pants. We're better informed too – all Roger had to go on were some vague directions and warnings issued over tea in Bernie's. Now, if we chose, we could have read a dozen different descriptions online, or even booked a guide to bring us here. Instead, I've scrutinised maps and watched the weather forecast and the river levels obsessively. There was heavy rain at home last night but apparently none here in the western Dales, and the uppermost gauge on the River Eden at Kirkby Stephen has not so much as twitched for days. We're good to go. Even so, the simple knowledge that this place was enough to turn the indefatigable Deakin back lends a frisson, and Orna, whom I've forbidden from looking at any account other than Roger's, admits to being slightly terrified.

We drive up Wensleydale, which, unusually, takes its name from a small village and not from the river running through it. This is the Ure (formerly the Yore), and we follow it to Hawes and then drive on to Garsdale Head and north into the broad dale known as Mallerstang, above which, on a soggy swatch of moor, lies the Pennine watershed. Rain falling here from one cloud might join either the flow of the Ure, bound for the North Sea via the Yorkshire Ouse and the Humber, or be diverted a few metres by a gust of wind into the headwaters of the Eden as they begin their journey to the Irish Sea. It is the top of the Eden we're bound for today. The name is derived from the Brythonic *Ituna*, meaning 'rushing water', rather than recalling the garden of creation – though stretches of it are divinely beautiful. It descends via Appleby-in-Westmoreland, where during the annual horse fair, animals are traditionally washed in the river to look their best after a long journey. Sam Lee, whose years of song collecting among the travelling community have taken him there, tells me it's an amazing sight, 'But I do flinch when I see all the shampoo in the water – I feel like going round handing out bottles of Ecover®!'

Mallerstang also crosses the borders of Cumbria and North Yorkshire, or Cumbria and Richmondshire to the traditionally minded. All three counties have welcome signs on the road at Aisgill, but between the signs is a gap, a few paces of no-man's-land. Precisely in this gap there is a track, and the track leads to a fissure that is a true boundary, a place where no signage and no local authority bureaucrat can do anything about the fact that the jigsaw pieces of the land don't quite meet. At surface level there is this side, and there is that side, and in between there is a space that is neither one place nor the other. Down in the bottom you can stand with one foot in Yorkshire, the other in Cumbria, and a hand braced against the sculpted edge of each. This waterworn chasm, 400m long, 20m deep but in places less than a metre wide, is Hell Gill.

We cross the Gill on an old stone bridge whose parapet is too high to allow us to see very much of what lies below, then continue uphill past a small woodland, beyond which we find the beck, with water shallow and light gold, slipping quietly over grey and pale terracotta bedrock. On either side the cropped turf of the banks is starred with tormentil and thyme, and the raggedy, lemon sherbet faces of mouse-ear hawkweed.

Amongst all this, the beck begins to drop quietly and undramatically away, one step at a time. After a last-minute wee in the bog cotton, we follow it, stepping down over sill after sill. Pool and drop, cup and fall. The pools are rounded and shallow to begin with and they brim with champagne-coloured water. But as the drops increase in height, the pools deepen and the water in them darkens to the colour of weak black tea.

We're between walls now, and they get higher and closer together with every sill. The rock of the walls is not smooth, but curiously dimpled – presumably by the kind of chemical 'alveolar' weathering, which might in other places result in deep pits or honeycombs, but here, with regular abrasion by high flows, the pits are smoothed into scalloped gouges. The dishings vary in diameter from thumbnail-ish to teaplate-y but those packed together on a given surface tend to be evenly sized, giving the impression of a diligent craftsman at work. In places the more sheltered downstream facing surfaces are heavily latticed, but the more exposed faces, subject to greater erosive force, are smoother. They remind me both of the beautiful adzed tabletops created by the Yorkshire furniture maker Robert 'Mouseman' Thompson, and of the reticulated pattern of light on the floor of the Afon Cothi gorge.

The bed of the beck is much smoother, the central channel almost perfectly so, and in its scoured surface there are fossils: lots of small coin-sized discs and ovals, sections though the stems and arms of ancient crinoids – relatives of starfish and sea urchins, which still live in oceans worldwide

and are known among other things as sea lilies and feather
stars. There's a marked difference in colour between the wet
bed and the dry: where water flows the rock is stained green
with algae while the dry surfaces are pale dusty terracotta.
The distinction suggests the beck has been running
consistently low for some time.

We're descending more steeply now and drops can no
longer be stepped down, but must be climbed or slithered
over. Between them, the water flows along its green bed, a
malachite serpent. I remember Nan Shepherd's description
of water emerging from holes in the Earth 'like the ancient
snake'. Further down, this flow becomes the River Eden, so
perhaps it is apt that the scaly trickster should have found his
way up here. Perhaps primed by thoughts of the Biblical
garden and its sinuous maker of mischief, I look up and see
a row of vulvas. They're not small or subtle vulvas either, but
disarmingly huge labial openings in the rock walls, deep
enough that you could reach an arm in, and more than a
metre tall. And now I've noticed them, I see many more,
all the way down the gorge. I think of the sacred women's
sites I was told about in Australia, places charged with
feminine power where visitors were not permitted. Often
they are honoured as the birthplaces of deities. And while
I'm wondering I think again of the name of this place.
Deakin suggested that 'Hell' in this case was not a direct
reference to the fiery pit or even to any perceived
unpleasantness, though it has undoubtedly served as a
deterrent to the idly curious. In Old Norse, Hel was the
underworld home of the dead, but its name meant 'hidden,'
and it could be that trait that gave this cryptic fissure its
name. What Deakin didn't mention is that in Old Norse
Hel is also a dour and fearsome giantess who rules that same
grim underworld. She's a daughter of Loki and the
giantess Angrboða and thus a sister to both the giant
wolf Fenrir, and the world serpent, Jörmungandr. The sagas
present the whole family as a bad lot. So much so that in

2017, a ruling by the Icelandic Naming Committee explicitly excluded Hel from the list of culturally acceptable forenames citizens are allowed to give their children, on the basis that it was likely to cause embarrassment or damage to its bearer. Perhaps I don't want this to be Hel's place after all.

But the idea is hard to shift. The entrance to Hel's realm is described in the *Prose Edda* (the thirteenth-century text on which most modern understanding of the Norse myths is based) as the 'stumbling block'. There are plenty of water-worn blocks to stumble over here and they are getting bigger as we descend. We come to one where a knotted rope has been slung around the base of a small tree rooted in a crack to help with climbing down – or more likely, to assist anyone desperate to get back up. Somewhat discouragingly, the tree is entirely dead. I ease down without the rope. Beyond this drop the walls close in further – there are places where we can reach out and touch both sides at the same time. They are slightly overhanging, swelling out above us like corpulent thighs, and there are spiders' webs across some of the crevices – some no more than a foot above the water. I suppose the spiders will quickly sense vibrations made by rising beck levels and scurry upwards to safety.

We're in deep shade in the canyon despite the late June sun being very high. The sky is a crack, high above us, and from this brightness comes a sudden flurry of tiny white flakes. They sprinkle down on us like confetti and I realise they are the petals of small rowans growing from crevices all along the upper parts of the walls. Rowans have a powerfully protective and feminine mythology, and were often planted at the entrance to dwellings in order to cast their reassurance over all who lived there. Hel's place or no, we'll be OK.

As the walls close in and the drops get bigger, the pools become deeper and colder, and I'm glad of the neoprene. I comment on how comfortable I am in it. Orna, an

Iron-distance triathlete who hardly ever enters the water uninsulated, raises an eyebrow.

'You know, I'm pretty sure that's why wetsuits were invented?'

There's wood sorrel on a mossy rock shelf and I tell Orna we can eat it.

'Oh, that's good, we can survive here a while then,' she deadpans back.

On higher ledges there are ferns and herb Robert, and further on, lush growths of wild garlic still in flower a month later than at home.

We reach the biggest of the stumbling blocks, the 'point of no return'. It was here that Roger turned back, and it's not hard to see why. From the lip there's a near-vertical chute dropping a couple of metres down into an oval pool four or five metres long, and at the far end another lip – over which the water slips out of sight, though we can see the gorge walls continue on, with a series of shapely buttresses projecting on either side. There is a fixed line bolted to the wall above us – you could clip to it for security or if you wanted an option to climb out, but without it, getting back could be a fearsome challenge.

We take the plunge – Orna goes first, swims the pool to peek beyond and the grin she flashes back is one of pure glee. I clip together the bags and lower them down for her to tow across. It's my turn. I slither part way down the chute and half jump, half slide, holding my nose.

The few brief seconds of submersion feel long. I go deep, but not deep enough to touch the bottom. From beneath the aerated water turns brown to greenish gold as I rise back to the light. It's cold, too. No place to get stuck in your Speedos®.

I reach the downstream edge of the pool and peer over a dam wall shaped like a wonky horseshoe. The water is pouring over the lowest point in the horseshoe into another small cup from which it spills again into a larger pool. I climb out and perch my bum on the wall. The noise is extraordinary. There's the constant white-noise rush, but within it an irregular thunderous crashing – I can't understand where it is coming from. Orna is laughing and shouting something but it takes a few repeats for me to make out the words:

'Yer arse is blocking the entire River Eden!'

And it's true. By obstructing the bottom of the horseshoe with my body I'm damming the flow. When I shift position the released water crashes into the cup below – the intermittent thundering is this sound bouncing around the walls so that it seems to come from everywhere at once. Orna wants a go at this too, so we swap places and she perfects the move, adopting a seated perch on the rim for five seconds then standing up so the river bursts out between her legs like epic birth waters. We whoop and cackle like a pair of sorcerous hags.

The next pool has a partial roof, supported, or so it seems, by two sculpted stone pillars. There is something arborescent about the way they splay outwards and downwards like the roots of Yggdrasil, the world tree. Swimming behind the roots we pass under the roof to part of the canyon where direct light never falls, and the water goes dark. If this is Hell, or Hel, then neither is what we might imagine.

This place is not infernal. Not today, anyway. It's amniotic.

We tread water for a few minutes, floating and listening to the throb and rush of Earth's circulation. But it's getting chilly, we can't stay long. It takes just a few swimming strokes to bring us back out into unroofed shallows. And from here the gradient begins to ease up, and we're mostly walking again rather than clambering, sliding, or wading. The floor of the canyon is littered with boulders – some wobble as we step over them. I try to envisage the flows that have brought them here over centuries. The noise when they tumble and roll in high water, as they evidently do, must be stupendous. The lower several metres of the gorge walls are free of mosses where they have been regularly or recently scoured and the force of those torrents is hard to imagine.

We can see brightness ahead now, as well as above, and the walls open out, become stepped and well vegetated. Herb Robert and speedwell are flowering prettily on the ledges and above them the banks are lined with rowans, whose fallen petals have formed halos in the shallow water around smaller boulders and cobbles. There are grey wagtails here, and a dipper bobbing on a rock in the sun.

The flow has found its way through, and us with it.

Epilogue

Three days after the trip through Hell Gill I'm reviewing some clips of video I shot in the canyon and I see something I didn't notice when we were there. It's wobbly hand-held, low-resolution footage – I was using the camera to take notes rather than shoot a quality movie. In a 14-second clip recorded to remind myself about rowan petals and the spiders' webs, the view pans briefly down the river. And there, on the wall, is the pale grey form of a slim young woman. She is wearing a dress with puffy sleeves, a nipped-in waist and full skirt. Her hands are clasped at her waist. She has a prominent nose, a small chin and her eyes are deep set under a thick fringe. Her hair is long, or maybe she's wearing a veil. The detail is all so distinct it takes my breath. When I show it to Roy, he points out that the woman is standing next to the snout of a huge green dragon with frowning eyes and a downturned mouth. Which is proof, I suppose, that you don't have to look hard to find faces in rocks. Our minds are so primed to recognise important patterns that we see them all the time. But I wonder all the same who she is, and if she is still there.

We come from water, and water runs through us. It carries our chemistry and our stories. It shows us more than itself: all the colours and none. We are mostly water for all of our lives, but water is only us for a short time before it becomes something else. Perhaps we leave something of ourselves with it. What might that trace be like? A chemical fingerprint? A voice? A gleam? A shadowy figure on a damp rock wall? Or perhaps a slight dimple in the surface flow, as though someone had touched the water and it remembered.

Author's note and acknowledgements

Otters are totem animals for me, and ever since the publication in 2017 of Robert Macfarlane and Jackie Morris' *The Lost Words*, the line 'Enter now as otter, without falter into water' has been a mantra for those times when I need to be a bit brave. The day I lost my phone and we saw the otter in the Cram Beck (see page 121), was also the day I signed a contract with Bloomsbury for this book. It was a good sign. My thanks to the whole Bloomsbury team, especially Jim Martin who saw book potential in *The Flow*; the amazing, unflappable Julie Bailey for nurturing it (and me) from there; Jenny Campbell for saintly patience; and also to Liz Peters for her generous and thoughtful copy-editing.

This book began as a submission to an extraordinary anthology, *Women On Nature*, curated and edited by Katharine Norbury. That piece, which became the prologue to *The Flow*, marked a huge transition for me, from writing about non-human nature to writing about real people. Katharine went out of her way to encourage and support me and I'm hugely grateful. I must also thank two other early readers of that piece, Derek Niemann and Patrick Limb, for their wonderful encouragement.

So many people helped me find and refine this stream of words and ideas. Some are identified in the pages, others contributed in ways too varied to list (I tried, but there aren't enough pages). They include: Polly Atkin, Mark Barrow, Cath Bashforth, Janet Batty, Will Boyd Wallis, Barbara Bray, Kirsty Breaks-Holdsworth, Lindsay Bryce, Nigel Bunce, Peter Cairns, Christa Campbell, Roisin Campbell-Palmer, Eliza and Martin Carthy, Darren Clarkson, Kester Clegg, Erlend Clouston, Edmund and Anne Collins, David Craven, Liz Doherty, Ben Eardley, Matthew Edgeworth, Mark Elliot, Paul Farley, Duncan Ferguson, Johnny Flynn, Matthew Francis, Mel Fox, Alison Fure, Elaine Gathercole, John Gent, Derek Gow, Malcolm Green, Lisa and Piers Guy, Roy Halpin, Jeremy Harte, Nick Hayes, Val Hazel, Robert Hellawell, Geoff Hilton, Chris Jones, Steve Knightley, Brian Lavelle, (David) Barney Learner, Jim Leary, Sam Lee, Paul Lister, Jim Lockyer, Tom Lord, Kitty Macfarlane, Robert Macfarlane, Dave Mann, Lynn Martell, Mo MacLeod, Kate Merry, David Miller, Nick Milsom, Andrew Mindham, Gwylim Morus-Baird, Patrick Moseley, Alan Mullinger, Coco Neal, Mervyn Newman, Elliot Newton, Terry O'Connor, Alice Oswald, Alistair Oswald, Chris Park, Jack Perks,

Martin Phillips, Paul Powlesland, Rob Rose, Alex Swift, Lee Schofield, Ben Seal, Steve Serowka, Caroline Shah, Feargal Sharkey, Merlin Sheldrake, Owen Shiers, Guy Shrubsole, Veronica Strang, Fred Strickland, Edwin Third, Wynne Thomas, John Till, Jon Traill, Samantha Walton, Barbara Webb, Norman West, Selina and Rob in Glen Feshie. Further thanks are due to the estates, executors and publishers of RS Thomas, Nan Shepherd and Roger Deakin. Thank you to all who've given permission for their words to be used here, and to the few I've not been able to reach for permission, I hope my representation is fair. Two of the stories here (my visits to Old Malden and Buscot) I have told before in shorter form in my Country Diaries for *The Guardian*. To any others whose contributions I may have neglected here, please forgive me.

I am lucky to have some amazing associates on social media and in real life − creators and activists, most of whom probably have no idea how much their art, action and solidarity has meant over the last few years − special shout out to Jamie Normington, Nicola Chester, Nick Acheson, Melissa Harrison, Nic Wilson, Rob Cowen, Stephen Moss, Chris Packham, Megan McCubbin, Ben Hoare, George Monbiot, Harry Whinney, Caspar Henderson, Hugh Warwick, Dara McAnulty, Patrick Barkham, Matt Gaw, Natasha Carthew, Ginny Battson, Jackie Morris, Nicola Davies, Tanya Shadrick and Sophie Pavelle. You inspire me week in, week out. A special mention to two particular stars in my firmament − Rob Macfarlane for the writing that made me wanna; and Sam Lee, for lighting my way back to an England (and a Britishness) I can love with my whole heart.

To the whole dear gang at New Networks for Nature, an organisation that changed so much for me, thank you, wonderful humans, and to the excellent Right To Roamers… let's do this. Reader, please follow @ Networks4Nature and @RightToRoam.

Special thanks to my favourite woad-smeared river pirate, Nick Hayes for his instinctive understanding of the heart of this book and for interpreting it so gloriously on the cover.

York Canoe Club in the noughties was more than just a canoe club. It was companionship, coaching, guidance, rescue and the best of times. Thank you to that extraordinary family and its affiliates including: Helen K, PK, Clare, Ian, Orna, Lyndon J, Lewis, Sarah, Jon, Jo K, Indy, Driller, Cat, Sara, Rob, Badger, Jen, Vicky, Alice, Sally, Nick, Fiona, TB, Tim, Cathy, Sue, Simmo, Lyndon S, Gunny, Jack, Rachel, Bev, Niki, Bill, Sanne, Ruth, Nige, Frank, Pete T, Paul B, Jo B, Mike, Becky, Christian, Stu, Jill, Ade, Jo C, Pete M, Chris, Ruth, Craig S, Gladys, Sean, Sam, Karl, Emily, Dan, Shaun, Pete W, Adam, Karine, Jay, Helen S, Jess, Craig G, Stevie,

James, Smurf, Saira, HTB, Tony, Weed, Els and Ted. A lot of you pulled me out of pickles, sometimes it was the other way around, but for that rope on the Clough, Dan Toward, special thanks. To Anne Raper – while we're still here, Jason is too, somehow. To those with Kate on that awful day, who did all they could, my love and deep respect. We all thought we were choosing rivers, but maybe the rivers were also choosing us.

Close to home, love and thanks to Paul, Badger, Jen, Orna, Ian, Matt, Lucy, Robin and Helen for your stalwart friendship, the extra childcare that has allowed me to roam, and the places to stay. Love you all.

Profound gratitude to my dear mum Sally, for being half of the dream team that gave me a childhood I appreciate more every day, to Dennis for stepping up to stepdad-hood with such heart and generosity, and to my beloved sister Nic whose wisdom and kindness arrives so gently as I racket about making dust and noise or go too long without calling.

To my dearest and best boys, Roy and Lochy, who through no fault of their own ended up with a writer for a wife and a mum, respectively. Thank you for coping with my physical and psychological semi-presence, and for being my first and most loyal readers. I'm blessed.

And lastly, my love, gratitude and deepest admiration to the family of that force of nature, Catherine (Kate) Stainsby – especially Paul, Hannah, Diane, Alan, Rob, Jonathan and Matt. She sparkles in you all.

A Note on the Author

Dr Amy-Jane Beer is a biologist turned naturalist and writer. She has worked for more than 20 years as a science writer and editor, contributing to more than 40 books on natural history. She is currently a Country Diarist for *The Guardian*, a columnist for *British Wildlife* and a feature writer for BBC *Wildlife* magazine, among others.

Amy-Jane campaigns for the equality of access to nature and collaboration between the farming and conservation sectors. She is a member of the steering group of the environmental arts charity New Networks for Nature and the land rights campaign RightToRoam.org.uk, and honorary President of the national park society Friends of the Dales.

Further reading

Chapter 1: Fresh and yet so very old

Deakin, R. 2007. *Wildwood: A Journey Through Trees*. Hamish Hamilton, London.

Eddy: Snow Dome

Martell, L. 2019. Interview between Lynn Martell and Bob Sandford. https://culturallymodified.org/bob-sandfords-decades-long-fight-for-fresh-water-video/

Chapter 2: Torrent

Baker, W. T. 1969. *They took the Lifeboat up the Mountainside: The Lynmouth Flood Disaster.*

BBC Radio 4. 2001. *The Day They Made It Rain*, broadcast 30th August 2001.

Cloud Seeding and Project Cumulus Paper. https://www.whatdotheyknow.com/request/89323/response/218495/attach/4/CloudSeeding.pdf?cookie_passthrough=1

Harper, C. 1908. *The North Devon Coast*. Chapman and Hall, London.Prosser, T. 2001. *The Lynmouth Flood Disaster*. Lyndale Photographic, Lynmouth.

Wordsworth, W. 1815. 'To M. H.' in *Poems Vol II.*

Chapter 3: Oak-water

Bradley, T. 1988. *Yorkshire Rivers No. 6: The Derwent*. Old Hall Press, reprinted from a series in *The Yorkshire Weekly Post* 1891.

Ogden, J. 1974. *Yorkshire's River Derwent*. Terence Dalton Limited, Lavenham.

Chapter 4: Fly while we may

Pryor, F. 2001. *Seahenge: a quest for life and death in Bronze Age Britain*. Harper Collins, London.

Chapter 6: The meanings of water

Edgeworth, M. 2011. *Fluid Pasts: Archaeology of Flow*. Bloomsbury Academic, London. Heglar, M. 2019. *But the Greatest of These is Love*. https://medium.com/@maryheglar/but-the-greatest-of-these-is-love-4b7aad06e18c

Leary, J. 2015. *The Remembered Land: Surviving Sea-level Rise After the Last Ice Age*. Bloomsbury, London.

Macfarlane, R. 2019 *Underland: A Deep Time Journey*. Hamish Hamilton, London.

Strang, V. 2004. *The Meaning of Water*. Routledge, Oxfordshire.

Eddy: Otter

Hughes, T. 1983. 'Visitation' in *River*. Faber and Faber, London.

Chapter 7: The Bell Guy and the Gypsey

Adams, R. 1971. *Watership Down*. Rex Collings.

Grahame, K. 1908. *The Wind in the Willows*. Methuen, London.

Chapter 8: A willow grows aslant a brook

Jefferies, R. 1883. 'A London trout' in *Nature Near London*. Chatto and Windus, London.

Millais, J. G. 1899. *The Life and Letters of Sir John Millais, Vol 1*. Methuen, London.

Mueller, L. 1996. 'Moon Fishing' in *Alive Together: New and Selected Poems*. LSU Press, Baton Rouge.

Webb, B. C. L. 1997. *Millais and the Hogsmill River*.

Chapter 9: The cry of the Dart

Doyle, A. C. 1901. *The Hound of the Baskervilles*. *The Strand* magazine.

Oswald, A. 2002. *Dart*. Faber and Faber, London.

Meander: Flow

Csikszentmihalyi, M. 2004. *Flow: the secret to happiness* (An introduction to Flow Theory). www.ted.com/talks/mihaly_csikszentmihalyi_flow_the_secret_to_happiness

Chapter 10: Trespassers will

Hayes, N. 2020. *The Book of Trespass: Crossing the Lines that Divide Us*. Bloomsbury, London.

Hayes, N. 2022. *The Trespassers Companion*. Bloomsbury, London.

Ogden, J. 1974. *Yorkshire's River Derwent*. Terence Dalton Limited, Lavenham.

Shrubsole, G. 2019. *Who Owns England?: How We Lost Our Green and Pleasant Land and How to Take It Back*. William Collins, London.

Eddy: Summer on the Nene

Watkins-Pitchford, D. 1981. *The Quiet Fields*. Michael Joseph, London.

Watkins-Pitchford, D. 1967. *A Summer on the Nene*. Kaye & Ward.

Eddy: Heron

Farley, P. 2011. 'The Heron' in *The Poetry of Birds* (edited by Simon Armitage and Tim Dee). Penguin, London.

Chapter 12: Land covered by water

Carstairs, I. 2007. *The Yorkshire River Derwent: Moments in Time*. Halsgrove, Wellington.

Jones, P. 2000. *Navigation on the Yorkshire Derwent*. Oakwood Press.

Eddy: High water

Editor of the York Press. 2016. *An open letter to Humphrey Smith*. York Press.

https://www.yorkpress.co.uk/news/14200874.an-open-letter-to-humphrey-smith/

Meander: Ghosts in the Willows

Deakin, R. 1999. *Waterlog: A Swimmer's Journey Through Britain*. Chatto and Windus, London.

Chapter 14: The silver fish

Francis, M. 2018. *The Mabinogi*. Faber and Faber, London.

Chapter 15: Light and water

Oswald, A. 2020. *Interview with Water*. The 2020 Oxford Poetry Lecture. https://podcasts.ox.ac.uk/interview-water

Chapter 16: Anadrome

Walton, I. 1653. *The Compleat Angler*. Richard Marriot, London.

Youngson, A. and Hay, D. 1996. *The Lives of Salmon: An Illustrated Account of the Life-history of Atlantic Salmon*. Swan Hill Press.

Chapter 17: Riverwoods

Dillard, A. 1976. 'The Death of a Moth'. *Harper's Magazine*. May, 1976.

Eddy: Flowover

River Hull Drainage Heritage Group. 2014. *Becks Banks, Drains and Brains: The Drainage History of the River Hull Valley*. East Riding of Yorkshire Council.

Chapter 18: Confluence and influence

Atkin, P. 2021. 'Pond Life' in *Much With Body*. Seren, Bridgend.

Hughes, T. 1998. 'The Earthenware Head' in *Birthday Letters: Poems*. Farrar, Straus and Giroux, London.

Macfarlane, R. 2019 *Underland: A Deep Time Journey*. Hamish Hamilton, London.

Plath, S. 1981. 'The Lady and the Earthenware Head' in *Collected Poems*. Faber and Faber, London.

Woolf, V. 1942. *The Death of the Moth and Other Essays*. Harcourt Inc., San Diego.

Meander: A river released

Schofield, L. 2022. *Wild Fell: Fighting for Nature on a Lake District Hill Farm*. Penguin, London.

Chapter 19: The Mucky Beck

Iklley Clean River Group. *Public Information on Swimming in Ilkley*. https://www.ilkleycleanriver.uk/water-quality-information-1

Laville, S. 2022. *River sewage discharged into English rivers 375,000 times by water firms*. The Guardian, London. https://www.theguardian.com/environment/2022/mar/31/sewage-released-into-english-rivers-for-27m-hours-last-year-by-water-firms

Chapter 20: Rodents of unusual size

Brazier, R. E., Elliot, M., Andison, E., Auster, R. E., Bridgewater, S., Burgess, P., Chant, J., Graham, H., Knott, E., Puttock, A. A. K., Sansum, P., Vowles, A. 2020. *River Otter Beaver Trial: Science and Evidence Report*.

Gow, D. 2021. *Bringing Back the Beaver*. Chelsea Green Publishing, Vermont.

Chapter 21: Heartland

Deakin, R. 1999. *Waterlog: A Swimmer's Journey Through Britain*. Chatto and Windus, London.

Minihane, J. 2018. *Floating: A Return to Waterlog*. Prelude.

Walton, S. 2021. *Everybody Needs Beauty: In Search of the Nature Cure*. Bloomsbury, London.

Chapter 22: A descent into Hell Gill (and out the other side)

Bandolier. *Risk of dying and sporting activities.* http://www.bandolier.org.uk/booth/Risk/sports.html

Deakin, R. 1999. *Waterlog: A Swimmer's Journey Through Britain.* Chatto and Windus, London.

The following further titles (among others) have undoubtedly infiltrated my thinking, provided pleasure and inspiration during the writing of this book – they may for you too:

Aalto, K. 2020. *Writing Wild: Women Poets, Ramblers and Mavericks who Shape how we see the Natural World.* Timber Press, Portland.

Gaw, M. 2018. *The Pull of the River: A Journey Into the Wild and Watery Heart of Britain.* Elliot and Thompson Ltd, London.

Gooley, T. 2016. *How to Read Water.* Sceptre, London.

Henderson, C. 2017. *A New Map of Wonders: A Journey in Search of Modern Marvels.* Granta, London.

Jeffs, A. 2021. *Storyland: A New Mythology of Britain.* Riverrun, London.

Laing, O. 2011. *To the River.* Canongate, Edinburgh.

Macfarlane, R. 2012. *The Old Ways: A Journey on Foot.* Hamish Hamilton, London.

Macfarlane, R. 2007. *The Wild Places.* Granta, London.

Norbury, K. 2015. *The Fish Ladder: A Journey Upstream.* Bloomsbury, London.

Norbury, K. (Ed.) 2021. *Women On Nature.* Unbound, London.

Shepherd, N. 1977. *The Living Mountain.* Aberdeen University Press, Aberdeen.

Some organisations worthy of your clicks:

BeaverTrust.org
Bradford-Beck.org
BritishCanoeing.org.uk
CitizenZoo.org
Friends of Bradford's Becks IlkleyCleanRiver.uk
FriendsoftheDales.org.uk
NewNetworksForNature.org.uk
OutdoorSwimmingSociety.com
RightToRoam.org.uk
ScotlandBigPicture.com
TheRiversTrust.org
WildlifeTrusts.org

Index

Page numbers in **bold** refer to definitions of hydrological terms.